AN EARLY EXPERIMENT
IN INDUSTRIAL ORGANISATION

An
Early Experiment in
Industrial Organisation

Being a History of the Firm of
BOULTON & WATT, 1775–1805

BY

Sir Eric Roll

With an introduction by
J. G. SMITH

Routledge
Taylor & Francis Group
LONDON AND NEW YORK

First published 1930 by Frank Cass and Company Limited publisher

2 Park Square, Milton Park, Abingdon, Oxon OX14 4RN
711 Third Avenue, New York, NY 10017, USA

Routledge is an imprint of the Taylor & Francis Group, an informa business

First issued in paperback 2016

First edition	1930
New impression	1968

Transferred to Digital Printing 2005

ISBN 978-0-7146-1357-4 (hbk)
ISBN 978-1-138-96811-0 (pbk)

TO

MY FATHER AND MOTHER

PREFACE.

This account of the Boulton-Watt partnership adds another item to the now growing series of writings on the history of individual firms or individual pioneers of modern business. The choice of this particular firm is due to three facts : the great importance of the enterprise ; the concentration in Birmingham of the bulk of its records (the completeness and state of preservation of which is almost unique), and the lack, notwithstanding the existence of several books on the subject, of any exhaustive history from the economist's standpoint of what must be regarded as the foremost engineering firm of the late eighteenth and early nineteenth centuries.

Several writers have been attracted by the great mass of information available on the development of the steam engine business at Soho. There is Muirhead's three-volume work, *The Mechanical Inventions of James Watt*, which is far from exhaustive, and which, as the title indicates, concerns itself mainly with the technical aspect of the subject. Then there is Smiles' biography of the two partners which, written as it is from the point of view of the author of *Self-Help*, cannot be considered very useful to the economic historian. A more recent small volume entitled *Capital and Steam Power*, by John Lord, which treats the subject from the desired point of view, is not sufficiently detailed ; for the author's main task seems to have been the assigning to the story of the Boulton-Watt firm its proper place in the general economic history of the time.

The Memorial Volume, *James Watt and the Steam Engine*, by H. W. Dickinson and Rhys Jenkins, published in 1927 as a consequence of the Watt Centenary celebrations in 1919, is very exhaustive ; but information of an economic character is scattered and subordinated to technical details.

The present monograph deals with the history of the Soho firm solely from the economic standpoint. It is based on a prolonged research amongst the records preserved in the Boulton & Watt Collection of the Birmingham Public Reference Library (referred to as : B. & W. Colln.) and the manuscripts of the Boulton family, now in the Birmingham Assay Office (referred to as : A.O. MSS.). The former of these collections came into the possession of Sir Richard Tangye, the successor of Boulton & Watt at Soho, and were presented by him to the City of Birmingham in 1913. The second collection was the property of Miss Boulton of Tew Park before it was handed over to the Assay Office, Birmingham.

Throughout the book emphasis has been given to problems of business organisation, and in a few instances only have attempts been made to show how the firm's history compares with the general economic structure of the time. More often, however, differences or agreements have been pointed out between the firm's organisation and the theories and practices prevailing to-day. Some of the material on which Part I. is based has been utilised before. It has been included not only in order to bring together hitherto scattered information and to amplify it in many details, but also in order to place the new material of Part II. in its proper perspective.

A word may perhaps be said on the difficulties encountered during the research. The very bulk of the material proved a great obstacle in the way of extracting the relevant details. On the other hand, since much of the information was gathered from correspondence between the partners, gaps appear when they were together ; for oral discussions on business policy were evidently not recorded. The important collection in the Birmingham Municipal Library has not yet been catalogued ; most of the material is, therefore, inaccessible to the casual visitor. This fact explains the great number of appendices, quotations, and references in footnotes. No bibliography is included since the principal authorities are documentary ; but where printed sources have been consulted references are given.

My sincere thanks are due to Mr. H. M. Cashmore, the Birmingham City Librarian, and Mr. Westwood, the Master of Assay, for giving me unique privileges and facilities for research among the collections in their care. Mr. Leonard Chubb and other members of the staff of the Birmingham Public Reference

Library have been very helpful and courteous on the many occasions on which I had to consult them; and my friend Mr. Bladon Peake has helped with many valuable suggestions.

Above all I have to express my gratitude to Professor J. G. Smith, on whose suggestion this research was undertaken, and under whose supervision it was carried out. Any merits this monograph may possess are largely due to his constant advice and criticism; but I alone am to be held responsible for all imperfections.

Lastly I have to acknowledge my indebtedness to the University of Birmingham for help in publication.

ERICH ROLL.

Birmingham,
July, 1930.

CONTENTS.

CONTENTS

PART TWO. BOULTON, WATT & SONS.

CHAPTER ONE.

———

LIST OF COLLOTYPE PLATES.

INTRODUCTION.

THE scarcity of monographs on what is known as Business History, and the consequent undue importance attaching to the few that are available, has led to generalisations by economic historians which have inadequate foundation on fact or else a strictly limited application to selected industrial districts. This is especially true of the accounts generally given of the introduction of machinery and of the origin of the factory system. By conclusions drawn principally from the records of the English textile industrial areas an impression is produced of great rapidity of growth in production by machines, of crudeness of system and of lack of common sense on the part of business managers (with significant exceptions) whenever questions of organisation and factory administration were involved; and it is further suggested that it was not until the second decade of the twentieth century (and then only by importation from the United States of America) that a science of industrial management began to interest British factory owners and supervisors. To students in industrial areas where these generalisations are inapplicable there has always seemed to be something lacking in this accepted account. On one point, a not unimportant one, Mr. Roll's work rectifies an omission and is for that reason worthy of notice by historians of the so-called industrial revolution.

The story, in a general way, of the firm of Boulton & Watt is fairly well known; for it has been already written several times in varying detail. The material consisting of the records of the firm and the correspondence of its members is now accessible in the City of Birmingham Municipal Library and the Library of the Birmingham Assay Office. In the latter the documents which are principally correspondence of the Boulton family are being carefully summarised, indexed and filed with cross references by the Master of Assay, Mr. Westwood; but by far the larger part, in the Municipal Library, is still in the boxes in which it was rather hurriedly dumped when it was sent there for safe-keeping. Unfortunately, it lacks order and system even in the boxes, and there is evidence that the story of visitors extracting letters with the signature of James Watt, senior, as mementoes when it was still in Heathfield House is only too true. Unfortunately, too, Municipal Libraries cannot devote any portion of their limited funds to the calendaring of such records however interesting; and the work, therefore, of investigators will continue to be extremely harassing and wasteful of time. There is scarcely any duplication of material between the two institutions; but the replies to letters in one are frequently to be found in files or boxes in the other. It is not thought that anything of importance referring to the period dealt with by

Mr. Roll has escaped his very careful and very prolonged search.

Two facts are clearly established by Mr. Roll,
that it was not James Watt, senior, and Matthew
Boulton who were responsible for the details of the
management of Soho Foundry, and that the sons,
James Watt, junior, and Matthew Robinson Boulton,
who took over this task, brought to the business an
intelligence and a capacity which are ordinarily associated only with modern scientifically trained business
managers. There is, in fact, nothing in the details
of the most progressive factory practice of to-day
that the two sons had not anticipated. Neither
Taylor, Ford, nor other modern experts devised anything in the way of plan that cannot be discovered
at Soho before 1805 ; and the Soho system of costing
is superior to that employed in very many successful
concerns to-day. This earliest engineering factory,
therefore, possessed an organisation on the management side which was not excelled even by the technical
skill of the craftsmen it produced.

The records of the firm continue until its disappearance in the middle year of the nineteenth century.
A preliminary survey of the later documents discloses
letters mentioning important contemporary social and
political events ; and reports from the firm's travellers
on the Continent indicate how wars and rumours of
wars affected the demand for steam engines. But
there appears to be little of importance to compare in
interest with the earlier period. It is hoped, however,
to work through these papers shortly, in order to

verify certain assumptions which would explain the virtual abandonment of the Midlands by the heavy engineering industry where it had its origin with this firm. With the publication of two short essays by other investigators on topics only briefly treated by Mr. Roll, and the further scrutiny of the post-1805 records, the way will be clear for an examination of certain business records, of other firms to which access has been promised. Then, it will be possible to present, perhaps, a fuller and truer picture of the problems of industry in the Midlands as they appeared to intelligent managers in the first half of the nineteenth century, and in this way modify or confirm some of the conclusions of economic historians which at present have but little documentary support.

J. G. SMITH.

University of Birmingham,
   July, 1930.

PART ONE.

BOULTON & WATT.

CHAPTER ONE.

INTRODUCTORY.

(a) THE STEAM ENGINE.

THE question as to whether steam power alone was responsible for the industrial revolution was debated even before the series of profound economic changes of the last half of the eighteenth century began to be known by that term. It is now generally recognised that the factory system, together with all the forces which moulded the modern industrial age, originated before and apart from the application of steam power to industry. At the same time it is admitted that without the existence of some such agent neither the rapidity nor the completeness of the development of the modern economic system can be explained. The evolution of the steam engine occupies, therefore, an important place both technically and economically in all discussions of the history of the industrial revolution.

Steam power was, of course, known to the ancient world, but even in modern times it was used earlier than the comparatively recent rise of its importance in industry would suggest. As early as the middle of the seventeenth century a practical device for its use was invented by the Marquis of Worcester, described in detail in his *Century of Inventions*.[1]

[1] Fleming, A. P. M., Brocklehurst, H. J., *A History of Engineering* (1925), p. 110.

The name of the Frenchman Soloman de Caus must also be associated with these early attempts to construct a steam " engine." The first name of real importance is, however, that of Dionysius Papin, also a Frenchman, whose experiments were carried out in this country. Although generally known mainly for his " digester," Papin considerably advanced the theory of steam power, but his practical experiments were not very successful. The first steam engine which worked at all satisfactorily was constructed by Thomas Savery, a Devonshire engineer of considerable ability, who was attracted to the subject by his experience of the difficulty of working the Cornish tin mines owing to the presence of water, a difficulty which was only partly overcome by the application of primitive chain pumps driven mostly by water power.

In 1698 Savery obtained a patent for an improved engine which did away with the required pumping apparatus through the alternate condensation of steam in two vessels, the water of the pit being sucked into the vacuum so caused. In spite of the generous description in the patent of an engine " for raising water and occasioning motion to all sorts of mill work by the impellant force of fire," [1] Savery's invention was not a practical success on account of the great waste of fuel ; and no further advance occurs in the development of the steam engine until the time of Newcomen. Newcomen's method was to inject cold water on to the cylinder into which the steam had been admitted, a vacuum being produced through the condensation of the steam. Atmospheric pressure then depressed the piston, thus obtaining the desired motion. In 1705 Newcomen and Savery took out a joint patent for this improved engine, and the first on this principle was constructed in 1712 at a colliery near Wolverhampton.

[1] Taylor, R. W. C., *The Modern Factory System* (1891), p. 104.

2

Newcomen's engine reigned supreme during the first half of the eighteenth century, and there can be no doubt that it greatly benefited the mines by enabling them to go deeper than had hitherto been the case. The great defect of the engine was, however, its high fuel consumption ; but this did not greatly affect the coal mines, which were thus enabled to dispose of their unsaleable coal. In Cornwall, however, where coal was scarce and expensive, this high fuel consumption was an important consideration, and prevented an extensive use of the engine. The problem, then, became one of reducing the fuel consumption of the Newcomen engine, and many engineers devoted themselves to the task of finding a solution to it. One must, however, also remember at this stage that the actual production of engines was not carried out in any systematic manner. Steam engines were not produced in factories, but were erected where they were wanted after the different parts had been made and worked by ironfounders, smiths and mill-wrights. The problem of advancing this great agent in material human progress assumed, therefore, a second technico-economic aspect.

The advance in both the technical and economic aspects is closely bound up with the name of James Watt, one of the few benefactors of mankind whose fame was established during his lifetime, and the value of whose work has usually been over- rather than under-estimated. Indeed, on account of the great importance of Watt's technical inventions the name of Boulton, the partner who was associated with him in his life-work, has often been overlooked ; and it is only recently that a reassignment of their respective merits has been made. It is now common knowledge that Watt entered into partnership with Boulton to market his improved engine ; and, although the rôle which this more powerful and more reliable engine

3

played in general industrial development is sometimes given less importance than it deserves,[1] on the whole, it is now recognised as having been one of the greatest powers of the period. With increasing technical improvements the Watt engine penetrated ever-widening fields of industrial application, which found its most striking form in the new cotton industry. Above all, it ensured the complete establishment of machine industry, and opened up an era of amazing technical, economic and social changes.

The part of Boulton & Watt was, however, not confined to the facilitating of the rise of modern machinofacture in other industries. By setting out to make steam engines they laid the foundations of the modern engineering industry, although it was left to their sons to establish the first steam-engine factory. The site of this development was Birmingham, and it forms one of the most interesting chapters in the varied history of that important industrial city. Birmingham was essentially unsuited to this new industry, and it is surprising, therefore, that it should have been chosen. " Engineering was hardly appropriately placed in Birmingham," [2] since the heavier iron industry had already become localised in South Staffordshire. The industries of Birmingham were largely concerned in the production of a great variety of highly-finished articles, " which required a great deal of skilled labour and in which the cost of materials and of transport made up only a small proportion of the total value." [3]

By the beginning of the eighteenth century the hardware trade was definitely established in the Birmingham district,

[1] Knowles, L. C. S., *Industrial and Commercial Revolutions* (1921), p. 73.
[2] Rees, J. F., in Introduction to G. C. Allen's *Industrial Development of Birmingham and the Black Country* (1929), p. xx.
[3] Allen, G. C., *op. cit.*, p. 17.

4

and the rise of the town's prosperity was very rapid. The nature of its trades and the independence of the highly skilled craftsmen employed in them made it the home of the small workshop and the small master. Throughout its history it has presented examples of prosperous small businesses, and even the combination movement of the most recent times has had far less effect in this district than in those with industries of a more homogeneous nature. Exceptions were, of course, in existence even in the eighteenth century ; and Soho itself was not typical of the district even before the establishment of the steam-engine business. The Soho works of Matthew Boulton were a factory in a district where sub-letting reached the highest degree of its development. Rich entrepreneurs came into existence, but their rôle was that of factors who purchased the raw materials which they sub-let for manufacture to small masters. It was on the whole nothing else but the domestic system applied on a much greater scale, but it had important consequences on the remuneration of the workers employed in the actual production. As a continuation to sub-letting, there arose the " journeyman " or " butty " system by which the small master would in his turn engage one or more journeymen, with a certain number of assistants, and pay him an agreed price for the job, leaving him to strike his own bargain with his men. In this way the resources of the capitalists trickled down through the various intervening strata until they reached the actual producers.

The objections to such a system are obvious, and have found expression in all historical studies of the period. Soho, however, was different. From its earliest days it combined, in a factory, all classes of workmen engaged in the manufacture of its various products ; and in the owner of this factory was vested the technical as well as the entire economic control over his employees. It eliminated the middlemen and, side by side with the possibility of more efficient production, it ensured a much better position for the workmen. Soho had all the characteristics of a factory, and it carried machine-production to a high degree, notwithstanding the unreliable power which it could command.[1]

If Soho had been unique in the district even before Watt became associated with his partner, its position under the direction of the generation that followed became, in many ways, unique in the whole world. It was, strangely enough, the newly-established steam-engine business, and not the grown-up hardware manufactory, which was to show the most surprising development. From modest and simple beginnings its organisation grew to such complexity that, by the beginning of the new century, it showed, in rudimentary or elaborate form, most of the characteristic features of modern mass production. Passing through different and more and more efficient stages of organisation a business finally emerged which continued to prosper until the middle of the nineteenth century. In the following chapters the story of the varying fortunes of the business will be told and an attempt made to show the changes which its organisation underwent, together with speculations on the causes of these developments. The limits of this essay are approximately set by the years 1775 and 1805, the former of these dates marking the beginning of the partnership of Boulton and Watt, the latter being chosen—perhaps arbitrarily—as the year when exceptional progress was likely to

---

[1] Dr. Clapham states in his *Economic History of Modern Britain : The Early Railway Age* (1926), p. 151 : " But power played a small part at Soho." Although the " fire engine " which Boulton had installed may not have been of paramount importance at Soho, the tendencies of the whole organisation of production were such as to make the part of power rapidly more important.

have reached its end. It is the date, moreover, of the complete withdrawal from the business of Matthew Boulton, who was the last of the old partners to remain associated with it.

(b) THE PARTNERSHIP.

At the time of James Watt's first visit to Soho in 1767 Matthew Boulton, then 39 years of age, was one of the most successful and best-known of Midland manufacturers.

On leaving school he had entered the business of his father, who was a silver stamper and piercer of Birmingham, and had very soon considerably extended its range by the introduction of improvements in the manufacture of buttons, watch-chains, sword hilts and other ornamental wares, including inlaid steel buckles which were of his own invention.[1] On the death of his father in 1759 he had inherited a considerable fortune ; and although, after his marriage a year later to a wealthy heiress, he had become a man of substantial means, his natural inclination for an active life of business prevented him from retiring. He planned for an even greater extension of his business, and after taking into partnership a Mr. John Fothergill, a man with a wide knowledge of foreign markets and great business ability, he removed in 1762 the whole of his plant and stock-in-trade from the old premises in Snow Hill, Birmingham, which had become too small, to the new establishment which he had built at Soho just over the county border in Staffordshire, and two miles north of Birmingham.

In the years that followed Matthew Boulton realised his ambition of making the name of Soho known all over the world as the hall-mark of excellent and artistic workmanship. It will be seen in the later developments of the organisation of the firm of Boulton & Watt that the personal element was of

[1] Shaw, S., *History of Staffordshire* (1798-1801), vol. 2, p. 117.

7

great importance. It seems desirable, therefore, to give some account of Boulton's business before his association with Watt.

Soho, entirely as a result of Boulton's enterprise and business genius, had by that time already become a populous area :

> " A beautiful garden, with wood, lawn and water now covers one side of this hill ; five spacious squares of building, erected on the other side, supply workshops or houses for about 600 people. The extensive pool at the approach to this building is conveyed to a large water wheel in one of the courts and communicates motion to a prodigious number of different tools. And the mechanic inventions for this purpose are superior in multitude, variety and simplicity to those of any manufactory in the known world. Toys and utensils of various kinds in gold, silver, steel, copper, tortoiseshell, enamels and many vitreous and metallic compositions, with gilded, plated and inlaid works, are wrought up to the highest elegance of taste and perfection of execution in this place." [1]

And even then Dr. Darwin hailed this transformation from a barren heath on which stood a hut, the habitation of a warrener, as " a recent monument of the effects of trade on population." On purchasing the lease of these tracts of land, which included Handsworth Heath, Monerbank Hill, Crabtree Warren, etc., from Mr. Edward Ruston, who held it from John Wyrley, Esq., the Lord of the Manor of Handsworth, Boulton proceeded to extend the existing premises and to rebuild the water mill served by Hockley Brook. In 1764 he completely rebuilt the manufactory. The building then erected, at a cost of £9000, was later also the sole home of the Engine Manufactory until the building of Soho Foundry.

---

[1] Dr. E. Darwin, in a letter to the Rev. Mr. Feilde of Brewood, who was then engaged upon a history of Staffordshire, 1768, Aug. 26. Quoted by Shaw, *op. cit.*, vol. 2, p. 117.

Power was a very important factor in Boulton's works and, although the use of machinery was still limited, it gave rise to a large degree of division of labour. It was possible for Boulton to lay the foundations of a well-organised business, largely machine-operated, divided into a great number of different shops, and providing employment for a total of between six and eight hundred workers. The second factor in the great success of Boulton's business, and one which was at least as strong as any other in bringing about the partnership between him and Watt, was the fact that Boulton, together with the establishment of a " factory," a unique exception at the time in the hardware industry of the Midlands, had trained a body of highly skilled craftsmen who were superior in the exactitude of their work to the usual type of workman engaged in these trades. This was brought about partly by Boulton's own desire for highly artistic workmanship, partly through his ambition to get rid of the bad reputation from which " Brummagem " goods were suffering, and partly through the nature of his products which were largely ornamental wares and, therefore, subject to considerable fluctuations of fashion. To some extent the skill attained by his workmen may also be attributed to the increased use of machinery [1] which would at that time necessitate a greater rather than a less degree of skill.

The methods of the firm of Boulton & Fothergill were recognised even by contemporary writers as an extraordinary departure from usual industrial practice. The firm had established a mercantile correspondence throughout Europe " by

---

[1] Watt tells us in his " Memorandum concerning Mr. Boulton, commencing with my first acquaintance with him," Glasgow, 1809, Sept. 17, that Boulton " was the first who had applied a mill to turn the laps." A.O. MSS.

which means the produce of their various articles was greatly extended and the manufacturer, by becoming his own merchant, eventually enjoyed a double profit." [1] In 1770 Boulton had arranged that weekly meetings of partners and managers at Soho should take place to examine the state of business, orders, prices and any other matters relating to the manufactory, and that questions regarding foreign trade should be discussed, a policy agreed upon, and important letters answered at these meetings only.[2]

All these extensions of the business operations necessitated a greatly increased capital ; and Boulton (who was obliged to find large sums of money for increased stocks, plant and credits) had to sell a great part of the property inherited from his father. He raised £3000 on his wife's estate and borrowed £5000 from his friend Baumgartner, who was again to help him indirectly at a later date. The gross returns of the business were £3000 in 1763 and had advanced to £30,000 in 1767,[3] but in spite of these figures it is doubtful whether it was really profitable. Boulton, it seems, was a man of great vitality and diversified taste, which found a suitable outlet in the manufacturing of a great number of different articles. He was not—at any rate until the later years of his life—a man of specialisation. He was continually introducing new manufactures into his works and into the district. Examples of these were : silver-plated articles, originally localised in Sheffield, and the manufacture of clocks. Boulton was also the first in Birmingham to manufacture complete services of plate and other large articles of silver.

This business, however, was not profitable " on account of

[1] Shaw, *op. cit.*, vol. 2, p. 118.
[2] Boulton's Memorandum, 1770, Nov. 27. A.O. MSS.
[3] Smiles, S., *Lives of Boulton and Watt* (1904), p. 142.

the great value of the material, the loss of interest on which was not compensated by the additional price put on it for workmanship and fashion. The withdrawing of so much capital from the staple articles of manufacture was very injurious." [1] New tools and machinery were necessary to work those materials that had become fashionable, such as mother-of-pearl, for this excellent reason : " in order to produce that rapidity of wholesale execution for which the manufactures of this country are distinguished." [2] Boulton himself, in writing to Adams, the famous architect, boasts of having

" . . . almost every machine that is applicable to those arts. . . . Through my correspondence with almost every mercantile town in Europe, I am regularly supplied with orders for the grosser articles in common demand, by which I am enabled to employ such a number of hands as to provide me with an ample choice of artists for the finer branches of work ; and I am thereby encouraged to erect and employ a more extensive apparatus than it would be prudent to provide for the production of the finer articles only." [3]

It seems certain that the productive capacity of the firm had been extended more rapidly than the nature of the business, the amount of capital invested in it, and the demand would have warranted. Boulton began to find difficulties in meeting the interest charges on the large sums of money borrowed, as in the case of a debt of £10,000 to a Mr. Tonson of London ; and his embarrassment was increased by the failure, during the panic of 1772, of Fordyce Brothers with whom he had deposited a considerable sum.

His two main qualities then—an astute business sense which, among other things, made him realise even at that time the

---

[1] James Keir, " Memoir of Matthew Boulton," 1809, Dec. 3. A.O. MSS.
[2] James Keir, *ibid*. [3] Smiles, *op. cit.*, p. 144.

value of novel ways of advertising,[1] together with a readiness to embark on almost any and every new venture, have to be taken into account when considering the origin of this most important of all industrial partnerships.

It was in 1763 that James Watt had conceived the idea of the separate condenser and, by thus improving the old New-comen engine, had virtually made it a new machine. The years that followed were occupied in putting his ideas into practice and in constructing a working model of the engine. During the long and costly experiments entailed through the lack of skilled workmen in Glasgow and through the general absence of machines capable of satisfying the demand for exactness Watt was assisted financially by his friend, Dr. Black ; and by the year 1768 his debt to the latter had risen to the sum of £1200. The successful end of the experiments was as yet not in sight and Dr. Black's financial resources proved unequal to continued assistance. It was imperative, therefore, for Watt to find another patron who would be willing to bear the cost of the experiments. A patron was fortunately forthcoming at this juncture, in the person of Dr. Roebuck of the Carron Ironworks, who, in a desire to secure the supply of his raw materials, had taken a lease of the coal mines belonging to the Duke of Hamilton. When Newcomen's engine was found insufficient to keep the mines clear of water Roebuck turned his attentions to Watt's experiments, about which he had heard from his friend, Dr. Black, and desired Watt to build an engine for him at Kinneil. Experiments with a small model engine pleased Roebuck so much that he decided to put his faith in

---

[1] Keir tells us in the above-mentioned memoir that Boulton was quite aware of the great advertisement value of the many visitors to Soho, who were invariably received with the greatest hospitality, in spite of the time lost in satisfying their curiosity.

Watt's engine and agreed to pay Watt's debt to Dr. Black, ensure the financial basis for future experiments and bear the costs of a patent in consideration of a two-thirds share in the invention. The first patent was obtained on the 5th of January, 1769, for fourteen years, and immediately afterwards Watt started on the erection of the Kinneil engine.

In 1766, when returning from London, Watt visited Soho, and, although Boulton was absent at the time, he was shown over the works by their mutual friend, Dr. Small.[1] Watt was naturally struck with the unique organisation of Soho, and above all with the excellent workmanship, which was in sharp contrast to that which he could command in Glasgow.[2] The next year Watt again visited Soho and met Boulton himself, who, interested for some time in the question of the application of steam power, had also heard of Watt's engine from Dr. Roebuck. Boulton expressed his great interest in the project and also his desire to be concerned in it. Watt replied to this offer after his return to Kinneil, giving a short history of his experiments and an account of the existing arrangement with Dr. Roebuck [3]; and a few months afterwards he expressed the opinion that it would be better to defer the bargaining till he and Roebuck were in England.[4] In the meantime the patent had been obtained and Watt's agreement with Roebuck had

[1] Dr. William Small (1734-75) was a native of Carmylie, County Angus, and became Professor of Mathematics and Natural Philosophy in the College of Williamsburg, Virginia. The climate did not suit him, and he came to England in 1765. He visited Boulton, to whom he had a letter of introduction from Benjamin Franklin, and he finally settled down in Birmingham.

[2] In his letters to Small, Watt is constantly complaining about " the villainous bad workmanship," and on the 24th of Nov., 1772, we find him writing : " The work done is slovenly, and our workmen are bad, and I am not sufficiently strict." A.O. MSS.

[3] Watt to Boulton, 1768, Oct. 11, *ibid.*

[4] Watt to Small, 1769, Jan. 28, *ibid.*

13

become definite. From that date began the long and protracted negotiations which, after five years, brought Boulton
into the partnership. Already, in his first letter to Boulton
Watt had stated that Dr. Roebuck, owing to the pressure of
his other business, which was then at the height of its prosperity,
was unable to give the necessary time to the executive part of
the engine project. Roebuck had seen Boulton soon after the
grant of the patent and had offered him the privilege of manufacturing Watt's engines in the three Midland counties—
Warwickshire, Staffordshire and Derbyshire—an offer which
Boulton refused.[1]

Throughout that year (1769) Watt was engaged on experiments for further improving the engine, and we find him constantly writing to Dr. Small about its progress and about the
problems of the patent specifications. His anxiety for Boulton
and Small to be in some way connected with the business was
undiminished ; in fact it increased owing to the disappoint-
ing results of local workmanship in Glasgow. Roebuck was,
therefore, prevailed upon to make another offer to Boulton and
Small, and we find the latter writing to Watt [2] that they had
accepted. Watt, apparently in ignorance of the exact terms,
acknowledged the result in the following words : " I received
yours and shake hands with you and Mr. Boulton on our connection, which I hope will prove agreeable to us all." [3] The
offer, however, was only an option to come in as partners,
within twelve months, holding a one-third share against a
payment to Roebuck of £1000. This option was never exercised. During the next three years, although friendship and

---

[1] Boulton to Watt, 1769, Feb. 7 : " It would not be worth my while
to make for three counties only, but I find it very well worth my while to
make for all the world." A.O. MSS.

[2] Small to Watt, 1769, Nov. 30, *ibid.*

[3] Watt to Small, 1769, Dec. 12, *ibid.*

correspondence continued, no progress was made in the negotiations. We do not even find any mention of experiments on
the engine during that time. These had, to a large extent, been
unsuccessful, and Watt had to look out for some source of
income, especially as Roebuck, whose business engagements
became more and more pressing, was less disposed to continue
further financial assistance. This other source was found.
Watt was engaged on survey work in connection with the
Monkland Canal, an occupation which, together with the
deepening of the harbour of the Port of Glasgow,[1] filled practically all his time until the year 1772. During that period,
however, another development had taken place. Roebuck's
affairs went from bad to worse, and during the crisis of 1772
he was seriously affected and became practically insolvent.
Work on the Monkland Canal, too, was discontinued, and Watt,
again deprived of a source of income, revived the old negotiations with Boulton and Small. On the 7th of November,
1772, he writes to Small regarding Roebuck's attitude in the
following terms :

> " He is now willing to part either with the whole or the
> greatest part of his property upon such terms as I dare say,
> in better times you and Mr. Boulton could have had no
> hesitation in accepting. . . . I think that you and Mr. Boulton
> ought to have a certain share without advancing to the
> Doctor or me, provided you took upon you the charge of the
> future experiments and of finding money to carry on the
> business in case of success." [2]

Dr. Roebuck's affairs, however, having taken this turn,
Small and Boulton did not entertain any thoughts of profiting

---

[1] Report concerning the harbour of Port of Glasgow made to the Magis-
trates of Glasgow by James Watt, Aug. 9, 1771, quoted by Dickinson
and Jenkins in *James Watt and the Steam Engine* (1927), p. 32.
[2] Watt to Dr. Small, 1772, Nov. 7. A.O. MSS.

by them, and we find the former refusing the offer.[1]   A meeting
of creditors was called in the early part of 1773, and Boulton
appointed Watt his attorney, stating that Roebuck's debt to
the firm of Boulton & Fothergill amounted to £630 11s. 3d.[2]
With the official letter of attorney there was also sent a letter
marked " private."   In this, Boulton stated that, apart from
the above sum, he had advanced to the Doctor some years
previously an amount equal to it without written agreement,
and, as it had never appeared in the books, he would not now
claim it even if he never received a farthing of it.   He suggested
that Roebuck should make over his share in the engine business
(two-thirds) to Boulton as a set-off against the above-mentioned
debt, and that if it turned out profitable, Boulton would be
bound by Watt's and Small's judgment as to how much more
to pay him.   On May 17, Watt had given a discharge to the
Doctor for all the sums owed by him under the partnership
" in consideration of the mutual friendship existing between
them," the Kinneil engine thus becoming his property.   On
May 31, Watt wrote that Dr. Roebuck had agreed to Boulton's
offer.   Boulton, however, refused to carry out the transaction
on the suggested basis.[3]   By then Dr. Roebuck had become
a bankrupt and Boulton had scruples about making a bargain,
as the creditors might think that he was making a capital
acquisition to their disadvantage.   Also, as his main purpose
was to assist and benefit Roebuck, he was afraid that any
explicit statement in the agreement of the advantages to the
Doctor in case of success might prejudice the latter in the eyes
of the creditors.   Lastly, he had difficulties with his partner,

[1] Small to Watt, 1772, Nov. 16. A.O. MSS. " It is impossible for
Mr. Boulton and me . . . to purchase . . . at a time when they might
be inclined to part with the commodity at an undue value."
[2] Boulton to Watt, 1773, March 29, *ibid.*
[3] Boulton to Watt, 1773, June 12, *ibid.*

Fothergill, who also had a claim on Roebuck's property but was disinclined to embark on the engine business. Boulton stated that he would, therefore, rather remain a creditor and buy the engine from the trustees if matters came to a head. It is somewhat tempting to question the disinterested motives of Boulton's action in first refusing to take advantage of Roebuck's situation, then making a definite offer, and lastly refusing the acceptance of that offer in the above terms ; for when, in August of that year, Roebuck was obliged to make a composition with his creditors, who, throughout, had not valued the engine as " worth one farthing," the final transfer of Roebuck's two-third share in the engine was made to Boulton against a discharge of all debts.[1] Nothing definite is known about an additional payment to Roebuck of £1000 out of the first profits of the partnership of Boulton & Watt, mentioned in July of that year ; [2] but even if, as would appear, that payment was made, it is certain that Boulton obtained his share on much better and more secure terms by holding out. Roebuck was evidently dissatisfied with the bargain, and in later years he often attempted to get some additional compensation.[3]

The transfer completed nothing was now in the way of a vigorous start on the erection of the Kinneil engine, which had been sent off to Birmingham as early as May of that year. Watt, however, was prevented for another twelve months from following it to Birmingham. He had been employed on survey

[1] See against this Smiles, *op. cit.*, p. 163.
[2] Watt to Boulton, 1773, July. A.O. MSS.
[3] Watt to Boulton, 1780, April 11, *ibid ;* also Boulton to Watt, 1780, March 8. B. & W. Colln. :—
" Dr. Roebuck seems to have lost all sense of justice and honour. He almost insists upon our taking his son John into partnership. Mr. Matthews has been very explicit with him to-day. The Doctor boasts of the great profits of his colliery, but in the same breath asks to borrow money."

work on the Caledonian Canal which was later finished by Telford ; and the death of his wife in September further delayed his departure. It was not until the 17th of May, 1774, that Watt finally set out for Birmingham, where he arrived on May 31.

Experiments on the engine were renewed and were largely successful, owing to the greater skill available. However, six years had already elapsed since the granting of the first patent, and Boulton, realising that the patent would expire before the business became barely profitable, would not invest any further capital until the monopoly had been extended for another term of years. Steps were immediately taken to secure an Act of Parliament,[1] which was cheaper to obtain than a new patent ; and, after a very stormy passage through the House, the Act granting Watt a monopoly in the manufacture of his improved steam engines for a period of twenty-five years in England, Scotland and Wales and the " Plantations " (the original patent had not covered Scotland) received the Royal Assent in May, 1775.[2] The partnership was then actually started on June 1, 1775, and was to run for the same number of years as the Act. The most important articles of the partnership are stated in a letter from Watt to

---

[1] In this respect, the practice then differed from that of to-day. Now applications for renewals of patents are granted by the Court of Chancery.

[2] The Bill was, of course, opposed on the old grounds of objection to monopolies. It is generally supposed that the patent laws of England were extremely helpful in fostering new inventions through the protection afforded to the inventors. Although the principle of the law was undoubtedly very strong its actual technical provisions were not sufficient to protect inventors from long, costly and harassing litigation in case of infringement. On this point Watt's own suggestions for improving the patent laws, mentioned later in connection with the firm's lawsuits against " pirates," are of the greatest interest.

Boulton, dated July 5, 1775, from Glasgow, and are as follows:[1]

1. I to assign to you two-thirds of the property of the invention on following conditions :

2. You to pay all expenses of Act or others incurred before June, 1775, and also the expense of future experiments, which money to be sunk without interest by you being the consideration you pay for your part, but the experimental machines to be your property.

3. You to advance stock-in-trade bearing interest, but having no claim upon me for any part of that further than my Intromissions, but the stock itself to be your property and security.

4. I to draw one-third of the profits so soon as any arise from the business, after paying the workmen's wages and goods furnished, but abstract from the stock-in-trade excepting the interest thereof, which is to be deducted before a balance is struck.

5. I to make drawings, give directions and make surveys, the company paying travelling expenses to either of us when upon engine business.

6. You to keep the books and balance them once a year.

7. A book to be kept, wherein to be marked such transactions as are worthy of record, which, when signed by both, to have the force of the contract.[2]

8. Neither of us to alienate our share without consent of the other, and if either of us by death or otherwise

---

[1] Dickinson and Rhys Jenkins state that they have been unable to find the actual deed of partnership, if one was ever executed, but mention should be made of a draft indenture of the partnership agreement, dated Sept. 5, 1777, kept in the Boulton and Watt Collection. The last page is missing, and it is impossible to state whether the deed was executed on that or any other date.

[2] Dickinson and Rhys Jenkins, *op. cit.*, p. 44. "The book . . . if kept, has not been found by the Editors." It has been impossible to trace this book. The draft indenture, however, makes no mention of it; only the usual provision for the keeping of proper account books is included.

shall be incapacitated from acting for ourselves, the other of us to be sole manager without contradiction or interference of heirs, executors, assignees or others, but the books to be subject to their inspection and the acting partner of us to be allowed a reasonable commission for extra trouble.

9. The contract to continue for twenty-five years from the First of June, 1775, when the partnership commenced, notwithstanding the contract being of a later date.

10. Our Heirs, Executors and Assignees bound to observance.

11. In case of demise of both parties, our Heirs, etc., to succeed in same manner and if they all please may burn the contract." [1]

On this basis, then, the partnership was entered into [2] and the business of the firm begun.

The characters of the two men who had thus come together were in many ways very different. Watt, the great inventive genius, was, through his quick temper and anything but jovial disposition, entirely unsuited for a business career ; and on his own confession he " would rather face a loaded cannon than settle an account or make a bargain." [3] Boulton, on the other hand, " was not only an ingenious mechanic, well skilled in all the practices of the Birmingham manufacturers, but possessed in a high degree the faculty of rendering any new invention of his own or others useful to the public by organising and arranging the processes by which it could be carried on as well as of

---

[1] Watt to Boulton, Glasgow, 1775, July 15. A.O. MSS.

[2] Of other provisions contained in the draft of the partnership deed may be mentioned one for disputes to be settled by arbitration ; another important provision not contained in Watt's letter was for the protection of Boulton in case of future claims against the patent, when Watt was to obtain any further Act or other protection required. He also gave an assurance that to his knowledge no other claim or right to the patent existed.

[3] Watt to Small, 1772, Nov. 24. A.O. MSS.

promoting the sale by his own exertions and by his numerous friends and correspondents." [1] Yet the combination of the two was so singularly happy that it has often been asserted—and it is hardly an exaggeration—that had Boulton not taken up the invention at a critical juncture the probability of its ever becoming practicable would have been very remote indeed. Watt himself pays a tribute [2] to Boulton's active and sanguine disposition which, through the whole of this business, served to counter-balance the despondency and diffidence which was natural to him. The chain of events which brought about so momentous a partnership is therefore a subject of interesting speculation. A great many factors contributed. There was, of course, first of all, the fact of their acquaintance together with the described difference of character, a difference which Boulton was not slow in recognising ; there was the extremely bad workmanship from which Watt suffered in Scotland, and, contrasted with this, the high development of organisation and skill of workmanship at Soho of which he had had an opportunity of convincing himself. [3] Yet another important factor was Boulton's own want of a greater and more stable supply of power, and the fact that he had been corresponding with Benjamin Franklin on the subject shows his great interest in any new improvements. Lastly, there was the fact that Dr. Roebuck, owing to his engagements, could not pay much attention to the executive part of the business. Watt himself wrote :

[1] Watt's " Memorandum." A.O. MSS.
[2] *Ibid.*
[3] It is characteristic of the unique position of Soho at the time, and also of Watt himself, that even his " Memorandum," written as late as 1809, begins with an account of his first visit to Soho that is entirely concerned with the organisation of Boulton's works and the articles manufactured there.

" the greatest part of which (the business) must devolve on me, who am from my natural inactivity, want of health and resolution, incapable of it." [1]

The climax came when Roebuck went bankrupt.

It is very tempting to place the emphasis on Boulton's want of greater steam power, and this indeed has sometimes been done.[2] Even contemporary writers stress this fact, and the following account is interesting :

" Mr. Boulton, finding from experience that the stream of water which had induced him to build a mill and transplant his manufactory to Soho was insufficient for its purposes, applied horses in conjunction with his water-mill, but finding that both troublesome and irregular and expensive, he made a Steam Engine on Savery's plan with the intention of returning and raising the water 24 feet high ; but this proving unsatisfactory to him, he soon after formed an acquaintance with his present partner and friend, Mr. James Watt. . . . The application of this improved steam engine at Soho to raise and return the water extended the powers of the water-mill, which induced Mr. Boulton to rebuild it a second time upon a much larger scale and several engines were afterward erected at Soho for other purposes, by which the manufactory was greatly extended, the source of mechanical power being thus unlimited." [3]

But this emphasis on the one factor seems hardly correct. It must be remembered that, although it was understood that the engine was first to be tested and applied at Soho, Boulton's idea throughout the negotiations was to manufacture Watt's steam engines on an extensive scale to supply the whole country and, indeed, the world. To Boulton it was essentially a new

---

[1] Watt to Boulton, 1768, Oct. 11. A.O. MSS.
[2] E.g. Smiles, *op. cit.*, p. 149 *sqq.*   [3] Shaw, *op. cit.*, vol. 2, p. 118.

business enterprise ; and, with his accustomed readiness to take up anything new, he was quite willing to embark on this, as it seemed, speculative venture. Boulton himself very clearly states the motives for his desire to be associated with Watt in the engine business :

> " I presumed that your engine would require money, very accurate workmanship and extensive correspondence, to make it turn out to the best advantage, and that the best means . . . would be to keep the executive part out of the hands of . . . empirical engineers . . . ; my idea was to settle a manufactory near to my own by the side of our canal, where I would erect all the conveniences necessary for the completion of engines and from which manufactory we would serve all the world with engines of all sizes. By these means and your assistance we could engage and instruct some excellent workmen (with more excellent tools than would be worth any man's while to procure for one single engine). . . ." [1]

It seems, therefore, a futile speculation to attempt to emphasise any one factor ; and we must accept the fact that it was the accidental but very happy combination of a great many factors that led to the establishment of the firm of Boulton & Watt.

---

[1] Boulton to Watt, 1769, Feb. 7. A.O. MSS.

CHAPTER TWO.

EARLY BUSINESS.

THE history of the firm, started in 1775, under the style of Boulton & Watt, can be divided roughly into two great periods. The first lasted for twenty years until 1795, the date of the building of Soho Foundry ; and the second, which presents a very sharp contrast, from that date onwards. Fothergill, Boulton's partner, having declined to take part in the new venture, and Dr. Small having died while Watt was obtaining his patent, Boulton alone was assigned a share in the Act of Parliament ;[1] and the partnership was set up ostensibly for the purpose of manufacturing Watt's engines. It is necessary to emphasise at this stage that for the first twenty years of their connection Boulton and Watt were not (with minor qualifications during the later years of that period) manufacturers of steam engines. A more appropriate description would be " consulting engineers." They made it clear in their answers to all the early enquiries that all they were prepared to do was to furnish suitable plans and drawings and supervise the erection of the engine, while the customer would be at liberty to have the engine parts made wherever he chose. Nor did they want to be executive engineers themselves,[2] being quite prepared to leave the executive part to local engineers,

[1] See p. 19.
[2] Watt to J. Hornblower, 1776, Oct. 17. " We have no plan of becoming executive engineers ourselves." Office Letter Books, vol. 1. B. & W. Colln.

a proceeding which was absolutely necessary in some cases owing to local opposition to their intrusion.

At this stage, too, another important character becomes closely associated with the new engine business. John Wilkinson, the famous Shropshire iron-master, had improved the method for boring cannon and had obtained a patent for his new invention in 1774.[1] The new practice of having the casting rotate instead of the boring rod, increased the exactness of the bore considerably. The importance of this improvement to Watt's experiments cannot be exaggerated. One of his greatest difficulties—that of obtaining an accurate bore—was at once removed and the engine advanced from the experimental to the commercial stage. At the same time the foundation was laid for a very successful business alliance. We find that, while Boulton & Watt undertook to furnish from Soho only engine parts which, owing to their new and original design, demanded special skill and care of workmanship, they usually recommended Wilkinson, and even insisted that while the purchaser was free to order such parts as boiler, piston and piston rods from whatever source he liked, the cylinder was to be made by the Salopian.

The reasons for this peculiar and strangely long-lived arrangement, which gave rise to an equally peculiar system of payment, are manifold. First of all, Boulton's well-established and extensive business in the hardware trade made great calls on his time ; and we find him writing to a customer [2] that the multiplicity of other business prevents him paying much attention to the engine. Although a change was bound to come (and we find Boulton writing to Watt shortly afterwards in an

[1] Ashton, T. S., *Iron and Steel in the Industrial Revolution* (1924), p. 63.
[2] Boulton to John Collet, 1775, Oct. 18. Office Letter Books, vol. 1. B. & W. Colln.

entirely different strain [1]), there is no doubt that the first few years on the part of Boulton were still mainly occupied with other business. Wilkinson—as mentioned already—possessed a monopoly in the improved method of boring; but most important of all was undoubtedly the lack of sufficient capital on the part of the new partnership for extensive foundry works.

Thus we find that all the original attractions that had made Watt come to Soho—a well-established, large business undertaking and an abundance of skilled labour—were really only of importance in bringing about the partnership, and did not continue to be of any particular advantage in the early years of the business; for the main use of Boulton's capital and supply of skilled workers was to finance Watt through the experimental stages, and this (a most important point) included the provision of materials and assistants.

A consequence of this arrangement, by which the part of Soho was mainly confined to the furnishing of plans, was the very peculiar price policy adopted. The system, which probably owes its origin to Watt's initiative, is outlined in the answer to one of the first enquiries which appear in the letter book of the firm.[2] They were, Watt wrote, unable to give any estimates as yet. As regards their own profit, however, they would not demand any on the prime cost but would require as reward for their plans and supervision, as well as for the licence to work the engine, a one-third share of the savings in fuel effected by the adoption of the new engine

[1] Boulton to Watt, 1776, Feb. 24 : " . . . as we will keep them (i.e. condensers) ready fitted up and then one engine can be turned out of hand in two or three weeks. I have fixed my mind upon making from twelve to fifteen reciprocating and fifty rotative engines per annum. I assure you that of all the toys and trinkets which are manufactured at Soho, none shall take the place of fire engines in respect of my attention." A.O. MSS.

[2] Watt to Ralph Lodge, 1775, June 12. Office Letter Book, vol. 1. B. & W. Colln.

instead of one of the old type. Being certain of the smallness of the extra cost of the new engine, they were also prepared to forego their share of savings until any such extra cost had been paid off. He also hints at a repair system adopted later by stating : " In this way it will be my interest to take care that the engine is kept in good order and be improved from time to time if capable of it."

This system, ingenious, honest and, as it proved to be later on, most difficult in its practical application, can, however, not claim to be an original one. The first engines, being pumping engines mainly applied to mines, it was natural that a similar system of payment to that used before by suppliers of steam engines to collieries should have been adopted. " The Proprietors of the Invention for raising Water by Fire," a company formed in London in 1715 which supplied engines to collieries in many parts of the country, had required the purchasers of their licence to order their own cylinders and other engine parts and pay for the cost of erection, while they were to be paid an annual rent amounting sometimes to as much as £300. In one case a colliery paid £200 a year and half the net profits " in return for their services in keeping the engine going." [1] This company, towards the expiration of their patent, also adopted the practice of accepting a lump sum which we shall later encounter in the case of Boulton & Watt.

The first engine that was ordered on these terms was one for the Bloomfield Colliery of Messrs. Bentley & Co., near Dudley. In June, 1775, an enquiry was received, and very shortly after their answer to it [2] we find Boulton & Watt

[1] Ashton and Sykes, *The Coal Industry of the Eighteenth Century* (1929), p. 38.
[2] Boulton & Watt to Bentley & Co., 1775, June 15. B. & W. Colln.

writing to Wilkinson that Bentley & Co. had agreed to
order a cylinder.[1] This was a large engine, 24 feet high with
a 50-in. cylinder and a 52-in. pump, and the cost of the various
parts came nearly to £2000.[2] An engineer named Perrins
had originally been engaged to erect an ordinary atmospheric
engine at Bloomfield, but Boulton persuaded the proprietors
to adopt one of Watt's, the arrangement being the usual one
and Perrins being left in charge of the erection. Again, only
some parts, such as valves and nozzles, were made at Soho,
and Boulton & Watt guaranteed to refund any extra cost out
of their share of savings. A guarantee as to repairs was
included in this contract. Several prospective buyers had
previously mentioned the possibility of the new engine requiring more repairs than the old one,[3] but Watt had replied to
the contrary and had estimated the life of the new engine at
from forty to fifty years. Doubts in the minds of their customers were, however, not dispelled, probably owing to the
allegations on the part of rival engineers as to the very complicated nature of Watt's engine ; and the firm had to adopt
some measure to counteract this serious drawback to an increase in the popularity of their engines. Consequently they
undertook, for the first time in the case of the Bloomfield
engine, to execute free all repairs, at least of their own work,
during the first year ; [4] and, later on, this undertaking was
extended to cover free repair of any damage, provided it was not
caused through the carelessness of the buyer's servants.[5] The
Bloomfield engine was not set to work until the first days of
March, 1776. It proved highly satisfactory and for the first

[1] Boulton & Watt to J. Wilkinson, 1775, June 27. B. & W. Colln.
[2] Watt to Garbett, 1776, Feb. 10, *ibid.*
[3] Watt to Burton & Wilbie, 1775, June 29 and Aug. 15, *ibid.*
[4] Watt to Garbett, 1776, Feb. 10, *ibid.*
[5] Watt to Cross, 1776, Oct., *ibid.*

time an account of the Watt engine appeared in the public
press.[1] The division of the work is set out :

"All the Iron Foundry parts (which are unparalleled
for truth) were executed by Mr. Wilkinson ; the condenser
with the valves, pistons and all the small work at Soho by
Mr. Harrison and others, and the whole was erected by
Mr. Perrins conformable to the plans and under the directions of Mr. Watt."

The performance of the engine is then praised, the fuel consumption estimated as one-fourth of that of a common engine,
and, finally, a short account of the Soho manufactory is given.

Although there were later difficulties in the way of a final
settlement of the annuity with the proprietors of the colliery
the success of the engine was of great advertising value to
Boulton & Watt, and we find them referring new clients to the
performance of this engine. About the same time Wilkinson
himself became a customer for Watt's engines. The first
engine at his works at Broseley, for blowing an iron furnace,
with a 38-in. cylinder, was also erected in March, 1776. It
is also the first blowing engine erected by Boulton & Watt
and its success was instantaneous, although the constant improvements soon made it more or less obsolete, a fact which
Wilkinson was not slow in bringing to Watt's notice, for we
find the latter acknowledging the defects two years afterwards.[2]
Watt himself recognised that they had undertaken the construction of large engines without sufficient experimental work,
and it is some time before the next big engines appear. By
the middle of the next year, however, the total number of
engines erected for Wilkinson amounted to four, one of which

---

[1] *Aris's Birmingham Gazette*, 1776, March 11.
[2] Watt to J. Wilkinson, 1779, Aug. 27. Office Letter Book, vol. 2.
B. & W. Colln.

was an engine with an inverted cylinder referred to as the
" Topsyturvy " engine. As is to be expected, the terms for
engines supplied to the iron-founder were quite different
from the usual, and are given explicitly in one of the firm's
letters to Wilkinson,[1] replying to his enquiry about the general
terms for engines erected for his own use. They grant him
and his successors a licence to use the two engines erected
at New Willey and the one he proposes to erect at Wilson
House, as well as a devil to be erected where he pleases, during
the time of the patent privilege upon payment of 1s. yearly
when demanded, provided he does not remove them to situa-
tions where coal is of much greater value. With regard to the
engine he proposes to erect at Snedshill, they will take the
premium in coals equivalent to one-third of the savings for
each hour the engine goes delivered on the spot, " when
demanded, which will not be the case if they are of no value,
and if they are, you certainly can afford to pay them." This
arrangement was certainly a very generous one, for it did not
demand a great deal from Wilkinson (the Snedshill engine
mentioned never paid any premium), while for two further
engines erected on the same terms at Bradley and Snedshill
the annual premiums were £34 and £57 respectively.

It was under these conditions that the stipulation about
the value of coal was introduced. Since the whole income of
the firm arose out of premiums measured on the basis of fuel-
saving the relative price of coal in the locality was naturally
of consequence. Already in 1775 Watt had suggested to
Boulton that where coals were very cheap they ought to charge
one half of the savings or ten years' purchase of such half ; [2]

---

[1] Boulton & Watt to J. Wilkinson, 1777, July 17. Office Letter Book,
vol. 1. B. & W. Colln. Part of the quotation in Lord, *Capital and Steam
Power* (1923), p. 159, is incorrect.
   Watt to Boulton, 1775. A.O. MSS.

and the same condition is mentioned a year later in a letter to a customer.[1] The actual standard adopted was a minimum price of coal of 5s. per ton.[2]

Another initial difficulty which appeared in many different forms later on was the type of engine to be adopted for comparison with Watt's engine. The usual engine chosen by Boulton & Watt was the ordinary fire-engine on the Newcomen principle, and the improved steam engine of Smeaton's construction, on which many customers insisted, was excluded except if the customer was willing to agree to pay one half of the savings.[3] Watt wrote to Smeaton himself in very courteous terms :

" In all these comparisons our own interest has made us except your improved engines unless we be allowed a greater proportion of the savings." [4]

At least on one occasion, however, did they depart from that practice. It was the Birmingham Canal Engine, ordered in 1777 and set up in 1778, that excited Smeaton's admiration so much that he finally withdrew his usual charges against Watt's engine. The engine went so well that Smeaton even relinquished to Boulton & Watt a contract he had obtained for the erection of an engine for Hull Waterworks. It was agreed that he was to be retained as the executive engineer, while they were to furnish the plans. The terms on which the engine was supplied were settled as follows :

1. Boulton & Watt were to be paid one-third of the savings as compared with the consumption of one of Smeaton's engines.

[1] Watt to Gilbert Mason, 1776, Sept. 13.   Office Letter Book, vol. 1. B. & W. Colln.
[2] Boulton to Charles Cook, 1776, July 26, *ibid*.
[3] Boulton to Garbett, 1776, Feb. 18, *ibid*.
[4] Watt to Smeaton, 1778, Jan. 17, *ibid*.

2. The premium was to be paid half-yearly for the term of the Act of Parliament or for so long as they shall use the engine.

3. Watt's counter (which had been invented to prevent frauds in the ascertaining of the engine's performance) was to be fixed to the beam to determine the annual number of strokes " unless the matter can be settled satisfactorily otherwise."

4. The engine was not to be removed off the premises without Boulton & Watt's consent.

5. Smeaton was to be judge in all differences that might arise, and lastly

6. The purchasers were to pay the expenses of the man who would supervise the putting together of the engine, which would probably last about a month.[1]

Condition 4, referring to the removal of the engine, is one that was adopted from the very beginning. In a letter to Garbett, Boulton had stipulated that Boulton & Watt were to be given notice of the sale or removal of the engine to any other place, and that the one-third of the savings to which they were entitled was to be assessed by reference to the value of coal of such place.[2] Previously they had made it a condition that the purchaser was not to be allowed to export the engine out of the Kingdom.[3] The insertion of the last clause in the Hull agreement had apparently become necessary through the great expenses incurred by engine erectors. To an enquiry from London Boulton had answered the year before :

" We will make it compleat at this place and send it you with one man to erect it, whose expenses you must pay for, we having lost all our profits in the engine we made

---

[1] Watt to Wright, 1778, April 16. Office Letter Book, vol. 2. B. & W. Colln.

[2] Boulton to Garbett, 1776, Feb. 16, *ibid.*

[3] Watt to Burton, Wilbie, 1775, July 15.

for Messrs. Cook & Co., by the repeated journeys of ourselves and men." [1]

The engine here referred to was the third one supplied from,
or rather through, Soho. It was a small 18-in. cylinder engine
for the brewery of Cook & Co., at Stratford-le-Bow, near
London, for which an enquiry had been received as early as
June, 1775.

As this was a small engine we find Watt for the first time
giving a definite estimate. He will risk erecting it for £200,
not including the firm's profits, which were to be paid on the
usual plan.[2] The proprietors of the brewery seem to have
expressed a preference for paying a lump sum instead of the
annual premium, and Watt agreed to grant them a licence for
twenty-five years in consideration of the sum of £150. He
also undertook to erect the engine " (except the house, pit-
work, fixtures for pump, cisterns and ropes for pulling) " for
£200, and defended the profit of £150, which was considered
too great, by saying that £50 was actually for the erection
while only £100 represented the premium.[3] A further innova-
tion was a guarantee that the engine, going at ten strokes per
minute, would not consume more than three bushels of the
best Newcastle coal in eight hours, otherwise a suitable reduction in the premium was to be made. The idea of compounding
the premium into a lump sum proved convenient in the case
of small engines and was applied on several occasions afterwards. The extension of the method in later years, however,
was due to entirely different causes and will be referred to
again. The agreement concerning this engine is of a rather

---

[1] Boulton to Beckett & Jonson, 1777, March 6. B. & W. Colln.
[2] Watt to Burton & Wilbie, 1775, June 29. Office Letter Book, vol. 1,
ibid.
[3] Watt to Burton & Wilbie, 1775, July 15 and Aug. 15, ibid.

exceptional character ; for, here, the firm of Boulton & Watt definitely contracted for the supply of an engine. The somewhat crude form in which Watt puts it is as follows :

ESTIMATE.

J. Watt
> The Cylinder, the boiler, the pumps and
>   all the machinery and ironwork . £200
> The Licence for 25 years .   .   . £150

B. Wilbie
> The House, the pit-work, the fixtures
>   for pumps, the Cisterns, the Ropes
>   for pulling.

In the ordinary way, however, the arrangement for the independent supply of the different parts from the various founders and smiths was adhered to. Of these, Wilkinson was, of course, the most important and was always recommended for the supply of the cylinder. To one of the earliest enquiries from Cornwall the following reply was given : [1]

" In the foundry part we must beg leave to recommend Mr. Wilkinson of Broseley, as he has, at our instance, provided very expensive apparatus for the accurate execution of the cylinders and we believe no other person can do them so as to answer the same good purpose."

In other cases the words chosen are even more insistent, and there is no doubt that they intended Wilkinson to have a monopoly in the supply of cylinders for their engines. It is evident that up to quite a late date he actually did have by far the largest number of orders for cylinders.

The high prices that Wilkinson demanded for his castings were often objected to. He had standardised the prices, which

[1] Boulton to W. Phillips, 1777, Nov. 16. Office Letter Book, vol. 1. B. & W. Colln.

were 30s. per cwt. for cylinders and condensers and 18s. per cwt. for plain pipes unbored.[1] In addition to this the transport charges to some localities were very high, e.g. from Bersham to London they were 15s. per ton. Price apart, Wilkinson's terms were considerably stricter than those of other makers ; for he insisted on quarterly settlement without discount. Some of Boulton & Watt's customers, therefore, were led to suspect a reason for this insistence on Wilkinson, and it was necessary for them explicitly to deny that they received any commission from him for preferring him but did so merely for his superior skill,[2] a denial which can be accepted very readily if both Wilkinson's character and temperament as well as his somewhat exaggerated idea of the merit of his rôle in the engine business is borne in mind.[3] The superiority of Wilkinson's workmanship and his virtual monopoly in the necessary machines were, no doubt, the main reasons for this preference ; for, from the very first, Boulton, and probably Watt more so, were most anxious to establish a good reputation for the new engine and for the firm. Boulton's policy in business had always been " quality," while Watt, as the inventor, was naturally eager to dispel by practical proof the flood of scepticism regarding the value of the invention.

The insistence, therefore, on a high degree of workmanship on the part of all suppliers of engine parts was the natural outcome of this. This concern for their reputation is seen particularly in the many cases in which they were asked to adapt existing " common " engines to the new design. It was only in those cases where this could be done profitably from the

---

[1] Watt to Magellan, 1778, March 24. Office Letter Book, vol. 2. B. & W. Colln.

[2] Watt to John Scott, 1777, Oct. 22. Office Letter Book, vol. 1, *ibid.*

[3] Ashton, *op. cit.*, pp. 70, 75.

point of view of the buyer that they agreed. In one particular instance, in reply to an enquiry,[1] Watt, after examining in detail the comparative profitability of an adaptation and a new engine, finally advised the customer to alter the old engine, " although," he wrote, " you would not do more work in proportion to the coals, yet you would do more work and that work, though done at a greater expense of fuel by the present engine, will be more your interest than laying out a great one of new construction when the interest of the first cost would pay for the very great quantity of coals." Another proposal that was frequently made to them, namely to attach their condenser to the "common" engine, did not receive their approval. The reasons are set out in a letter to Smeaton[2] and throw an interesting light on their business policy :

" Though it might have enabled them (the miners) to have gone deeper with their engines, yet the savings of fuel would not have been great in comparison to the complete machine. . . . By tacking the condenser to engines that were not in good order, it would have ushered our engine into that country (Cornwall) in an unfavourable point of view and without such profits as would have been satisfactory either to us or the adventurers . . . and thereby curtailed our profits and perhaps our reputation. Besides, where a new machine is to be erected and equally well executed in point of workmanship and materials I cannot find by my estimates the old kind of engine of the same power can be erected materially cheaper than ours, our boiler and cylinder being so much smaller."

Another reason advanced later against the suggestion of granting licences to Cornish engineers for adapting the con-

---

[1] Watt to Cannon & Co., 1776, Aug. 30. B. & W. Colln.
[2] Watt to Smeaton, 1778, Jan. 17, *ibid.*

denser to the " common " engine [1] was that there were very few engines in Cornwall, and they could, consequently, convert them all into Soho engines in one year. They did, however, grant Smeaton permission to employ a condenser, or rather to condense the steam separately, " in such a manner as he shall judge proper." He was to keep all accruing profits to himself ; but they requested that " he does not give them to his employers," which would, of course, have been considered unfair competition on his part. They suggested that he should use the same system of premiums.

No doubt this policy of establishing and keeping up a reputation for high quality was in some degree responsible for the slow development of their market, for it made for a rigid system of supply, higher prices and delays in delivery ; but the policy certainly proved to be the right one in the long run and the fruits of it became visible many years afterwards, when, with the lapsing of the patent, the door was opened to very strong competition.

Nor were they unaware of the great value of advertising a successful new engine extensively. Boulton, of course, had employed all existing media of advertising before in his old business. Open access to Soho for all visitors has already been mentioned. In addition, printed illustrated circulars were used extensively both at home and (in French and German) abroad, while newspaper announcements were also employed. All these channels were now available to the new branch, the engine business. It is interesting to note that Watt, who is habitually represented as a very bad business man and who actually did not take much interest in the commercial side, seems to have learnt at least the value of

---

[1] Boulton to Smeaton, 1778, March 14. Office Letter Book, vol. 2. B. & W. Colln.

advertisement from Boulton; for we find him giving the following suggestions for an announcement in the newspaper to one of his customers :

"We hear from Lawton Saltworks that Mr. S. has now completed his new works on the banks of the Staffordshire Canal, which are esteemed to be the most complete in their way of any in the country ; the reservoir of brine is situated 100 yards above the brine in the pit and higher than the canal. It is filled with brine by a small Fire Engine constructed by Boulton & Watt of Birmingham, which does its business with great ease and a very small consumption of fuel." [1]

We now return to the history of the business during the early years. Although the first engine in Cornwall was working in 1777 and the Cornish business continued to be the most important one until the late eighties when it began to decline, it has been thought desirable to consider the Cornish business as a whole in a later chapter ; for although, roughly speaking, the general complexion of the business was the same until 1795, as mentioned before, yet the consequences of the penetration of Cornwall were so great in various aspects that it is best to consider first and separately the early experimental years.

The fourth engine supplied by Boulton & Watt was again a pumping unit for a colliery. It was the largest engine yet made by the firm, having a 58-in. cylinder, and was set up in 1777 at Hawkesbury Colliery, Bedworth. This engine was, as were the previous large ones, not quite satisfactory, and frequent breakdowns occurred, although it worked well enough at first. Various parts had to be renewed, such as

---

[1] Watt to Salmon (Lawton Saltworks), 1778, April 9. Office Letter Book, vol. 2. B. & W. Colln.

the valves, nozzles, and the working gear in 1778. The owners of the colliery seem to have doubted the wisdom of having erected so large an engine and frequently complained about it. Boulton & Watt answered,[1] pointing out that as their work grew and the mine went deeper a smaller engine would have gradually become overpowered, while the present large one would be equal to the task. The determination of the savings of fuel presented considerable difficulties. Trials and comparisons were constantly delayed, and it was not until two years later that the colliery owners consented, after having thoroughly overhauled their old engine, to a trial. Although they had originally considered £30 per annum a just premium, Samuel Garbett, who was appointed independent arbitrator, awarded Boulton & Watt £217 per annum as well as £275 for time past. This settlement was announced to Boulton in the only sanguine letter of Watt extant.[2] A short time afterwards the Hawkesbury people demanded to be granted the further privilege of being allowed to remove the engine to any other colliery that may be or may become their property within four miles.[3] This permission was granted.[4]

The next engine (excepting engines for Cornwall) was quite a small one, for the purpose of domestic water supply, for which an enquiry had been received from Sir Harbord Harbord in the summer of 1775. The estimate given by Watt [5] amounted to £60, but it appears that the engine was not put in hand until late in 1777. Another large engine, which had been

---

[1] Boulton & Watt to Whieldon, Parrott & Taylor, 1777, July 6. Office Letter Book, vol. 1. B. & W. Colln.

[2] Watt to Boulton, 1779, June 31. A.O. MSS.

[3] Watt to Boulton, 1779, July 7, *ibid.*

[4] Boulton to Watt, 1779, July 8. B. & W. Colln.

[5] Watt to Sir Harbord Harbord, 1775, Aug. 4. Office Letter Book, vol. 1, *ibid.*

39

contracted for as early as 1776 but which was not set to work until the beginning of 1778, was one for Peter Coleville of the Toryburn Colliery in Fifeshire, and this was erected by Lieutenant Henderson, assisted by Symington the elder.

Another engine set up in Scotland at a later date was that for Wanlockhead Mine, near Edinburgh. Enquiries for this unit had come from Gilbert Meason, one of the partners in the mine, early in 1777. At first Watt replied giving only particulars of certain technical improvements he had carried out in order to make the engine better adapted to mines.[1] The engine would now draw the same amount of water if the mine were to sink from ten to fifty or one hundred fathoms. The coal consumption between one and five would be proportionate to the depth, while from five to ten it would be in increasing proportion. In a further reply,[2] setting out the conditions for the premium, Watt first mentions that they " will fix to the beam an unerring counter that shall show with certainty the number of strokes made in any given time and which shall not be capable of being put wrong by any person who has not the key to it, and by its account we will be judged." This engine was erected by William Murdock, whose first independent job it was.

A number of other engines were erected in these years, such as the one for the Lawton Saltworks already mentioned. Two engines were made for John Scott of Shrewsbury. In 1778 engines were also erected at Richard Reynolds' Ketley ironworks, for Wilkinson at Bradley, and one at Byker Colliery ; while an engine for a colliery in Ireland was erected in 1782 and one for Walker's ironworks at Rotherham in 1783. It is

[1] Watt to Gilbert Meason, 1777, April 24. Office Letter Book, vol. 1. B. & W. Colln.
[2] Watt to G. Meason, 1777, June 4, *ibid.*

interesting to note that the importance of collieries as potential buyers of Watt's engines was not very great. Altogether only six engines for collieries were made during the first ten years, whilst from 1785 to 1800 only twenty-five more colliery engines were supplied. The reason, as a recent investigation well suggests,[1] was undoubtedly the fact that the main advantage of the new engine over the old—the saving of fuel—did not weigh greatly with the colliery owners, who used their unsaleable coal for the purpose. Therefore, the pumping engine on Watt's principle was to find a far wider market in Cornwall, where its advantage would be very apparent indeed.

Other engines very important during the first ten years, not in number, but certainly by their nature and judging by the time and attention they absorbed, were those supplied to waterworks. Of these, six were made between 1775 and 1785, and six more during the next fifteen years. It was natural that Boulton & Watt should have looked for a potential market to waterworks, whose success depended on regular working. Reliable steam power only could make the raising of water to high levels possible. Consequently Watt, as early as the beginning of 1775, while in London on patent business, took the opportunity of visiting some of the waterworks there.[2] He recorded carefully the performances of those engines he saw, and came to the conclusion that the advantages of his new engine, as well as of the adaptation of existing units to the new design, could be made apparent to the proprietors of these works.

Negotiations were soon afoot, the first being for Chelsea Waterworks, but owing to the cumbersome bureaucracy

---

[1] Ashton and Sykes, *op. cit.*, p. 40.
[2] Watt to Boulton, 1775, Jan 31. A.O. MSS.

generally prevailing in those undertakings, nothing was done in 1775. In November of the next year Boulton & Watt replied to an enquiry by Shadwell Waterworks about the terms for alterations of the existing engine.[1] If these were to be carried out at the expense of Boulton & Watt they would demand one half of the savings of fuel, while one-third only was to be paid if the customer bore the expense of the alterations. A similar reply was also sent to West Ham Waterworks. Owing to the pressure of business in Cornwall, however, these negotiations were not taken up again until the beginning of 1777, when Boulton was in London and could personally attend the Committees of the Chelsea, Shadwell and also the Richmond Waterworks. It was first agreed with the Shadwell Committee that Boulton & Watt should erect an engine at their own expense and be allowed half of the savings of fuel, " which," Boulton writes, " I think is in our favour, as I suppose the two cylinders, the piston, the condenser and the nozzles with the valves will not cost us more than £250, and I suppose the addition to our third will not be less than £50 per annum, which, at ten years' purchase, will be £500." [2] He further suggested that a clause should be included for a proportionate increase in case the Company extended the sales of water and added : " I think we should reserve powers to enter and examine their engine from time to time." It seems, however, that, later, the conditions were altered and it was understood that the Shadwell Waterworks were themselves to bear the cost of erecting the engine.

This contract proved most difficult and troublesome, and although work on the engine was begun as early as November,

---

[1] Boulton & Watt to Shadwell Waterworks, 1776, Nov. Office Letter Book, vol. 1. B. & W. Colln.
[2] Boulton to Watt, 1777, Feb. 7, *ibid.*

1777,[1] the negotiations for a settlement were not carried to a satisfactory conclusion until well into 1779. The engine was set to work in August, 1778, by Joseph Harrison, and, although the new engine on first trial consumed less than one bushel of coal per hour as compared with two with the old engine, the proprietors were not at all satisfied. They alleged that they had been put to an extra expense of £600 owing to the additional work necessary, although Boulton & Watt's bill amounted to less than £200, including £112 for goods supplied by Wilkinson.

" It is rather hard," wrote Boulton, " to work without profit and then not get paid." [2] There were also difficulties about the charges of the erectors, and Watt advised from Cornwall that only Harrison's and Cartwright's wages and travelling expenses should be charged.[3] At last the Shadwell Committee paid £150 to Matthews, Boulton's London agent, on account of a total debt of about £220 ; but, as the engine was not yet perfect and the erection of new buildings had involved them in such great additional expenditure, Boulton did not then press for payment of the whole sum.[4] Boulton was soon able to report that the engine worked well and also that it had " shortened the men's day's work, as it only works from 6 to 6," [5] but even then it was difficult to get full settlement.

The Chelsea engine, too, provided protracted and troublesome negotiations. From the very beginning certain concessions had to be made. Boulton & Watt agreed to take the average price of coal for the last five years in computing the

---

[1] Boulton & Watt to Shadwell Waterworks, 1777, Nov. 1. Office Letter Book, vol. 1. B. & W. Colln.

[2] Boulton to Watt, 1778, Aug. 27, *ibid*.

[3] Watt to Boulton, 1778, July 20. A.O. MSS.

[4] Boulton to Watt, 1778, Sept. 12. B. & W. Colln.

[5] Boulton to Watt, 1779, Feb. 2, *ibid*.

value of the savings,[1] and although they at first refused to allow the buyer to be at liberty to discontinue the use of the engine after five years and revert to the old system, on the ground that Watt had guaranteed a performance at least twice as good as the old, they later agreed even to that condition, and work on the engine was started in the summer of 1777. The erection, however, was not complete until almost two years later and to obtain payment was again a matter of considerable difficulty.

The Richmond contract was the least troublesome of all. In 1777 the Company had agreed to pay £350 for the engine [2] and work on it was started at once. The engine was set up in the summer of the following year, and Boulton was able to report [3] that the " town of Richmond is now supplied exclusively by Boulton & Watt." In this particular instance Boulton & Watt had paid for the goods furnished by Wilkinson a bill amounting to £63 15s. 10d.[4] and had then drawn on Richmond Waterworks. The bill, however, was not accepted until the Committee was perfectly satisfied with the engine's performance.

With all these engines for waterworks which, it should be mentioned, were all on the " expansive " principle, we see that the firm had considerable difficulties first in securing the contracts and then, owing to the bureaucratic nature of these enterprises, in obtaining payment. Indeed, the profits arising from these contracts do not appear to have been at all commensurate with the time and energy spent on them, especially, as we shall see later, in view of the ever-increasing demands of

---

[1] Boulton to Chelsea Waterworks, 1777, June 1.   Office Letter Book, vol. 1.   B. & W. Colln.

[2] Watt to Boulton, 1777, April 22.   A.O. MSS.

[3] Boulton to Watt, 1778, July 28.   B. & W. Colln.

[4] Watt to Boulton, 1778, July 20.   A.O. MSS.

the Cornish business. We can, therefore, only assume that the great "publicity" value attached to the supply of engines for these public-utility undertakings was the main inducement to Boulton & Watt to carry out this work.

In a similar category fall also the three engines erected between the years 1775 and 1785 for the Birmingham Canal Company. The first engine (which, incidentally, is still in working order and was actually used until 1898) was ordered in February, 1777,[1] and was set to work at the Smethwick Locks early in 1778. The engine was tested by Smeaton, and its performance was greatly admired by him. In an account of the trial which appeared in a local paper,[2] the engine's fuel consumption is given as 64 lb. of coal per hour. This compared very favourably with 194 lb. considered necessary for one of Smeaton's improved engines.

The estimate for the total cost of this engine was as follows:[3]

"CANAL ENGINE			£	s.	d.
The Cut, Embankment, etc.	.	. .	166	19	8
House and all belongings	.	. .	451	17	9½
Engine :					
Wilkinson's Bill	.	. £165	5	5	
Boiler	.	.	28	0	0
Drink, etc.	.	. .	11	8	11
Putting together and all other things	.		346	12	11½
Licence	.	. . .	105	0	0
			£1070	10	5

Perrins' chain, say 30 guineas."

[1] Watt to Wilkinson, 1777, Feb. 21. Office Letter Book, vol. 1. B. & W. Colln.

[2] *Aris's Birmingham Gazette*, 1778, April 20.

[3] Boulton to Watt, 1778, July 28. B. & W. Colln.

The proprietors were so pleased with the engine that in 1779 another was set up at Spon Lane Locks, while a third, for Ocker Hill Locks, was ordered in 1783. A great number of enquiries were received during those early years for engines for different industrial purposes; but outside Cornwall the business remained considerably limited owing to a number of circumstances.

The general position of industry in England at that time was such that the possibility of applying one of Boulton & Watt's expensive steam engines was restricted to those enterprises that had already attained a definitely capitalistic character; and these were naturally to be found only in the newer industries, such as cotton. Here, however, it was the impossibility of applying Watt's invention to produce a rotary motion that prevented the engine being widely used until the year 1782. Boulton & Watt had produced a rotary motion by setting up a Steam Wheel at Soho, but the answers to enquirers for such engines show that they were not prepared to give either estimates for, or to undertake the erection of, them. Boulton did propose in one instance [1] that if he were given a return of the annual expense of horses, horses' keep and all other incidents thereto of the silk mill for which the engine was wanted he would erect a steam wheel equal in power at " such price that the interest of the first cost, the annual supply of coal and all other expenses shall not cost him more than half the expense he is now at." Notwithstanding the attraction of this proposal nothing came of it, and there is no evidence that a steam wheel was ever erected for an outside customer. From a general point of view the range of these early enquiries is of very great interest as illustrative of the

[1] Boulton to Samuel Rowe, 1775, June 29. Office Letter Book, vol. 1. B. & W. Colln.

economic history of that period shown during a recent research.[1]

On the whole, however, the pumping units remained the most important during the first years, and the total number of engines erected outside Cornwall from 1775 to 1785 was only forty-five, which number also includes a few of the new rotary engines. Foundry and forge works were the biggest customers in England and account for seventeen engines built during that period. From the point of view of the history of the firm itself it is not until the introduction of the rotary movement that the market was considerably widened and, as we shall see later in this connection, that the range of business had any influence on the internal organisation of the firm.

Another aspect of the business which must be mentioned here is the large number of enquiries received from abroad. The first definite foreign enquiry that reached the firm was one from Van Liender, of Rotterdam. In his reply[2] Watt, after explaining the technical advantages of his engine and the terms on which they would be supplied in Great Britain, stated that they were not willing to erect engines abroad unless they were granted an " exclusive privilege " by the State concerned. He emphasised the fact that " nobody can make them here for exportation without my consent." To a later enquiry[3] he replied that the firm would build an engine for £5000 to be paid " here on delivery." Similar mention is made of the requirement of an exclusive privilege in a letter to a Paris

[1] Lord, *op. cit.*, pp. 166-80.
[2] Watt to Van Liender, 1775, July 10. Office Letter Book, vol. 1. B. & W. Colln.
[3] Watt to Fred Lewis Kaller of Silesia (then in London), 1776, Nov. 10, *ibid.* Other negotiations mentioned were with Russia—Boulton to Watt, 1779, Jan. 26, *ibid. ;* and with the State of Venice and the King of Sardinia —Boulton to Watt, 1779, Oct. 4, *ibid.*

banker, and when Baron Steinitz, the Commissioner of the Bureau of Mines of Prussia, then in London, enquired through Magellan, one of Boulton's London agents, the same reply was given. Although the correspondence with Mynheer Van Liender is extremely voluminous, nothing came of the long negotiations. That gentleman was constantly making new proposals and it became evident that he was really concerned with the technical principle of the engine only. At last, when an honorary award by a Dutch learned society had been offered as an inducement for lower terms, Boulton was moved to write :

> "As Mr. Watt and myself are engaged in the Fire-Engine as a business or profession, we do not enter ourselves candidates for honorary awards, neither do we engage in any discussion upon theories or principles." [1]

About the same time an enquiry was received for two engines for Spain from a Señor Izquedo, one for the use of the docks at Carthagena and one " to raise water to water their lands"; but although Spain was the second Continental country to obtain a Boulton & Watt engine, this was not to be until a few years later. The only foreign contracts that materialised during this period (1775-85) were for France ; and, although only three engines were supplied, the importance of these contracts as an illustration of the difficulties in the export business is so great that they deserve more detailed mention.

Jacques Constantin Perier, who had obtained an exclusive privilege to supply Paris with water in 1777, came to England to contract for a fire engine. Through Wilkinson (who, later, obtained the order for the forty miles of cast-iron pipes required)

[1] Boulton to Watt, 1778, Aug. 27. B. & W. Colln.

48

he heard of Watt's new invention and entered into negotiations with Soho after being recommended by Sir W. Chambers.[1] He tried to induce Wilkinson to supply him with one of the new engines without Watt's licence, but he did not succeed. Watt, on this occasion, wrote to Wilkinson in the following terms :

"You will see your own interests connected with ours as sole Founder where we are sole Engineers. . . . In time, by bribery and experiment, they may learn to make our engines, but without your assistance they cannot make the goods, so that among us we have them pretty safe, as I doubt not but their own interest, if they see it, will force them to agree to such terms as shall be fixed for them at the next meeting of the ' Engine Parliament ' to be held when Mr. Boulton returns." [2]

Watt thought that the firm could produce the engines more cheaply if it were the sole patentee in France. The negotiations did not proceed any further at that stage, however, as Perier had to leave for France.

In the same year the Comte d'Heronville had enquired through Magellan for an engine to be erected on the " moeres at Dunquerque," and the firm, as usual, demanded that they be granted an exclusive privilege for France. The Comte succeeded in obtaining, on April 14, 1778, an " Arrêt de Conseil " through the good offices of the Comte de Chastenet. The *arrêt* grants Boulton & Watt a patent, provided they can demonstrate to the satisfaction of an Academy Commission the superiority of their engines over the common type.[3] This trial was to be held either at Dunkirk or Paris. The Comte

---

[1] Sir W. Chambers to Boulton, 1777, April 7. B. & W. Colln.
[2] Watt to Wilkinson, 1777, May 11. Office Letter Book, vol. 1, *ibid.*
[3] Arrêt de Conseil, 1778, April 14, *ibid.* The duration was to be " pendant l'espace de quinze ans."

d'Heronville urged them to come to Paris to conduct the trial for fear of losing the patent,[1] and also intimated that he was negotiating for the sale of the " moeres " to the Dutch, in which case there would be no order for an engine as the latter preferred windmills. A short time before they obtained their decree Boulton & Watt had also received an enquiry for an engine from M. Jary, " Commissionaire du Roi pour les Mines du Nord près de Nantes en Bretagne." [2] Among the conditions on which they were prepared to supply the engine was one to the effect that Jary was to seek permission to make the trial on his engine at Nantes instead of at Dunkirk. This was obtained and the negotiations concerning the terms proceeded. M. Jary seems to have been an extremely hard and shrewd negotiator and fully justified Boulton's maxim " not to trust a French politician." He considered Boulton & Watt's price of £50 annually for 22 years, to which figure they had reduced their demand, excessive on the ground that he was the first in France to order one of their engines, especially as Boulton & Watt ran no risk, made no advance, and that all was paid by him. He had thought that they would not ask more than what would represent a capital sum of between a hundred and a hundred and fifty guineas. The stipulation regarding an increase in the premium proportionate to the price of coal, in case of a sale of the engine, met also with considerable opposition. Lastly, he impressed upon them an extremely shrewd point of business policy. They ought to

---

[1] Le Comte d'Heronville to Magellan, 1778, May 17. B. & W. Colln. : " Il est fort à craindre que ces Messieurs, faute de faire l'épreuve de leur machine, ne perdent leur privilège." He also thought that the market for colliery engines was not too good in France, because " celles qui sont sur les mines de charbon dépensent fort peu parceque le charbon y est à fort bon-marché."

[2] Magellan to Boulton, 1778, March 12, *ibid*.

consider, he wrote, that the English foundries would always have an advantage over the French for cylinders and pipes, so that nobody would have them cast in France, at least if the high price asked by Boulton & Watt would not lead the French foundries to imitate their engines, so that " keeping the proportion " Boulton & Watt would assure themselves of their privilege. The above reasoning for a monopolist price policy seems to have impressed them ; for we find Boulton agreeing [1] to reduce the premium to £20 per annum although he thought it would not pay them.

The engine was completed but there were great difficulties in the way of obtaining a passport for a ship to go to Jary's mines at Nantes. Unless they could obtain an order from the Privy Council they would have to get a neutral ship which would clear out for Ostend and then call at a port in France.[2] Such a passport was obtained through the influence of Lord Dartmouth and, when Jary had fulfilled Wilkinson's condition to pay his bill before the goods were shipped, the engine was sent off. There is no evidence that Boulton & Watt ever made any profit out of that transaction. On their own evidence and that of the firm's account books Jary never paid for his engine licence.

The second engine for France again proved unsatisfactory from the firm's point of view. Perier had returned to England in 1778 and had once more entered into negotiations with Soho. The previous year he had formed a company authorised to raise by way of shares the sum of 2,400,000 livres tournois.

The articles of this company are still in existence and are of considerable interest. The following may be mentioned here :

---

[1] Boulton to Watt, 1778, July 25. B. & W. Colln.
[2] Boulton to Watt, 1778, Jan. 22, *ibid.*

One half of the profits were to go to Perier and the other half was to be divided between all the shareholders. There were to be 2000 shares of 1200 l.t. each, and provision was made for a guaranteed interest of 5 per cent. per annum and a " prime de bénéfice " of one per cent. Coupons were therefore attached for 60 l.t. interest per annum and 12 l.t. bonus. There was a provision for new issues to be authorised on the same basis and foreigners were allowed to hold shares.

Perier had ordered two engines [1] and had expressed the desire to have the usual third of the savings compounded into a lump sum.[2] He offered Boulton & Watt twenty shares in his company (24,000 l.t.), but they showed him from calculations that their share of the savings would probably amount to £1300 per annum and that his offer was therefore not equal even to one year's payment. A further offer of twenty-five shares was again refused. Perier did not hesitate to threaten that he would order two engines of the old type, since, having a monopoly of the water supply in Paris, any extra cost would be made up by an increase in the price of water. Boulton & Watt would also, for that reason, lose the Paris market, and, finally, he even threatened to prevent their exclusive patent for France being granted. It appears that Boulton was in this way intimidated, and, being advised generally to close with Perier so as not " to bring about a general engine war," [3] he signed an agreement on the following terms :

" We are to be given directly twenty shares, each share of the value of 1,200 livres, and whenever there are any additional shares created (be they more or less) we are to have twenty more, viz. forty in all, or at our option in lieu

[1] Perier to Boulton, 1778, Nov. 24. B. & W. Colln.
[2] Boulton to d'Heronville, 1779, Jan. 9, *ibid*.
[3] Boulton to Watt, 1779, Jan. 29, *ibid*.

thereof, we are to receive the value in money, viz. £1,000 now and £1,000 more whenever there are any additional shares created."

Here again advertisement was thought important, for Boulton adds :

"This engine will raise us up to the publick view, show us in a conspicuous point of light to make our merits or our faults evident even to all Europe."

Perier would have preferred them to take shares, but Boulton's own opinions were against it, and they decided to take the first £1000 in money and the second in shares.[1]

Early in May, 1780, when 9600 l.t. had been paid, the following account was sent out from Soho :

PERIER, FRÈRE & CIE.

Dr.				Cr.
To amount of sundry articles in 1779 and 1780, including charges . . £151 2 1			1779 June 11th	By produce of a draft drawn by Mr. Boulton in favour of John Motteux, Esq., for L.T. 9,600 negotiated at 28¾d. per French Crown £383 6 8

More than a year later the remaining debt of 14,400 l.t. had not been paid, but Perier authorised Boulton & Watt to draw on him for the debt of £151 2s. 1d.[2] By the end of the year the company was in difficulties and had to raise loans in Paris ; and payment of Boulton & Watt's debt was again delayed on the ground that new shareholders had not yet approved

[1] Boulton to Watt, 1779, Feb. 2. B. & W. Colln. He shrewdly remarked : " Although the plan is a very good one, yet there may in such a publick concern arise many obstacles, which we can't foresee, and if there is no money in the purse of their Company you can have none because you cannot sue any individual."

[2] Perier to Boulton & Watt, 1781, May 27, ibid.

53

their claim. In fact it has been impossible to ascertain at what date the debt was finally settled.

The French business had thus been very far from successful, and, when in 1786 Boulton & Watt visited Paris and applied to the King for a confirmation of the Decree by His Majesty's Letters Patent, they declared that they had been discouraged in proceeding with the French business because they had been informed that certain formalities in the Decree had not been fulfilled.[1] Notwithstanding this fact and tardy payment by the Paris Waterworks, they had consented, on Wilkinson's representations, to erect an engine for the forges of Mont Cenis ; and they pointed out that they had acquired far greater experience than anybody in the making of these engines (of which they had erected about two hundred). It may seem that too much space has been devoted here to the French engines ; but it was considered important to describe the first experiences of the firm in foreign trade in some detail.

Wilkinson himself had not played too noble a part in these transactions. It was with great difficulty, it seems, that he managed to refuse Perier's demand for an engine without Watt's consent. He was indeed suspected on more than one occasion by Boulton & Watt,[2] and in 1777 Boulton had even written to Watt :[3]

"It certainly is in Wilkinson's interest to be open with us and behave as becomes a man of honour. So long as that is the case we shall, I am sure, throw every reasonable advantage in our power into his hands, but if ever he assumes the character of Judas, I will sell all my old clothes and everything else but what I will erect a foundry and everything else necessary to do without him."

[1] Copy of petition in B. & W. Colln.
[2] Boulton to Watt, 1778, Dec. 20, *ibid*.
[3] Boulton to Watt, 1777, May 3, *ibid*.

Wilkinson, however, did " assume the character of Judas " ; for he made an engine for Perier[1] a few years later, and many other piracies were to follow, undetected by Boulton & Watt until nearly twenty years afterwards.

It is interesting to note that it was at that time the practice, in some instances, for the purchaser of an engine to pay Wilkinson's bill to Boulton & Watt, who sometimes, as mentioned, had already paid it. On the whole, however, it was usual for the engine firm to forward money so received to the iron-founder. In the case of Salmon's engine for Lawton Salt-works, Boulton & Watt definitely instructed Wilkinson to charge the goods supplied to their account.[2] These isolated instances, however, made no difference to the general system ; for it was undoubtedly true that Boulton & Watt did not, in the vast majority of cases, contract for the supply of an engine at a certain figure, and the buyer was indebted to Wilkinson for any goods supplied, although the payment was sometimes effected through Boulton & Watt.[3]

In the case of Perier's first engine Wilkinson's bill was paid in shares of the Waterworks Company, and he certainly made a good bargain ; for in 1815 his heir collected £10,000 interest and principal for these shares.[4] As regards the supply of other engine parts it was in many instances left entirely in the hands of Boulton & Watt. Valves and nozzles, of course, were in almost all cases made actually at Soho ; but other parts, such as pistons, piston rods and castings, were given out to various iron-masters. Wilkinson himself seldom received

[1] Boulton to Watt, 1783, Feb. 11. B. & W. Colln.

[2] Watt to Wilkinson, 1777, Feb. 24. Office Letter Book, vol. 1, *ibid*.

[3] Watt to Wilkinson, 1777, Dec. 27, *ibid*. Has received bills to the value of £256 16s. in settlement of Peter Coleville's account with Wilkinson. Invites the latter to draw on B. & W. for the sum.

[4] Lord, *op. cit.*, p. 212.

orders for anything but cylinders and condensers. Regular suppliers of pistons were Spedding, Fisher & Co. of White-haven, to whom a trial order had been given in 1776,[1] and Spedding, Hicks, Senhouse & Co. of Seaton. Piston rods were often supplied by Jukes Coulson of London and Rother-hithe. Castings were supplied from many different sources, sometimes from Carron, Joab Parsons of Burton-on-Trent, or Nicholas Ryder of Marston Forge ; while orders for barrels for pumps were often given to Coalbrookdale. Reynolds of the Ketley Ironworks, who had installed one of their engines, supplied pipes, and Richard Dearman and Feerth were regular suppliers of castings.

The firm obtained their pig iron from Isaac Spooner of Bir-mingham or from Wright & Jesson. In a letter to Hornblower,[2] the Cornish engineer, Watt mentions that they worked only upon the best tough scrap iron made at Wednesbury which, in the bar, cost them 20s. per cwt., or upon the best gun barrel iron at the same price. He explains how their screws were made (with solid heads), and maintains that they were far stronger than the common sort, but that, owing to the extra workmanship, they were unable to sell them under 6d. per lb., adding that they " have hitherto been losers at that price." He goes on to state that " as the whole iron work we mean to execute here is at least as much labour as these screws we must charge it at the same price."

There can be no doubt, therefore, that the Soho prices were generally very high, for Watt reports from Cornwall [3] that their prices so far exceeded those on the spot that he

[1] Watt to James Spedding, 1776, June 2. Office Letter Book, vol. 1. B. & W. Colln.
[2] Watt to Hornblower, 1777, Jan. 20. Office Letter Book, vol. 1, *ibid.*
[3] Watt to Boulton, 1777, Sept. 10. A.O. MSS.

considered it advisable " to give up the manufacturing of any parts of the large engines." While in the case of Wilkinson's goods the firm did not make any profit, it is interesting to note that, as regards other parts, their usual assurance that they would not require any profit on the " initial cost " was not carried out in practice. Boulton writes : [1]

> " Dearman charges the Heating Cases 14/- per hundred, but I have charged them 16/-, for I think we should take a profit or commission upon everything we take the trouble to provide."

The criterion in this respect seems then to have been, on the one hand, the extent to which the particular part was of original design and, on the other, the actual placing of any particular order with Soho by the customer. While in the case of Wilkinson's cylinders (Boulton & Watt were, of course, rewarded for their design by the premium) the fact that the customer was in debt to Wilkinson did not justify an extra profit, any other engine parts ordered from Soho and executed according to the firm's design by any of the ironmasters ought, it was considered, to bring in a profit.

One of the most striking facts noticeable in the foregoing account of the execution of some of the earliest contracts is the long delay that occurred almost inevitably from the time the plans for an engine were first put in hand until its final successful erection. One of the reasons for this is, of course, the fact that the production of the various component parts was not under the direct control of the Soho firm and that Boulton & Watt were dependent on the speed, efficiency, technical perfection and goodwill of the many suppliers. Wilkinson was sometimes a bad offender,[2] for the nature of the parts

[1] Boulton to Watt, 1778, July 1. B. & W. Colln.
[2] Watt to Wilbie, 1776, July 23. Office Letter Book, vol. 1, *ibid.*

57

supplied by him made speed in his case doubly necessary. On the whole, however, Wilkinson's improved methods and extensive organisation proved equal to the demand for cylinders and his supply was as a rule speedy enough. For a foreign order one delay was caused through his insistence on payment in advance, and it is quite possible that similar strict conditions were responsible for other delays recorded against him. Other suppliers were often slack and the Soho firm had to take the blame for all delays; and although Boulton optimistically stated, in answer to several enquiries,[1] that they would reserve three to four months for delivery, none of the first engines were finished in that time.

Transport, too, proved difficult, and delays on that account were another obstacle to an extension of the market. The great revolution in the technique of transport had already begun, but its fruits were at the time obviated through minor difficulties; and although the Grand Trunk Canal, which was " to open up the industrial centres of Staffordshire and Worcestershire, hitherto accessible only by road," [2] was opened in 1777, the transport of cylinders to Cornwall, Boulton & Watt's most important market, was impeded by more trivial obstacles such as the size of the hatchways on ships, which were, as a rule, too small to let the cylinders pass.

Usually engine parts had to be transhipped several times before reaching their final destination. Those from Soho and the Midlands were shipped along the canal to Stourport, thence to Gloucester, Chepstow or Bristol and from there, on a coasting vessel, to their destination. Wilkinson's goods from Bradley were shipped on canal barges from the foundry and

---

[1] Boulton to J. Cross, 1776, July 3. B. & W. Colln.
[2] Brentano, L., *Geschichte der Wirtschaftlichen Entwicklung England's* (1927), vol. 2, p. 429.

those from Bersham were sent by road to Chester, whence they were shipped usually to Falmouth. Matters were further complicated by the state of war with France when English waters were full of French pirates. Ships and cargoes were always insured in London, but the captains were also given ransom money.

The lack of suitable agents to receive and forward the goods in transit was another difficulty. Here the old-established connections of Boulton & Fothergill were of value. Goods destined for Cornwall were usually shipped to John James, Boulton & Watt's agent in Bristol, who forwarded them on to their destination.[1] It seems, however, that his service was not entirely satisfactory; for we find Watt writing to Boulton in 1779 : [2]

> " . . . some more regular mode of conveyance to Bristol should be adopted and some person employed there who will advise us when he receives the goods and who also will enquire after them when they do not arrive in time."

John James became bankrupt in the summer of that year, and Watt secured John Lean, a merchant, who would take care of their business for the time being. We also find that the " unbusinesslike " Watt had some very practical suggestions to make in order to overcome the transport difficulty. He writes : [3]

> " With every parcel of goods which is sent, there should go an open note mentioning the weights and parcels and the day they went from Birmingham, with directions, that

---

[1] Boulton to Dearman, 1777, Nov. 28. Office Letter Book, vol. 1. B. & W. Colln.
[2] Watt to Boulton, 1779, Oct. 4. A.O. MSS.
[3] Watt to Boulton, 1779, Sept. 30, *ibid.*

at each change of vessel the person who forwards should mark the date of receipt and forwarding and the person at Bristol should advise Soho and Cornwall of the receipt and also of the forwarding."

It is not known, however, whether this system of checking, which would at least have done away with the ignorance of the whereabouts of cargoes, was ever adopted.

Undoubtedly the most important reason for delays in the erection of the first engines was the lack of labour, both skilled enough for the new technical inventions and steady enough for the growing factory routine. In the case of Boulton & Watt the second factor was of less importance during the early years when the quantity of goods manufactured at Soho was almost negligible ; but the lack of skilled and reliable engine erectors who could be sent out on the firm's business was very keenly felt as soon as the business was started. Not only had Boulton & Watt to make a highly complicated mechanical contrivance a successful commercial proposition in the face of the opposition of popular prejudice, professional scepticism and above all the lack of exact machinery, but they had to educate a new class of skilled worker in the engineering industry, to which task was to be added, at a later stage, that of organising this industry and its workers on the basis of the factory system. There is no evidence during the early years of any of those labour difficulties which are associated with the results of the introduction of the factory system ; and, although Boulton is often taken as one of the typical " homines novi " of the industrial revolution, there is no evidence until 1791 to show that there can be applied to the workers in the steam engine business at Soho these words of a Marxian historian : ". . . but they knew that they suffered, they saw that new men had appeared, men who, dominated by greed, had introduced a hitherto unknown inanimate power that was robbing them of their bread and was reversing all traditional institutions." [1]

We will have to decide later whether Boulton & Watt were indeed exceptional employers, or whether the absence of an extensive manufactory of steam engines during the years 1775 to 1795 is responsible for the absence of dissatisfaction among their workers. Although the records of the firm might tend to give a somewhat one-sided picture in this respect, it is a safe assumption that the balance of dissatisfaction was, during the earlier years, on the side of the employers, and it is as a strange incident that Boulton reports a strike at Hawkesbury Colliery.[2] Complaints about the lack of skilled engineers are constant, and Watt, writing to Smeaton,[3] states :

> " We wish we could join you in saying that we can easily find operative engineers who can put engines together according to plan, as clockmakers do clocks—we have yet found exceedingly few of them. . . ."

At Soho, it appears, only the partners themselves were dealing with enquiries,[4] and Watt informed a customer that " nothing in the planning way is done in my absence." [5]

The usual failing of workmen was that of drunkenness, and few were free from it. The engine erectors who gathered round Boulton & Watt were got together in different ways.

---

[1] Rothstein, Th., *Beiträge zur Geschichte der Arbeiterbewegung in England*, 1929, p. 9.

[2] Boulton to Watt, 1779, Oct. 18. B. & W. Colln. " A spirit of mutiny and rebellion seized all the colliers, they being determined to bring the ton weight down to its proper standard, and they thought the best time to do it was when the winter was so far begun that there remained not a single hundred of coals upon the bank."

[3] Watt to Smeaton, 1778, April 4. Office Letter Book, vol. 2, *ibid*.

[4] Stuart to Cross, 1776, July 30. Office Letter Book, vol. 1, *ibid*.

[5] Watt to G. Meason, 1777, Nov. 11, *ibid*.

Usually they were engine smiths who had had experience with the common engine and who were trained by Watt in the erection of the new improved machine. The principal assistant during those early years was Joseph Harrison, sometimes referred to as " faithful Joseph," who erected the first engine at Soho and some of the earliest engines, such as those at Bow, Richmond, Shadwell, and Chelsea. Though not free from the common complaint he worked better than most others, was often sent out to repair mistakes and was certainly one of the mainstays of the Soho staff. Perrins has been mentioned in connection with the Bloomfield engine. He was afterwards concerned in the erection of several others, but his name disappears at an early date. Isaac Perrins, one of his sons, however, was later employed by the firm. Other names of workmen at Soho were Johnson, Dickson and Horton, smiths employed in the engine yard, while Peplo, Cartwright, Law, Carless and Webb were employed as engine erectors. Most of these were given to drink in a greater or less degree, and much delay in the erection of engines and damage to those already erected resulted. Even the tolerant Boulton was often moved to strong terms, and the following is a typical instance of complaints that were usually made : [1]

" Sam Evans and young Perrins at Bedworth are two drunken, idle, stupid, careless, conceited rascals and have used the engine and their masters so ill that they wish to change them, but these two fellows say, and their masters seem to believe, that it requires the learning and knowledge of a University man to keep an engine in order."

William Murdock is the most important of those assistants who joined the staff a few years later, and he quickly gained a very prominent position in the firm. The story or rather

[1] Boulton to Watt, 1778, Sept. 1. B. & W. Colln.

legend of Murdock's "Timmer Hat" and ensuing acquaintance with Boulton & Watt has often been told. Whatever
there may be in it, it is doubtlessly true that already in 1777,
the year of his entry into the business, both partners were
impressed with his ability. He was soon sent out on important and independent jobs, and the customers, too, were not
slow in recognising his capability and often definitely demanded
his services. Another important assistant was Lieutenant
Logan Henderson. He had offered Boulton an invention for
creating a circular motion and, although it was never proceeded
with, he himself joined the firm and until 1783 did very
valuable work. A number of other engineers were connected
with the firm in the Cornish contracts and these will be mentioned later; but apart from engineers, clerks and draughtsmen
were also difficult to get. Pearson and Buchanan were cashier
and clerk respectively. Pearson remained with the firm until
1817 when he retired on a pension, and, although during the
first few years Watt complained that he "does not understand
our business," [1] he was an extremely capable employee if one
is to judge him by the books he kept.

Very early Watt had found pressure of work very great,
for not only had he to leave Soho very often but he had also
to produce all the plans. Boulton often urged him to get
assistants. Playfair, who had acted alternately as draughtsman,
engineer and clerk, was not very capable and left the firm in
1781. The next year sees John Southern at Soho as assistant
draughtsman, and he continued as a valued assistant of the firm
until his death in 1815. In 1779 James Lawson had joined
the firm. He acted first as engine erector and draughtsman
and we shall meet him again in later years as one of the firm's
most important agents.

---

[1] Watt to Boulton, 1780, Sept. 20. A.O. MSS.

Not only the outside men gave grounds for complaint through drunkenness and lack of skill. At Soho, too, things were not as yet well organised, and we find Boulton writing in 1782 : [1]

> " Our forging shop wants a total reformation ; it is worse than ever. Peplo has been drunk ever since his wife's death almost. Jim Taylour has been drunk for nine days past."

And

> " Jim Taylour has been drunk for some time past on account of a girl . . . "

It was some time until matters finally mended at Soho, for the establishment of the new factory discipline was not completed until the end of the century.

The history of rates of payment and of systems of wages used at Soho will be treated at length later. At this stage let it suffice to state that, although, even at a very early date, the comparative advantages of piece rates over time rates were discussed, most of the work-people during the period 1775-95 were paid a weekly wage. This varied for ordinary employees at Soho from 2s. 6d. for apprentices up to 20s., while engine erectors were paid anything from 10s. to 2 guineas William Murdock was paid 15s. a week when he first entered the business and two years later his wages were raised to 1 guinea. When, one year later, he applied for an increase to 2 guineas, this was not granted ; but he was given a present of 20 guineas, half of which was paid by one of the Cornish mining companies. Usually three to five years' agreements were entered into with the engine erectors (a fact which again illustrates the great scarcity of labour) and usually the agree-

[1] Boulton to Watt, 1782, March 26 and April 6. B. & W. Colln.

ment provided for a rise every year. John Webb, engine smith, who has been mentioned before, had his contract renewed in 1786.[1] He was engaged for five years with wages rising from 14s. per week during the first year to 15s. during the second and third, and 16s. during the fourth and fifth. Richard Cartwright's contract of the same year [2] provides a wage of 16s. during the five years. A usual provision in all these contracts was that regarding absence from work. In cases of justified absence no wages were to be paid, whilst for the times a worker was absent without suitable reason he was to serve his employers after the expiration of the five years' agreement, two days for each day so absented at the rate of wages payable at the time he absented himself. Normally engine erectors also got $2\frac{1}{2}$d. per mile extra when away from Soho ; and Cartwright was, in addition, allowed 2s. a week extra expenses when travelling. Apprentices were in many cases poor children of the parish who were taken on until they reached the age of 21. The usual provisions were that Boulton & Watt were to provide all food, lodging and clothing and to see that they did not become a charge on the parish. Apprentices were generally also given from 5 to 7 guineas a year.

One must emphasise the fact that, at that stage, engine erectors were paid by the customer buying the engine and not by Boulton & Watt, though in some cases the latter advanced the money and were afterwards reimbursed. Difficulties arose sometimes on that account. In one instance [3] Boulton assured his customer that " as to Joseph Harrison's time, we will not charge you more than it and his journey has cost us." In

[1] Agreement with J. Webb. B. & W. Colln.
[2] Agreement with R. Cartwright, *ibid.*
[3] Boulton to John Scott, 1777, Dec. 27. Office Letter Book, vol. 1, *ibid.*

later years it was the practice to pay the erectors and then to charge the sum on to the customer's account, a procedure largely made necessary by the changed nature of the market ; for the new customers were not like the mine-owners, who were themselves disposed to take charge of the erection, but left everything in the hands of Boulton & Watt.

The great scarcity of skilled labour is also shown by the many attempts made to " entice artificers away," and Boulton & Watt suffered greatly, especially from foreign offers to their work-people.[1] Mention must also be made of the firm's troubles with what they termed " spies " (English and foreigners, but mostly the latter) interested in the invention, who, by bribing the firm's work-people, endeavoured to discover some of the secrets of the invention. It would seem, however, that too much has been made of this : in one case, that of the crank movement, Cartwright's indiscretion is sometimes supposed to have led to Pickard's patent ; but despite Watt's strong and frequent complaints, often in hysterical language, the firm did not suffer greatly from these attempts. The reason is not far to seek. Even if the principle of the new invention had become known to a stranger he would have found it impossible to construct an engine without the combination of advantages possessed by Boulton & Watt, namely, superior technical knowledge, superior workmen and, above all, superior suppliers of the main component parts.

[1] Watt to Boulton, 1777, May 3, quoted in Smiles, *op. cit.*, p. 196.

CHAPTER THREE.

CORNWALL.

It has already been stated that Boulton & Watt had little prospect of supplying many of their engines to collieries where coals were cheap and where the saving of fuel was of little importance. The first engines, however, were all pumping units, and it was necessary, therefore, to find mines other than coal mines as a market for them. Further, it was imperative that this market should be fairly extensive and stable in order that the firm could proceed with the building up of their business on a sound basis.

That market was found in the Cornish tin and copper mines. The far-seeing Boulton had, from a very early date, this prospective market in view, for we find him writing the following : [1]

> " Mr. Papys seems very friendly disposed and promises to render us all the service he can in Cornwall. He hath given me a list of all ye engines in that county with their respective names, which I have deposited amongst the archives of our Engine. The whole number in the County of Cornwall are exactly forty, but there are only eighteen of 'em in work on account of ye high price of coals."

and some years later Watt refers to Cornwall as " our richest mine." [2]

[1] Boulton to Watt, probably 1775, Sept. A.O. MSS.
[2] Watt to Smeaton, 1778, Jan. 17. Office Letter Book, vol. 1. B. & W. Colln.

By the end of the eighteenth century, the drainage of the mines in Cornwall had become a very difficult problem, and the contrivance most widely used, and most effectual at the time, was still the old water wheel.[1] Steam power had, of course, already started to penetrate the industry, and New-comen's fire engine was certainly in use very early in the eighteenth century. The power of the machine was, however, as yet insufficient and, what was most important, the expense of working it, especially in deep sinkings, was enormous, owing to the high price of coal. It is natural to find, there-fore, that the adventurers [2] in the Cornish mines were con-stantly on the look-out for an improved machine, and, in the middle of 1776, a deputation came to Soho less for the purpose of negotiating the purchase of a Watt engine than for that of gleaning some information about the new invention.

Enquiries soon followed, and in the same year Watt reports the first of these to Wilkinson.[3] This was from Thomas Dudley, an engineer in Cornwall; and Boulton & Watt showed the importance they attached to the new potential market by announcing their willingness to depart from their usual terms. Where a shaft was already sunk, for " otherwise it would keep us in suspense for a year or more," they were prepared to erect an engine at their own expense in order to demonstrate the improvement over the old engine, in spite of the fact " that we do not look for our profits in erecting engines . . . besides it is incompatible with our scheme in business to advance money for all the erections we make."

---

[1] Hamilton Jenkin, A., *The Cornish Miner* (1927), pp. 98, 99.

[2] " Adventurers " or " miners " is the term used at the time to describe the owners of the Cornish mines, and the term " working miners " is used to distinguish the workers from these.

[3] Watt to Wilkinson, 1776, Oct. 3.   Office Letter Book, vol. 1.   B. & W. Colln.

In order to overcome any opposition from the vested interests of local engineers, they impressed on Dudley the fact that he would promote his own interests by promoting their engines as they would endeavour not to introduce other engineers but give the local engineers preference in this province.

The same offer to erect an engine at their own expense was extended to another Cornish engineer, Jonathan Hornblower,[1] and it appears that, not having yet received an order from that county, they were extremely anxious to obtain a foothold there. A few days later (Nov. 30, 1776) the first order from Cornwall was received[2] and Watt was hopeful that soon more would follow. This order was for a 52-in. cylinder engine for Tingtang mine and was given by Hornblower, the mine's engineer. The plans for this unit were soon made and were sent on to Wilkinson for execution early the following year. The speed with which this order was dealt with indicates to some extent the importance attached to it. The distribution of the work for the various parts was clearly set out in a letter to Hornblower[3] and is worth quoting in full :

" LIST DISTINGUISHING WHERE DIFFERENT PARTS ARE TO BE MADE.

Bersham.   Inside and outside cylinder, bottoms, piston, lid and stuffing box, the condenser, cast-iron work complete.

Bradley.   The nozzles and short pipe, the gudgeon and bed, the plummer blocks and brasses, cast-iron chains for cylinders end.

---

[1] Watt to Hornblower, 1776, Nov. 8. B. & W. Colln.
[2] Watt to Boulton, 1776, Nov. 30. A.O. MSS.
[3] Watt to Hornblower, 1777, Jan. 20. Office Letter Book, vol. 1. B. & W. Colln.

Soho. The regulators brass and iron work, the plug frame, chains for condenser pumps, gearing, the buckets and clacks of condensers, two round piston rods. All the screws and burrs for the two cylinders, condensers and boiler steam pipes. Screwed ends for holding down screws, the iron work for the great piston rod top, the piston rod itself, three two-inch diameter adjusting screws and burrs for top of piston chains, three dtto. for pump chains (if you choose them), four screwed ends to shoot to martingale bolts.

Tingtang. The boiler, fire doors and grates, the pumps and ye appurtenances, pithead iron work, the poise beam, the pump chain, the screw bolts and arch plates for beam. The catch pins. The two glands that keep down the gudgeon. The stirrups for dto. excepting the screwed ends, which will be brought ready to shoot to the martingales. The house and all the woodwork."

Work on this engine was started at once and was speedily executed, the piston rod made by Coulson in London, for example, being ready in May, 1777. However, delays occurred in the transport of this engine on account of the small size of the hatchways on the ships, and it was not until January, 1778, that the goods reached Falmouth. The engine itself was set to work in the summer of that year.

In the meantime, however, the first enquiry from Dudley had been followed up by a second one from Thomas Wilson of Wheal Busy,[1] Chacewater. Watt, as usual, anxious to secure an order, replied in the following terms:

[1] " Wheal " is the Cornish term for mine.

"... but as we have not the happiness to be much known in Cornwall and it being our wish and intent to give every encouragement to Gentlemen adventurers in mines in your country, we will so far deviate from the terms we have established, as mentioned to Mr. Dudley, as to propose the following : We shall erect your company one of our engines of equal power to a 40-in. cylinder of the old kind on condition of our receiving two-thirds of the savings while it actually works. When our premium at that state hath augmented to what we should have got in five years by our first proposal [1] we shall permit you or the proprietors to work the engine for the remainder of the term of five years from its first erection without any premium, but the gentlemen in whose possession it then is, to become accountable for one-third of the savings as usual while the engine is worked during our patent of twenty-five years." [2]

As will be seen later, these initial proposals were seldom adopted —Tingtang mine, for instance, ordered an engine at their own expense—but it is of importance to mention the various attempts and experiments made by Boulton & Watt during the beginning of their Cornish business to ensure that the terms should be as attractive as possible. Boulton himself never doubted the eventual success of the engine in Cornwall. He was optimistic too about the gradual recovery of the copper industry. " I think," he writes on one occasion, " there will be more miners employed as the consumption at home will be greater and new markets opened abroad, and this will put adventurers in mines upon schemes of economy and therefore will have our engine in lieu of the common ones." [3]

---

[1] Watt to Hornblower, 1776, Nov. 8. Office Letter Book, vol. 1. B. & W. Colln. " If it answers, we demand the price of the articles furnished and the third of the savings for twenty-five years."

[2] Watt to Wilson, 1777, March 1, *ibid*.

[3] Boulton to Watt, 1778, July 25, *ibid*.

71

A 30-in. cylinder engine for Wheal Busy was ordered and put in hand, and this was actually the first engine erected in Cornwall. Dudley was the engineer, but Watt himself went down to Cornwall to supervise the erection, and, although his letters of that period contain constant complaints about the incapacity of the workmen, including Dudley himself, the engine, when set going in the autumn of 1777, proved an immediate success. The Tingtang engine was the second in order of erection. This engine caused a great deal of trouble and, owing to delay in the transport of the parts, the proprietors of the mine had even rejected it,[1] but in the end were persuaded to change their minds.

The distribution of the work for this engine has already been given. The reason for a great number of parts being made locally was the high price of the Soho goods as compared with those prevailing in Cornwall. Watt had made it clear that they would leave everything " which a workman would reckon a beneficial job " to be done in Cornwall. The engine was set to work at the end of July, 1778, and proved successful. Difficulties, it seems, were encountered in the attempt to get the accounts for the engine materials settled, and Boulton answered [2] the argument of the mine proprietors, who wanted to return to the original proposal of letting Boulton & Watt bear the expense of the engine and only paying for it after exhaustive trials, to the effect that the spirit of their offer to Hornblower's Company related to theirs being the first engine in Cornwall. Now that there were so many proofs of the superiority of their engine in England and also one in Cornwall (Wheal Busy), he hoped they would not keep Boulton & Watt

[1] Boulton to Turner, probably 1777, Aug. 30. Office Letter Book, vol. 1. B. & W. Colln.
[2] Boulton to Watt, 1778, July 25, *ibid*.

out of their money. Shortly afterwards Watt was in a position to forward from Cornwall Tingtang's remittance for £386 10s., which was the amount of Wilkinson's account paid by Boulton & Watt.[1] The bill for the Soho goods, however, was not settled for some time, and Boulton, justly indignant, wrote to Watt :[2]

" If it is not customary for engineers to give credit, pray why should not Tingtang pay for our work."

About that time a third engine was set to work in Cornwall.[3] This was a very large 63-in. cylinder engine for Wheal Union, belonging to Edwards & Co., which had been ordered by the company in September, 1777, for their mine at Tregurtha Downs. The original engineer for this mine was Budge, or " old Bouge " as he is often referred to. Not having the necessary confidence in Watt's engine he gave up his contract and Dudley was entrusted with the erection of this engine. The latter does not seem to have given great satisfaction for Watt continuously complains about his workmanship, and the connection with him was severed some time afterwards.

Another engine was set to work during August of that year—a reconstructed engine of Smeaton's—at Chacewater mine. Although they had repeatedly refused to consider the alteration of common engines, Boulton & Watt were eventually persuaded to adapt this large engine, retaining Smeaton's 72-in. cylinder as the outer cylinder for the one supplied by them, which had a 63-in. diameter.

The year 1778 was an extremely busy one in the development of the Cornish business, and even at the beginning of the year

[1] Watt to Boulton, 1778, Aug. 8.   A.O. MSS.
[2] Boulton to Watt, 1778, Aug. 27.   B. & W. Colln.
[3] Boulton to Watt, 1778, Sept. 1, *ibid.*

Boulton & Watt had stated that now the loss of an order was no grievance, for "we have more to do than is in our power." [1] A smaller engine with a 40-in. cylinder was set to work at the end of the year. This was the Hallamanin engine and its success was not immediate. Harrison had to be sent to Cornwall to correct certain mistakes, and trouble threatened owing to the proprietors' attempt to make Boulton & Watt responsible for the delay. The firm had not yet entered into an actual agreement with the proprietors, and Boulton thought that they would therefore have to have recourse to the original letters that passed between them.[2] He advised Watt to adopt a conciliatory attitude; for, although they were in a position to dictate the terms for engines still to be erected, they would have to make the best terms they could as regards those already finished. He impressed, however, the following arguments on the proprietors of the Hallamanin mine, arguments which illustrate Boulton & Watt's point of view and policy in all the frequent disagreements. He asked them to consider whether the damage arose from any blunder of Watt's in the plan of the engine or from the blunders of the mine's engineers; whether Boulton & Watt had undertaken to erect an engine for them, or whether the undertaking was to grant them a licence to erect one after Watt's plans and upon his principles; thirdly, whether the engine would or would not perform better than a common engine; and fourthly, whether they had not agreed to pay Boulton & Watt one-third of the savings caused by this superior performance.

Two 63-in. cylinder engines followed during the next year. The first of these was for Poldice mine, and the terms for it

---

[1] Watt to Dudley, 1778, Jan. 31. Office Letter Book, vol. 2. B. & W. Colln.

[2] Boulton to Watt, 1779, Nov. 6, *ibid.*

were settled in 1778 during Watt's stay at Redruth. They were as follows : [1]

1. Boulton & Watt were to receive one-third of the savings per month, as long as the engine was used at Poldice.
2. The premium was to increase as the strokes do, and to increase one-twelfth for every additional five fathoms of depth reached beyond sixty fathoms.
3. No extra premium was to be paid during the time of forking the pool at the beginning.
4. The books of the mine were to be liable to Boulton & Watt's inspection, and the latter were also at liberty to appoint at their own expense a supervisor or checker of coal.

Boulton & Watt further reserved to themselves the absolute power of displacing engine men, of rejecting bad coals and of inspecting and directing repairs of the engine. A new agreement was to be made if the engine was sold off the premises, and Boulton & Watt were to have a veto on the bargain. In addition to this Boulton & Watt secured the order for about £580 worth of goods, to be supplied by them and Wilkinson, and it should also be mentioned that the practice which they had only recently adopted of charging for plans and drawings was applied in this case, the sum involved being £26 5s.

The proprietors of the Poldice mine were apparently in great difficulties over their inability to drain the mine and sink it deep enough for profitable working, and were losing nearly £150 a month.[2] They were consequently very anxious to get Watt's engine, and Watt too seems to have considered this contract as one of the most important in Cornwall. He asked for speedy work, and it is interesting to note that in this

[1] Watt to Boulton, 1778, Sept. 16. A.O. MSS.
[2] Watt to Boulton, 1778, Sept. 24, *ibid.*

75

connection he advised that Murdock should be sent for " who understands patterns." [1] Budge was the engineer of the mine ; but, as he had not altered his opinion of Watt's engine, the actual erection was in the hands of James Law, one of the Soho men. The other 63-in. cylinder shipped together with the Poldice engine was that for Wheal Chance. This engine was ordered in January, 1779.[2] The proprietors were appointing Budge as their engineer, and Boulton advised Watt to require him to state that he had changed his views regarding the engine, for " it would not be prudent to trust the conduct of so important a machine into the hands of a man who has shown such manifest prejudices against it." [3]

Early in 1780 another engine was put up at "Ale and Cakes " mine which had a 58-in. cylinder. This engine was erected by Jethro Hornblower and proved a great success, a fact which shows the higher degree of skill that had by that period been acquired by the Cornish engineers and workmen. Boulton's report from Cornwall at the time was very cheerful, and he emphasised the " neatness, exactness and quietness " of the two engines at United Mines, of which the " Ale and Cakes " engine was one, and of that set up at Tresavean mine. " It seems," he said, " that they have at last succeeded in raising a spirit of emulation amongst the Cornish engine men." [4]

During the year 1780 they also secured a contract for five engines at Wheal Virgin and Wheal Maid (Consolidated Mines). These had cylinders of between 50 and 60 ins. in diameter and were all at work towards the end of 1782. Poldice mine, too, had ordered a second engine which was ready in 1782 and was referred to as " Poldice Western." Business had by

[1] Watt to Boulton, 1778, Oct. 2. A.O. MSS.
[2] Watt to Boulton, 1779, Jan. 20, *ibid.*
[3] Boulton to Watt, 1778, Dec. 26. B. & W. Colln.
[4] Boulton to Watt, 1780, Sept. 7, *ibid.*

this time increased considerably, and at the end of 1783 twenty-one engines had been erected in Cornwall by the firm ; and Watt was able to write that in the whole county only one New-comen engine remained.[1] It is really at this stage that the importance of Cornwall for Boulton & Watt engines declines ; for this year sees the introduction of the rotary movement which removed the old limitations of the market. During the following thirteen years, twenty-two engines were erected in Cornwall, and the number erected after that, until the connec-tion of Boulton & Watt with Cornwall ceased entirely, is put at eleven.[2] The total number, therefore, is fifty-five, and it is a significant fact that twenty-one of these were erected during the first six years.

One of the most interesting aspects of Boulton & Watt's business in Cornwall is the fact that there the usual difficulties, which we have previously met with in the settlement of the annual premium by ascertaining the actual savings of the engine, took a very complicated and sometimes violent form, and it is certainly not surprising that the great number of disagreements over the premiums continued to a greater or less degree throughout the whole period of Boulton & Watt's connection with the district. Not only was there the usual objection to continue paying for an engine which had already been bought ; but the very importance of the consumption of fuel, which had originally placed the Watt engine on a better competitive footing, proved to be a great obstacle to the pleasant settlement of annual royalties, measured to some extent in terms of this fuel consumption. The great advan-tage derived from the introduction of Watt's engine seemed to the miners to be obviated by the terms of payment, and we

[1] Watt to Boulton, 1783, May 18. A.O. MSS.
[2] Dickinson and Jenkins, *op. cit.*, p. 329.

77

should expect the degree of objection to them to vary with the varying fortunes of the Cornish mines.

In most cases where a Watt engine was set up it was expected to do more work than had hitherto been done, i.e. to go to greater depths and to raise more water. The comparison with the performance of the old engine, necessary to establish the amount of savings, became, therefore, more complicated, and the consumption of Watt's engine had to be compared with that of a hypothetical Newcomen engine capable of doing the same work. The actual coal consumed was easily ascertained. It was an old practice in Cornwall to measure it, owing to the requirements of the Customs authorities who allowed a drawback of the duty on sea-borne coal used in the Cornish mines. The calculations for ascertaining a ratio of comparison for the new engine with one of the old type were not only very difficult, but obviously open to objections and wrangling. Watt, however, succeeded in establishing very detailed statements of comparison based on a series of highly technical calculations.[1] The standard of comparison for each individual engine was embodied as one of the articles in each agreement. Naturally the objections on the part of the miners to this mode of assessment were great ; for the tables, based on difficult calculations, were incomprehensible to the layman and it was difficult for him to check them. Again, by their very nature the premium would be highest for those months in which the performances of the engine in pumping the water was highest ; and it was exactly in those months that the working of the mines was most expensive and least productive.

In face of the frequent suggestions to change this method,

[1] For a detailed exposition of these, see Dickinson and Jenkins, *op. cit.*, p. 332 *sqq.*

Watt adopted an intransigent attitude ; for, naturally, he took a great pride in these ingeniously devised tables which he also considered scrupulously honest. Boulton first supported him in this attitude. He would not be bullied, he wrote, out of a single sixpence by rascals, or stand the loss of reputation.[1] His inclination was not to alter the general table, for that would throw them into confusion. To him it was clear that the table was just, according to the engines from which it was deduced. The Wheal Union proprietors, objecting to the high royalties, were told that this was caused through their own mistake for not having sufficient confidence in the new invention and ordering a larger engine than was necessary. In this case, although they recognised to some extent the justice of the demands for a reduction, Boulton & Watt were exceedingly anxious not to set up a precedent in Cornwall which would affect their interests. It seems, however, that Boulton himself soon recognised the necessity of coming to terms, and, as he first expressed it in a letter to his partner, he thought they ought to secure peace and goodwill.[2]

When difficulties arose with the Wheal Chance proprietors, we find Boulton already disposed for bargaining.[3] He wanted to know Watt's idea as to how low he could go with the miners, provided they chose to pay a lump sum per annum. In his estimate, however, he wanted Watt to consider the average price of coal, the difference between the Eastern and the Western Wey, and the average quantity of water raised. At last he came to the conclusion that the tables were too complicated. " The fewer columns," he writes,[4] " and the fewer figures,

[1] Boulton to Watt, 1779, Oct. 21.   B. & W. Colln.
[2] Boulton to Watt, 1779, Nov. 6, ibid.
[3] Boulton to Watt, 1780, Sept. 11, ibid.
[4] Boulton to Watt, 1780, Oct. 2, ibid.

the less will they be puzzled and the less room for cavilling."
Boulton, as a business man, was obviously awake to the exigencies of bargaining, and he recognised the justice of the
miners' demand for the payment being made in a fixed annual
sum based on the size of the engine. Watt came round to
this view, and when Boulton reported [1] that Wheal Virgin
wanted to pay an annual sum so that they could be free " to
draw the water as deep as they pleased and as much as they
pleased," the first contract on this basis was concluded. Boulton agreed with the Consolidated Mines for an annual payment
of £2500 on the basis of £63 per month for an engine with
a 63-in. cylinder and a 9-ft. stroke and others in proportion.
The astuteness of his business policy is clearly discernible in
the letter communicating his decision to Watt.[2] Although he
had at one time thought that as the mines went deeper so
Boulton & Watt would get higher premiums on the basis of
the tables, now he had come to the conclusion that in this
case " their expenses will be greatly augmented and the mine
will consequently be less able to afford it, so I think it would
be prudent in us not to discourage these mines from continuing
during your term " (of patent). Nevertheless, he gave Watt
detailed instructions for a letter in which he was to inform
the adventurers that " they had got the better of the bargain."
But he asked him also (and this is characteristic of the opinion
he had of Watt's ability for diplomatic negotiations) : " Don't
say anything rigid in your letter about punctuality in payments,
it will be time enough when we settle the draught of the articles."

It was likely that agreement on this basis would appeal
to the mine owners, and Poldice mine and others were expected
to follow soon with a similar agreement. With Poldice mine

[1] Boulton to Watt, 1780, Oct. 7. B. & W. Colln.
[2] Boulton to Watt, 1780, Oct. 7, *ibid.*

an agreement was, in fact, arrived at shortly afterwards ; and Boulton wrote [1] that the two Poldice mines now came to about £1500 per annum. It seems that after some time the rate was reduced to £55 per month and certain minor variations were from time to time introduced. Another concession which Boulton & Watt were obliged to make in the course of their Cornish business was that regarding the clause forbidding the sale of engines. The usual fate of the engines, however, was constant removal from one mine to another, largely according to their state of comparative prosperity, and the opposition to this restriction was so strong that Boulton & Watt considered it advisable not to insist on it.[2]

Another very important problem often arising in Cornwall was the frequent opposition on the part of local engineers and the difficulty of reconciling the different vested interests in the allocation of orders and contracts. The usual practice was for each mine to have its own engineer, and we have already met some of the most important, such as Hornblower, Dudley and Budge. Often, however, these would be unwilling or unable to erect one of the new engines ; and Soho men had to be called in, either as assistants or as sole engineers. Boulton was well aware of the difficulty of dividing the work of erection in such a way that all parties would be pleased. In the case of the Consolidated Mines of Wheal Virgin the adventurers were disposed to leave the matter entirely in Boulton & Watt's hands.[3] Boulton proposed to employ for the erection of the five engines, Hornblower, Dudley, Murdock and Law, paying them a commission and wages, with Henderson to control and supervise the whole work. The adventurers were to pay to each £60, and, out of the common fund of

---

[1] Boulton to Watt, 1780, Oct. 21. B. & W. Colln.
[2] Boulton to Watt, 1780, Sept. 7, ibid.
[3] Boulton to Watt, 1780, Oct. 11, ibid.

£300 into which these sums were to be paid, the men were to receive their wages and the rest was to be divided amongst them and old Hornblower as Boulton & Watt should judge equitable.

The Cornish adventurers had, it seems, little confidence in their engineers, and Boulton reported [1] that Hornblower and Dudley had applied to Wheal Virgin without success. The adventurers argued that as Boulton & Watt had contracted to furnish plans and directions they required working engineers only, and in that capacity they were willing to employ Hornblower and Dudley, or anybody approved by Boulton & Watt, but no one else. They also insisted, and this was agreed to, that either Boulton or Watt should attend the erection in person ; [2] and an outcome of this anxiety over the care to be bestowed upon the erection of their engines was the inclusion of a further clause in the agreement stipulating that the adventurers should be entitled to adopt any improvement which Boulton & Watt might make on their engines during the term of their licence, at their own expense and without having to pay a further premium.

The question of the time of delivery was naturally a very important one for the Wheal Virgin miners, and Boulton undertook to furnish them the five engines by September of the next year, impressing on Watt and on the various suppliers the fact that this contract was very important and that " their honour and interest " were at stake. The details of the supply of the various parts received careful attention. Wilkinson was, of course, always recommended and Boulton tried to secure for Wilkinson a good share of the castings [3] but he realised

[1] Boulton to Watt, 1780, Nov. 16. B. & W. Colln.
[2] Boulton to Watt, 1780, Nov. 13, *ibid.*
[3] Boulton to Watt, 1780, Sept. 7, *ibid.*

that he would not be able to get all because of strong local competition, expecially from Derby of Truro. Some castings were done at Coalbrookdale, but did not prove satisfactory. Boulton intended to show one of the adventurers a broken pump cast at Coalbrookdale, probably to convince them of Wilkinson's superiority, but with his usual diplomacy he had to do this " accidentally " ; for, he wrote, " we must not apparently enter into parties, nor make Coalbrookdale our enemy, as they will probably pay us a better annuity than Snetshill." Again, the smith's work for the Consolidated Mines, which was left entirely in the hands of Boulton & Watt, both respecting the foundry of engines and pumps, had to be distributed in such a way as not to cause enmity ; and Boulton suggested that the brass working barrels should be made by Wilkinson and the rest divided between him and the " Dale Company, otherwise the Dale, Reynold, Philips, and Fox may think us too partial." Much of this smith's work had to be done outside Cornwall as there was a great scarcity there of skilled smiths.

However, these minor difficulties were of little importance compared with the increasing demands from the adventurers for a reduction in premiums ; and examples of the granting of such reductions are frequent until quite a late date.[1] Whenever trade was very bad or expenditure of the mines heavy, Boulton & Watt usually acceded to the requests for abatements ; for they realised that the premiums paid to them, which in time amounted to a considerable sum, were really a heavy tribute exacted from the Cornish mining industry, and however much they were justified intrinsically, the interests of good trade connections as well as the sometimes very precarious state of the mines demanded a certain degree of consideration.

[1] See Appendix VII.

There is no definite evidence regarding the total premiums received from Cornwall. In 1782 Boulton had compiled a statement of all engines erected in and out of Cornwall from which an annual income was expected.[1] The total annual income for all Cornish engines was then stated to be £2960, the highest being £720 for Dolcoath mine and the lowest £70 for Tresavean mine, but the income was expected to rise to £8560 when all the engines were working to capacity, and this sum included £2560 for the five engines at Consolidated Mines which were " erected but they will not set to work till the price of copper is advanced and the price of coals lower and certain of being supplied." A detailed statement exists [2] showing the annual receipts for the years 1780 to 1791 inclusive, the total of which is £76,000 ; while in another statement [3] it appears that from the beginning of 1781 until the end of September, 1800, £139,400 had been collected for Boulton & Watt's account by Thomas Wilson, who had become their agent in Cornwall with a commission of $2\frac{1}{2}$ per cent. These sums show the heavy burden of engine premiums on the mining industry ; but they also illustrate the extent to which Boulton & Watt's business in Cornwall had grown.

It must have been gratifying for them to see how their initial expectations had been realised ; and the importance attached to Cornwall is conclusively shown in the fact that the firm took a house in Cornwall for the use of the partners when business demanded their presence there. Watt had already in 1778 enquired about the possibility of taking a house for at least one year,[4] but it was not until two years

---

[1] Boulton to Watt, 1782, Sept. B. & W. Colln.   [2] *Ibid.*
[3] " Statement of the Commission paid Thos. Wilson at sundry times by Boulton & Watt," *ibid.*
[4] Watt to Wilson, 1778, Nov. 28. Office Letter Book, vol. 1, *ibid.*

later [1] that Boulton, during his stay in Cornwall, rented Cosgarn House, five miles from Truro and five miles from Penryn, at 15 guineas per annum. The difference in the business-like qualities of the two partners is shown most clearly in their letters reporting the progress made in Cornwall during their alternate stays. Although, of course, things there were constantly improving with time it is nevertheless a noteworthy fact that while Watt's reports during the first two years show him sometimes in a very despondent mood indeed, Boulton's later reports are of a much more cheerful and optimistic character. Reports about the incapacity of workmen, so frequent during Watt's sojourn, became less and less so; and the agreements with the various mines, which Watt had almost despaired of ever seeing concluded, were signed soon after Boulton had taken the negotiations in hand.

Smiles is certainly right in saying that Boulton knew how to handle men. This is evident from the bargains he struck and from the fact that he got the best out of the Cornish workmen when Watt's superior technical knowledge and inventive genius were apt to make him impatient and, at times, contemptuous. Boulton was, throughout, the business man; and one of the most important and, for that time, most interesting innovations which he proposed and later introduced was the manufacture for stock of duplicates of certain engine parts such as buckets and clacks for air and hot-water pumps and piston rods; " for if any misfortune should happen, the mine might be ruined before a piston rod could be made." [2] Thus the idea of manufacturing " spare parts," which would, of course, demand a certain degree of standardisation or at

[1] Boulton to Watt, 1780, Nov. 13 Office Letter Book, vol. 1. B. & W. Colln.
[2] Boulton to Watt, 1780, Nov. 18, *ibid.*

least gradation of engines, arose in this case through the peculiar necessities of the working of deep water-logged mines.

Although Boulton & Watt had originally entered Cornwall solely as suppliers of steam engines, yet the combination of the nature and the state of the copper-mining industry on the one hand, with the character of the man at the head of the commercial side of the firm on the other, was such that the connection was, in an amazingly short time, to become a very much closer one. Watt had, in 1778, occasion to report the bad state of the mines owing to the low price of ores. " Mr. Wilson," he wrote,[1] " continues in very bad spirits . . . in short, if the price of ores does not rise, Chacewater Mine will not be workable," and, he added, with a very true understanding of the position, " nothing will effect that rise so readily as the stoppage of Wheal Virgin and some others which the present price will accelerate." A short time later the first intimation of the impending new departure came when Watt reported [2] that Budge and another adventurer had given up their shares in Wheal Union and that Boulton & Watt had been invited to take them up. He pointed out that there would be no outlay except for the money required for their share of the running expenses as they became due ; for the rule was for those giving up their shares not to receive their part of the value of materials until the mine ceased working. At that time the total capital invested in the mine amounted to £6000. Boulton replied : [3]

" I should like to take some shares in some of these companies that have been evaporated to a consistency by the flying off of some of the partners, but the want of money is the want of power, of sense, and of spirits of enterprise."

[1] Watt to Boulton, 1780, July 16. A.O. MSS.
[2] Watt to Boulton, 1780, Aug. 22, *ibid.*
[3] Boulton to Watt, 1778, Sept. 1. B. & W. Colln.

However, the state of this mine continued to be very bad and the prospect of having to cease working it became menacingly real. Watt, it seems, was more eager than Boulton to obtain a foothold in some of the mines, for his early letters on the subject contain very detailed accounts of the financial organisation of some of them. Wheal Union, which comprised the Owen Vain copper mine and the Tregurtha Down tin mine, with a Watt engine, employed nearly six hundred miners, and one quarter of the shares were held by Blewett & Co. One-tenth of the shares had been given up.[1] Wheal Maid had been combined with Wheal Union, and through this combination the position had become even worse. One of the shareholders, who owned one-sixteenth, had had to sink his profits, amounting to £2000, into the mine again, and Watt considered a stoppage of the mine as very likely, in which case nearly two thousand people would be thrown out of employment.[2] Poldice mine, too, was in a bad position, and £150 a month was being lost before the setting up of the Boulton & Watt engine. Two years later, after Wheal Union had only just managed to get along with difficulty, Boulton was informed by Mr. Edwards, one of the shareholders, that unless they could raise a new corps of adventurers the mine would be given up. He again invited Boulton to take some shares in the adventure, and Henderson, who was on the spot, assured Boulton that if the mine were stopped the engine would be sold to Dolcoath mine. Boulton, who was then somewhat easier in money matters, found, no doubt, a great deal of attraction in this new field of activity for his restless interest in business. This aspect has, however, been rather over-emphasised, and the main reason for the eventual embarkation on this new

[1] Watt to Boulton, 1778, Aug. 29. A.O. MSS.
[2] Watt to Boulton, 1778, Sept. 6, *ibid.*

venture was certainly his apprehension regarding the fate of the engine business in Cornwall in case of a collapse of the copper industry.

In short, it seemed absolutely essential for him to secure the market—and Cornwall was then still by far the most important—for his engines. His opinion, as expressed at the time, was as follows : [1]

"What strikes me at this time is this : If the engine is stopped, we gain nothing. If they will sell for the value of the materials that are upon the spot and if they will accept of our payments from our monthly savings, we may venture to buy to that extent, because if the mine does not turn out profitable we may gain nothing, and if the mine does not go on at all we are sure to gain nothing, and as to Dolcoath, they may have another engine. . . . If Mr. Edwards can buy the Marezion shares for the mere value of the materials and the Marezion Corps will accept of our payment by £40 per month, which the engine will pay, then and in that case we may venture."

In other words he was prepared to have the monthly premium transformed into a share in the mine. In the end Boulton & Watt bought a one-sixteenth share in Wheal Union and this became the first instance of the new policy to take up shares in the mines. In all cases where this course had been forced upon them, through the menace of the mine closing, their position was that "in the case of stopping, we gain nothing and in the case of going on, we stand a chance of gaining without the least risk of losing." [2] In the second instance they took a share in Wheal Virgin ; but here the reason was that the mine enjoyed a good reputation and was expected to be profitable. Wilkinson too became interested and stated

[1] Boulton to Watt, 1780, April 19. B. & W. Colln.
[2] Boulton to Watt, 1780, April 28, *ibid.*

that he would take a sixty-fourth share in the mine on condition that he could be the Founder for all the plain work as well as for the engines. This, of course, was not guaranteed to him ; but as Boulton's influence secured him a large share of the orders and as the demand for shares was very great he finally took up a share in the concern without insisting on this condition. This again is an instance of a manufacturer securing some control over his market by means of taking a share in the undertaking. For Boulton & Watt it had become a definite policy to overcome difficulties with the purchasers of engines by taking themselves an interest in the mines. As a minor consideration they would " by these means . . . gain ascendancy over malicious captains," and when Boulton was invited by Sir Francis Bassett, a wealthy landlord and mine adventurer, to take up a thirty-second share in Pool mine, he consented.

By the end of the year 1780 Boulton & Watt held shares in five mines,[1] and in another mine, Polgooth, which had not been worked for twenty-five years, they later took up five sixty-fourth shares. Many of Boulton & Watt's friends were also induced to become interested, and Wilkinson and Wedgwood, too, held a similar share in the last-mentioned mine. This policy was indeed adopted by many contractors who supplied the mines with materials, and in some instances it developed into a sort of parasitism,[2] the shareholders " reserving a large part of the merchant's interest to themselves " and afterwards disposing of their share.

One of the first results of Boulton's interference in Cornish mining was the introduction of more efficient methods of internal management. This aspect had been very neglected

[1] Boulton to Fothergill, 1780, Dec. 11. A.O. MSS.
[2] Boulton to Watt, 1780, Sept. 25. B. & W. Colln.

89

indeed ; and on a very early occasion Boulton had prepared a definite agenda for a meeting of adventurers which, hitherto, it had not been the practice to do.[1] He also succeeded in abolishing the old custom of dining before the meeting and thus beginning " after the sixth glass of wine." [2] But the main trouble of the copper industry at this period was of an external nature. The price of ores had been falling for some time owing largely to the flooding of the market by the enormous output of the Parys mine in Anglesea,[3] which, having a favourable structure, could compete easily with the deep, water-logged and, therefore, expensively worked Cornish mines. The ore was easily quarried, no shafts had to be sunk, no hydraulic machinery was needed for drainage, and the mine, therefore, was able to supply the market with an enormous quantity of copper. Moreover, this mine was very efficiently managed by Thomas Williams, who seems to have been a man with a natural talent for business enterprise similar to that of Boulton. Like Boulton he made considerable use of travelling agents, both for the home and export trade, and he was also successful in finding important new uses for copper, such as for the manufacture of forged and rolled nails. He also became a customer for Boulton & Watt's steam engines, and that fact, together with the similarity of the range of their business, brought the two firms into contact. But, along with the dangerous competition from Anglesea, another very serious obstacle to the recovery of Cornish copper mining was the relation between the adventurers and the smelting houses.

The story of how the difficulty was finally overcome by the establishment of a type of combination which seems

---

[1] Boulton to Watt, 1780, Sept. 25. B. & W. Colln.
[2] Boulton to Watt, 1780, April 18, *ibid.*
[3] Hamilton Jenkin, A., *op. cit.*, p. 157.

strangely modern is largely bound up with the growing influence gained by Boulton & Watt in the industry. It is worthy of short mention (although not quite within the scope of this monograph) since it illustrates, in the first place, the great repercussions which followed the introduction of the Watt engine in Cornwall, but above all, because it throws an interesting sidelight on the growing range of the business enterprise of the steam engine firm.[1]

It was Boulton who realised most clearly that salvation could come to the Cornish adventurers only through some sort of understanding with the smelters on the one hand and with their competitors of Anglesea on the other ; and in 1785 he succeeded, after having previously discussed certain schemes with Williams and with Wilkinson, in inducing a meeting of Lords and adventurers to pass a resolution to establish a company in order " to maintain and keep the price of the copper ores at a proper standard."

The Cornish " Metal Company," as this new concern was called, resembled very closely that form of combination known as Cartel. It was formed at Truro on September 1, 1785. Of the £500,000 capital, divided into £100 shares, £130,000 was to be subscribed at once. The voting power of each individual shareholder was limited to six votes, and the Governor and thirty-six Directors were empowered to enter into agreements with any copper producing company. On the

[1] The following is based largely on the detailed research of Dr. G. C. Allen, embodied in an unpublished thesis in the Birmingham University Library, an abstract of which was published in the *Economic Journal* of March, 1923. More recently, the subject has been dealt with in Hamilton, *The English Brass and Copper Industries to* 1800 (1926), while shorter summaries are also contained in Witt Bowden, *Industrial Society in England towards the End of the Eighteenth Century* (1925) ; and Levy, *Monopolies, Cartels and Trusts in British Industry* (1927).

same day the Cornish adventurers agreed with the Metal Company to sell to it all their ores from the beginning to the expiration of the contract at such prices as the Company should direct, but with the stipulation that prices were to be so fixed as to leave a clear annual profit of £15,000 and 8 per cent. on capital, the former sum to be put aside as a Reserve Fund against all future losses.

Boulton took a considerable number of shares in the new Company, and by inducing some of his friends, such as Wedgwood, to do so also and by entering into an alliance with another powerful group of shareholders, he secured very great influence in the management of the Company, together with the power to choose twelve of the directors, of which he himself was one, and all the officials. Most of the shares were held by adventurers, many of whom were also contractors to the mines and thus already closely connected with the copper industry. The Metal Company also entered into an agreement with five smelting houses to smelt its ores at certain prices, and it proceeded to negotiate an agreement with Anglesea so as to secure complete control of the copper market. Actually a price agreement with Anglesea was reached and the markets were pooled. This agreement was originally intended to last from 1785 to 1792, but great difficulties arose during the first few years. The rise of the price of copper caused production to increase to an excessive level. The interests of the adventurers which were strongly represented in the Metal Company, were, naturally, not always those of the smelters nor, indeed, of consumers of copper generally. Stocks which could not be disposed of profitably began to accumulate and, again, owing to competition from outside English producers and from foreign producers, it was difficult ultimately to maintain the price. It was even suspected that Anglesea had broken the price agreement and undersold the Cornish Company. The new combination, so optimistically begun, had not brought the desired salvation and the mines were, in 1787, still losing large sums.

These years were critical ones in Boulton & Watt's business connection with Cornwall. As usual demands were made to them for abatement of dues ; and Boulton, although a share-holder in mines, could, as the supplier of steam engines, adopt the undoubtedly correct but somewhat long view that any such concession would only make matters worse, " because anything which could enable them to get more copper would certainly decrease the value of what is already got. . . . At present the best thing that can happen to the County is half of the mines stopping till better times, and as neither we nor anybody can dictate who shall stop, the weakest must go to the wall. . . ." [1] The workers, however, could not be expected to take this long view ; and in the years 1787 to 1789 a series of riots occurred which were, in many cases, directed against Boulton & Watt. To Boulton the only remedy seemed to be the deliberate closing down of some of the least efficient-producing units and the raising of prices by curtailing production.

All proposals for schemes involving any such measure, however, met with determined opposition, partly owing to fear of further rioting on the part of the working miners and partly for fear of throwing the great number of unemployed thus created on the parish, in which case the burden would again fall on the Lords and adventurers in the mines. Of course another very important reason for this obstinate opposition was the large capital of a fixed nature sunk in the

---

[1] Boulton to Wilson, 1787. Hamilton Jenkin, A., *op. cit.*, p. 158, quoting from manuscripts in the possession of the Royal Cornwall Polytechnic Society, Falmouth.

93

mines which, in the event of closing down, would be lost. The original agreements with the Company were therefore first rescinded and then altered considerably, and there was at one stage a suggestion, apparently emanating from Boulton, for securing the desired unity in the industry through the usually much despised Government interference. In the end the old Metal Company was reconstructed and Williams secured almost absolute control.

It would seem, however, that the recovery of the copper industry was less due to the activities of the combination than to the gradual working out of economic tendencies. Some of the weaker mines were forced to cease working, and gradually the market recovered. The inevitable consequence of this industrial crisis, to which so many modern analogies could be formed, was that the immediate, as well as the ultimate, sufferers were the working miners.

The last fifteen years of the century constitute one of the most distressing periods through which the Cornish working miner ever had to pass, and it was not until the beginning of the nineteenth century that prosperity again set in. As already stated, the Cornish Metal Company was finally wound up in 1792. The recovery of the market and the beginning of prosperity was a stimulus to the individual profit seeker and competition was restored. Boulton, whose part in this development of the industry had been so important, had, some time before 1792, begun to lose interest in mining. Cornwall as a market for Boulton & Watt's engines had considerably declined in importance, and Boulton's recently erected coining mill at Soho made him a large purchaser of copper. His interest, therefore, in the maintenance of its price and his connection with the Cornish copper industry, ceased.

This chapter must not be concluded without reference to

a somewhat similar organisation in Birmingham in which Boulton again played an important part, namely, the Birmingham Brass House. Up to 1780 Birmingham had been dependent for its brass supply on the manufacturers of Cheadle and Bristol ; and these, acting together, had often put up the price against the brassfounders. In 1780 an advance of £13 per ton was actually made, and the Birmingham brassfounders were obliged to put up the price of their products by 7½ per cent.[1] On October 9, 1780, there appeared in *Aris's Birmingham Gazette* "A Serious Address to the Merchants and Manufacturers of Hardware," urging them not to bow down to the arbitrary raising of prices by the brass manufacturers but to make their own brass instead. Aitkin, one of the earliest historians of the brass trade, suggests that Boulton was himself the author of this " Serious Address." It is, however, certain that Boulton, who was at the time in Cornwall, did not take the initiative in this matter. The author was actually Peter Capper, a copper merchant of Bristol, who had corresponded with Boulton for some time previously on the subject of copper and brass prices and their manufacture, and who later became one of the principal shareholders in Polgooth mine. He informed Boulton of the initiative he had taken in the matter,[2] and assured him that all manufacturers were ready to join in a subscription and that there would be no difficulty in raising £50,000 if needed. If Boulton approved of the idea, he asked him to take the lead in proceeding further with the scheme.

Another advertisement appeared later convening a meeting for November 28, of all interested manufacturers to consider

[1] Aitkin, " Brass and Brass Manufacture," in S. Timmins, *Birmingham and Midland Hardware District* (1866).

[2] Capper to Boulton, 1780, Nov. 2. A.O. MSS.

plans for founding a Company for the making of brass.[1] Boulton was not very favourable to the scheme. He expressed his opinion in detail when informing Watt of the invitation he had received to take over the management of this proposed new Company. " I showed him (Peter Capper)," he wrote,[2] " that all their efforts are vain and that we shall do that business for them more effectually than they could do it for themselves with £100,000, and have recommended patience for eighteen months as in that time there will, in all probability, be double the ore raised than at present in this County." To the official invitation extended to him by the above-mentioned meeting, he replied advising " the formation of a company with a capital of £20,000 divided into 200 shares to be known as the ' Birmingham Metal Company,' to manufacture brass and spelter." No shareholder was to be allowed to hold more than four shares, and each was to undertake to purchase one ton of brass per annum for each share he held. Boulton advised them to invite tenders for copper, and did not miss the opportunity of asking the privilege that, in case of equality of prices, Chacewater mine should be preferred because of superior quality and more regular supply.

The shares were oversubscribed when the list was opened in February, 1781, and soon a bonus of £5 per share was offered. Boulton's advice to extend the number of shares was rejected, and further friction arose later over the question of site. Boulton and Capper recommended Swansea as the most suitable site, but the Committee of the new Company decided on Birmingham, and the erection of the works was actually started in August, 1781,[3] on a site beside the canal, off the

---

[1] *Aris's Birmingham Gazette*, 1780, Oct. 16.
[2] Boulton to Watt, 1780, Nov. 26. B. & W. Colln.
[3] Boulton to Capper, 1781, Aug. 13. A.O. MSS.

present Broad Street. Boulton was embittered and resigned from the Committee,[1] and Capper soon followed. The Company continued with increasing success for many years, but Boulton's connection with it grew weaker as time went by. Throughout, his conduct had been of a rather selfish character ; for the advice he gave was usually coloured by his interests in the Cornish Copper Companies to which he hoped the new Brass Company would prove an important customer. The success of the Company, formed as it was by consumers, and having thus a secured market for its output, proved Boulton's gloomy prophecies of its future fate to be wrong. There is no doubt, however, that these prophecies were caused to a large extent by hurt vanity over the rejection of his advice, as well as by a certain amount of jealousy of the success of the company at a time when the Cornish Metal Company's affairs were in a very bad state.

[1] Boulton to Brass Committee, 1781, May 21. A.O. MSS.

CHAPTER FOUR.

CHANGING FORTUNES.

WE have so far followed the history of the business of
Boulton & Watt during the first ten years of the firm's existence,
but we have been concerned only with pumping engines. This
was necessary because not only were these the firm's only
product of importance during the greater part of that period,
but also because the introduction on the market of engines
other than pumping engines—rotative engines which could be
applied to a great number of industrial enterprises—definitely
marks the beginning of another era in the fortunes of the firm.
Before considering the changes following upon these technical improvements and inventions, it is necessary to deal
first with another aspect of the great difficulties which has
not yet been discussed and which presented serious problems
during the whole period so far reviewed. This was the serious
lack of capital which, perhaps, even more than all the external
difficulties attendant on the introduction and marketing of the
new engine, hampered the growth of the business and more
than once presented the partners with the prospect of immediate ruin.

Although entirely a new firm the partnership was financially,
at any rate, based on the resources and the reputation of the
already existing hardware business of Boulton & Fothergill.
The old firm had, for some time past, been working at a loss,
and in 1780 the cashier estimated that the accumulated losses

during the past ten years amounted to £11,000 on a capital of £20,000.[1] One of the reasons for this business proving so unremunerative is undoubtedly to be found in the fact that the firm had expanded its productive capacity far beyond the limits justified by the fluctuating nature of the demand for its products. The extensive foreign business in particular was anything but profitable ; and Fothergill, who was himself responsible for its development, and who had never been of too optimistic a nature, was ready to stop payment and agree to the business being wound up. Boulton was, however, averse to such a course by nature and had already entered into many and heavy commitments, especially in the new engine business, faith in which he never lost. Only the most unprofitable side of the business, that of painting and japanning, which had been carried on at an average annual loss of £500, was closed down, while the hardware side still continued to work.

In addition to all the financial stress which it experienced, the old firm had also to finance to some extent the new engine business, although Fothergill had refused to take any part in this. The expenses of the new business were heavy in spite of the fact that the manufacture of the most expensive foundry parts was not undertaken. They included first of all expenditure on materials, labour, and tools for the parts manufactured at Soho, and the travelling expenses of the partners and engine erectors. Some capital was sunk in the erection of a new forge and engine shop at Soho, while Boulton himself had already contributed £2200, paid to Roebuck and his creditors, and had, according to the terms of the partnership, borne the expenses of the patent and of all the initial experiments. In addition to his expenses Watt also drew, until

[1] Statement by Zach Walker. A.O. MSS.

the business began to pay, the sum of £330 per annum [1] which was paid by Boulton & Fothergill. Boulton's private resources were considerable, but were heavily drawn on, and of the £28,000 brought him by his wife, he was forced to sell the Patkington Estate for £15,000, and he also sold and mortgaged some of his father's property.[2] Day, Wilkinson, and Wedgwood, amongst other friends, had assisted him with loans, and his engagements were beginning to be very embarrassing. The income on those engines which had by that time been erected was small and very slow in coming in ; and difficulties were even experienced in the settlement of accounts for goods furnished.

Boulton was, at this time, banking with the London bankers, Lowe, Vere, Williams & Jennings, and he had borrowed large sums from them. In 1778, when he was in London, he attempted to settle matters. His bankers accepted his bills, but they were refused at the Bank of England.[3] Boulton found other means of placing them for the time being ; but when a week later he tried the Bank of England again unsuccessfully, he learnt that the suspicion was not against him but against Lowe, Vere & Co. The junior partner of that house, Jennings, had absconded after having accepted bills for an Irishman to the amount of £180,000 without the knowledge of his partners. When the bills became payable he took £500 and went off to France. Fortunately no run was made on the bank because it was known that at the time these transactions took place Sir Charles

---

[1] See Appendix I. The total of the sums paid to Watt by Boulton & Fothergill during the years 1776 to 1779, amounted to £1119 2s. 6½d. The following interesting item appears on the 4th of March, 1780, in Watt's private expenses account : " Cash given to a certain person by Mr. Boulton's consent for services done . . . £10 10s. od." *Muirhead Papers*, B. & W. Colln.

[2] Smiles, *op. cit.*, p. 234.

[3] Boulton to Watt, 1778, July 1. B. & W. Colln.

Raymond was a partner in the firm and therefore was responsible for his share of the losses ; but the misfortune of the banking house was great, and although Boulton considered it possible that it would pull through if the West India Fleet, on which many of its securities depended, arrived safely, he thought it desirable to look out for a new banking connection.[1]

Lowe, Vere & Co. were pressing for repayment while Boulton & Watt required greater advances for their growing business ; and Boulton urged his partner to secure the speedy settlement of all outstanding Cornish accounts. " It is better," he wrote, " to be pressing for the payment of our just debts than to be pressing and importuning cold friends to lend their money." He hoped that Watt would be able to obtain payment for the bills which he enclosed, amounting to nearly £700, but only that part of the accounts which represented Wilkinson's goods for Tingtang mine was paid shortly afterwards. To Boulton's anxious enquiry about the possibility of bankers' advances in Cornwall, Watt replied with characteristic frankness and pessimism :

" The principal banking house here is Elliot & Praed. . . . They are remarkably cautious, and I think there is not the least chance of their accepting any security we have to offer." [2]

Opinion concerning the engine was very unfavourable in Cornwall, and nobody would advance £500 on a mortgage except their friend Wilson who, however, had no money himself. If Boulton could only weather the storm for a little longer, Watt thought that the performance of the large engines, which would then be working in Cornwall, might help them to obtain a credit there. Boulton received £3000 during July, 1778, from various sources on account of his hardware

[1] Boulton to Watt, 1778, July 3. B. & W. Colln.
[2] Watt to Boulton, 1778, July 8. A.O. MSS.

business, and he succeeded, moreover, in persuading Lowe, Vere & Co. to continue his credit, though it was reduced from £14,000 to £10,000. In this way the situation was eased.[1] This credit in face of the prevailing scarcity of money was undoubtedly due to Boulton's high commercial reputation. He had always paid punctually, and as regards Lowe, Vere & Co. he had, in his own words, " never suffered them to be in advance for us 1s., and have had a resting cash in their hands of £500." At the same time, although some damage was done by a fire at Soho, only part of which was covered by insurance,[2] the financial situation became slightly better during the rest of July, and Boulton could even write that he was in a position to wait a few weeks for money.[3]

The next few months saw things getting worse again, and it soon became obvious that this day-to-day struggling would have to cease and the financial position of the firm be put on a sounder basis. Some time before, Watt had suggested that, disagreeable though the idea was to both partners, Wilkinson's often-expressed wish to become a partner in the engine firm might be considered ; for " rather than founder at sea, we had better run on shore." [4] Nothing came of this suggestion, however, and money matters continued stringent until the end of the year, when Boulton & Watt's commitment to Lowe, Vere & Co. stood at £8400,[5] a balance which the latter would not increase. Boulton had to search for someone who would be prepared to grant him a large long-term loan. He entered into negotiations with a Mr. Wiss, a rich merchant, to whom he had been introduced through one of his correspondents,

[1] Boulton to Watt, 1778, July 11. B. & W. Colln.
[2] Boulton & Fothergill to Watt, 1778, July 25, *ibid.*
[3] Boulton to Watt, 1778, July 28, *ibid.*
[4] Watt to Boulton, 1778, July 8. A.O. MSS.
[5] Boulton to Watt, 1778, Sept. 25. B. & W. Colln.

Mr. Baumgartner. The proposal was·that Wiss should advance them £7000 repayable in annuities which they were to guarantee him by assigning to him their agreement for one of the Cornish engines, the premiums on which were equal to the annuities. Wiss was not disposed to invest money in the Cornish Copper industry (that is what this plan would virtually have amounted to) unless the prospects were good and the firm of Boulton & Watt remained under some obligation.[1] The result of the negotiations was very doubtful for some time, and Boulton expressed the following opinion :

" It would be better to mortgage than sell agreements ; but all agree that money will be this winter more scarce than ever it was known." [2]

Wiss demanded a definite allotment of certain engine premiums, and his lawyer drew up a plan by which Boulton & Watt assigned over such a sum payable to Wiss per annum as was proportionate to the sum advanced, payment being made to Wiss direct by the engine owners. Naturally, Boulton & Watt objected to this plan, which would have dealt a serious blow to their reputation and authority in Cornwall, and the negotiations dragged on.

In the meantime, the monetary situation had gone from bad to worse. The old hardware firm was still losing money, and had, in addition, to bear the burden of the still unprofitable engine business ; and although Boulton had succeeded, during his stay in Cornwall, in obtaining a loan of £2000 from Elliot & Praed, the Truro bankers, which had at once been sent to London for the relief of the firm, the other obligations weighed heavily on him. Of these, the most important was the mortgage on certain engine royalties together with

[1] Baumgartner to Boulton, 1778, Sept. 17. A.O. MSS.
[2] Boulton to Watt, 1778, Dec. 17. B. & W. Colln.

the personal bonds of the two partners which had been granted to Lowe, Vere & Co. as security for the firm's debt. Watt made matters even more difficult not only by constantly demanding to be released from his personal bond to Lowe, Vere & Co.[1] which he had given very reluctantly, but also by refusing to execute any mortgage to Wiss unless it were applied in relief of the debt to Lowe, Vere & Co.[2]

The end of 1780, however, saw the beginning of a certain degree of recovery, and by May of that year, after having reached a climax, matters were soon on a fair way of being settled. Wiss demanded that Boulton & Watt should assign to him, as security for the annuities payable on the debt, a number of engines both in and out of Cornwall. At that time Boulton had received £4000 for silk reels[3] which he had manufactured for the East India Company in partnership with Rehe and the assistance of his friend Keir. Of this sum £1000 was paid to Rehe, while Boulton proposed to pay the rest, which was held by Wiss as security until the deed of assignment was executed, to Lowe, Vere & Co.[4] He hoped to get their release for £7000, i.e. to be able to prevail upon them to release Watt from his personal bond and take Boulton & Fothergill's personal security for the remaining £7000. If he succeeded, he proposed that Watt should either receive of Boulton & Fothergill one-third of £7000 or accept an assignment from Boulton for several engines to the value of such third in return for handing over to Boulton & Fothergill sufficient engines to meet the demands of Lowe, Vere & Co.

[1] Watt to Boulton, 1780, May 1. A.O. MSS.
[2] Watt to Boulton, 1779, Jan. 15, *ibid.*
[3] " Reels used in organising silk . . . which Mr. Boulton undertook, and by the assistance of the late Mr. Rehe made considerable improvements in." Watt's " Memorandum," *ibid.*
[4] Boulton to Watt, 1780, April 18. B. & W. Colln.

In May, Boulton repaid Wiss £1000, agreeing to pay him another such sum in December, 1781, and 1782, so that the annuity only amounted to £400 per annum [1] secured by a mortgage agreement between Wiss and Boulton & Watt. The latter, whose conduct throughout these negotiations had been, to say the least, very ungenerous, refused to execute this mortgage, which, in his opinion, should have been between Wiss and Boulton & Fothergill. At the same time, still concerned only for his own skin, he continued urging Boulton to obtain his release from the personal bond to Lowe, Vere & Co. Watt saw at last that any assignment which left him, the inventor of the engine, out, would be unacceptable to Wiss, and he agreed to execute a mortgage for the engines,[2] though still insisting that Wiss should accept Boulton & Fothergill's personal bond in place of his. To his demand for a release from the bond to Lowe, Vere & Co., Boulton replied that he had not been able to approach them on the matter until he had reduced their acceptance to half of Boulton & Watt's security, and this he could not do until, by executing the agreement with Wiss, he had obtained the £3000 held by the latter as security. Watt himself, he maintained, was responsible for the delay caused. He had insisted that only the Chacewater engine should be assigned to Wiss instead of several smaller ones [3] on the ground that Boulton & Watt had made concessions to the owners of Chacewater mine in order to get the premium liquidated into a fixed sum which could be put into the hands of Wiss, and when the latter had agreed to that, he had delayed the execution of a mortgage with a personal bond. However, Boulton persuaded both

[1] Boulton to Watt, 1780, May 17. B. & W. Colln.
[2] Watt to Boulton, 1780, June 9. A.O. MSS.
[3] Boulton to Watt, 1780, June 3. B. & W. Colln.

Wiss and Lowe, Vere & Co. to waive Watt's personal bond. The bankers agreed to relinquish the security they had of all the three shares in the engine business upon condition that Boulton assigned to them his own two shares. After all this, Boulton hoped that Watt would not put any more obstacles in the way of a speedy settlement, and would agree to assign to him as much of Chacewater engine as would cover the annuity to Wiss, while he would assign to Watt half of the sum upon any other engine. The agreements were at last settled, and the gradually increasing incomes from the erected engines were applied to the paying off of debts.

Throughout, Watt had failed to appreciate his, at least moral, obligation under the partnership, and his conduct had been rather shabby in the face of a partner such as Boulton. His complaints led to Boulton desiring him to take over the accounts of the firm, and one of the first things that Watt did was to arrange for all profits of the engine firm, which had hitherto been paid into Boulton & Fothergill's account, to be banked separately with the Birmingham Bank and to be applied to wiping off the debt to Lowe, Vere & Co. Pearson, who was keeping the accounts of both firms, was instructed to transfer Watt's account to the books of the engine firm,[1] and careful instructions were given regarding the keeping of accounts according to the partnership agreement.[2] The main points to be observed were as follows :

1. All expenses incurred prior to the patent were to be charged to Boulton's account.
2. As all expenses incurred in experiments on engines were to be charged to Boulton and all such engines or models were to remain his property, his account

[1] Pearson to Watt, 1782, March 2. B. & W. Colln.
[2] Watt to Pearson and Buchanan, 1782, Feb. 20. A.O. MSS.

was to be debited with the cost of all engines erected at Soho, while his account with Boulton & Fothergill was to be credited with the value of these engines " which were applied for the use of the manufactory," and with the cost of their maintenance.

3. All expenses incurred in the manufacture of engines for sale were to be charged to the respective engines, and " interest of money rents, clerks' salaries, travelling expenses, etc.," were to be charged to General Expenses.

Watt was still worried about the debts, and advised Boulton[1] to wipe off the sum he owed to Lowe, Vere & Co., either by raising money on bond or mortgage of any of his property or by selling his share in Boulton & Fothergill, or, lastly, by disposing of so much of his property in the engine as would relieve him. Watt's main concern was still to be released from any obligation on his own part. The end of the financial year 1781 found the firm again in a precarious position, and it was not until Fothergill's death in June of the following year that the financial recovery set in.[2] The income from Cornwall increased, and Boulton was able to pay off the debt to Lowe, Vere & Co. ; and, in 1784, Matthews, the firm's London agent, took over its banking.[3] The engine business was now firmly established and Watt ceased to draw his salary of £330 per annum. The main reason for this increasing prosperity is, however, to be found in the introduction of the rotative engine, and to this we must now turn.

The idea of attaching some mechanism to the steam engine for the purpose of producing a circular motion had been in the minds of both Boulton and Watt for some time, but the

[1] Watt to Boulton, 1782, March 16. A.O. MSS.
[2] Boulton to Ingram, 1782, June, *ibid.*
[3] Boulton to Matthews, 1784, Dec. 16, *ibid.*

first practical contrivance of this kind—the Steam Wheel or "rotary engine," which has already been mentioned, was never put on the market. The same idea formed at the time the general preoccupation of engineers and a great number of inventions were tried. It was to an engine of the old Newcomen type that a mechanism for rotative motion was first applied. This was done by Matthew Wasborough, a clockmaker of Bristol, who had on several occasions made nozzles for the Soho firm. He patented his invention in 1779, and in that year he set up [1] an engine at his works in Bristol with the new mechanism ; but he had to work on an engine of the old type, since Boulton & Watt would not allow him a licence for their engine with the application of his new invention.[2] In the same year he erected another engine with the new mechanism at the metal grinding mill belonging to James Pickard of Snow Hill, Birmingham.[3]

The next step in the development of the rotative motion was the introduction of the crank, and in this connection the tradition, following Smiles' biography, maintains that the invention, or rather the application of the crank to the steam engine, was stolen from Watt by James Pickard who succeeded in having it patented first. It is, however, clear from the chronology of the events as revealed by the correspondence that this was not so.[4] Wasborough replaced his own invention, which did not turn out successful, by the single crank ; [5] and it seems that Watt did not object to that, for he did not consider it a patentable improvement as it was " like taking a knife

---

[1] Wasborough to Boulton, 1779, April 3. B. & W. Colln.
[2] Dickinson and Jenkins, *op. cit.*, p. 149.
[3] Watt to Chapman, 1779, April. B. & W. Colln.
[4] The technical details are discussed at length in Dickinson and Jenkins, *op. cit.*, p. 150 *sqq.*
[5] Watt to Boulton, 1780, Nov. 19. A.O. MSS.

to cut cheese which had been made to cut bread." In 1780, however, Pickard had obtained another patent,[1] for the exploitation of which he had entered into partnership with Wasborough. It was to the granting of this patent, which combined the crank with an arrangement of counter-weights, that Watt strongly objected ; and he maintained that it was this combination which had been stolen from him. From a statement drawn up by Dick Cartwright,[2] one of the Soho workmen, it appears that Watt had been experimenting with this contrivance for some time and had actually constructed a working model at Soho. Cartwright, talking with fellow-workmen about engines at an ale-house, was guilty of an indiscretion, and in this way Pickard was alleged to have obtained knowledge of Watt's new invention.

It is difficult to ascertain the truth in this matter ; and the fact that Watt, usually over anxious to secure patents for the slightest improvement, had not done so for this, speaks certainly against him. At any rate his annoyance over Pickard's patent was quite futile, at least from a commercial point of view ; for this particular appliance proved useless and was soon abandoned. The application of the crank was considered by Watt not to be patentable ; and he threatened to use it without regard to Pickard's patent. Wasborough had offered Watt a free licence in return for the right to use the new engine for which he was willing to pay ; but Watt would not agree. In the end, Watt recognised that in attacking Pickard's patent he would set up a dangerous precedent regarding his own ; and he therefore turned his mind to other devices which would be patentable and by which he would be able to evade Pickard's

[1] Dated 23rd of Aug., 1780.
[2] "Cartwright's confession of what he told Sam Evans about the Crank Engine, 1780." B. & W. Colln.

patent. On October 25, 1781, he was granted a patent, the specification of which was signed on February 23, 1782, comprising five different mechanisms for producing a circular motion, but of these only one, the " Sun and Planet " gear method, was adopted in practice. It seems that William Murdock had some share in the invention,[1] and he was considered by Smiles, among others, as having been its original contriver.[2] The patent, however, was taken out in Watt's own name ; and there is no evidence that Murdock got any remuneration for whatever his share in the invention may have been.

Enquiries for rotative engines were very numerous at the time. As Watt expressed it : " the devil of rotations " was afoot.[3] Calculations and experiments on the new rotative engine kept him very busy during the year 1782 ; but, as he stated in reference to an enquiry for an engine for their old customer Reynolds of Ketley, he did not consider the new scheme commercially remunerative. His mind was occupied with other projects, and on July 4 of the same year, he took out an additional patent, which, among other improvements, contained the principle of the double-acting engine. The first Sun and Planet gear was applied at the end of 1782 to an engine erected at Soho the previous year to work a forge hammer ; but the first engine on the new rotative principle supplied to a customer was for Wilkinson's forge hammer at Bradley, which was set to work in March, 1783. Soon the new double-acting principle was combined with the rotative motion, and the first engine of this construction was put up at Soho at the end of 1783. The number of iron mills, however, to which

[1] Watt to Boulton, 1782, July 3. A.O. MSS.
[2] Smiles, *op. cit.*, p. 281.
[3] Watt to Boulton, 1782, Sept. A.O. MSS.

the new engine could be sold was small, and Boulton thought
that business would increase only if the engine could be introduced as a motive power in corn and flour mills. A corn
mill was therefore set up at Soho to demonstrate this application. Boulton also hoped that a considerable market could
be found for the new engine for the purpose of winding coals
or ores. As a matter of fact one of them was set up in Cornwall in 1784.[1]

An extensive field for the application of the steam engine
in this new form soon opened up, and the types of industrial
enterprises by which it was adopted grew more and more
numerous. In the year 1784 engines were erected for two
London breweries, Goodwyn & Co. and Whitbread. Another
engine erected at the same time was for an oil mill belonging
to Cotes & Jarrat at Hull ;[2] and during the next few years
engines were erected for such divers enterprises as starch
manufactories, oil mills, distilleries and, after the erection of the
Albion Mill, for corn and paper mills also. During the years
1790 to 1800, engines were erected for cotton mills and sugar
mills on the plantations : while the press of orders after 1786 was
very heavy indeed, and Watt found it increasingly difficult to
cope with the work and to find sufficient suitable men to execute
the orders. It is worthy of note as illustrating the increasing
range of the business that about the same time an unsuccessful
attempt was made by the firm to obtain a patent in the United
States.[3]

One of the main reasons for the increasing popularity of
the new engine was the performance of the Albion Steam

[1] Boulton to Watt, 1784, July 8. B. & W. Colln.
[2] Watt to Boulton, 1787, Oct. 21, quoted in Muirhead, J. P., *The
Mechanical Inventions of James Watt* (1854), vol. 2, pp. 202-3.
[3] Dickinson and Jenkins, *op. cit.*, p. 65.

Flour Mill. This enterprise deserves, therefore, a little more than passing mention.[1] The idea for this undertaking was certainly the outcome of Boulton's firm belief that corn mills would eventually prove the best customers for the new rotative engine, which, by a patent of 1784, had been still further improved through the introduction of the " parallel motion," a device for communicating the vertical motion of the piston to the angular motion of the beam. The scheme for the erection of a large steam flour mill in London was put forward as early as 1783, and Boulton & Watt at once showed great interest. The project, however, met with great opposition from those London capitalists who were approached ; and it became evident to Boulton & Watt that they themselves, in conjunction with a few interested friends, would have to find the money necessary to launch the scheme. A number of shareholders were got together, and in 1784 a charter of incorporation was applied for, the opposition being renewed with increased vigour. The millers and mealmen argued that the new undertaking would prove an unfair competitor to the existing wind and water mills and would, it was asserted, throw a great number of workers out of employment and reduce the price of bread. Boulton replied with his characteristic, well-founded academic arguments. The reasons put forward by the opposition, he maintained in a letter to Matthews,[2] could be carried back much farther :

" So all machines should be stopped, whereby men's labour is saved, because it might be argued that men were

---

[1] The history of this, virtually the first steam flour mill in England, is of considerable interest, and it awaits comprehensive reconstruction from the plentiful material available in the Boulton & Watt Collection and the Birmingham Assay Office.

[2] Boulton to Matthews, 1784, April 30. A.O. MSS.

thereby deprived of a livelihood. Carry out the argument and we must annihilate water mills themselves, and thus go back again to the grinding of corn by hand labour."

Apart from the fact that he was himself the supplier of the new motive power, he pointed, with his usual cold logic and complete detachment, to the inevitable march of scientific progress, ridiculing the inertia of an industry satisfied with existing power available to it, and conveniently forgetting that the changes following upon the introduction of the earlier inventions he enumerated, had already afforded considerable time for readjustment. Opposition to the Charter was, however, too strong, and the Albion Mill at Southwark was floated on the existing principles of partnership.

For the erection of the engine and mill work, Boulton & Watt secured the services of John Rennie, the famous engineer and builder of Waterloo Bridge. The building was in charge of Sam Wyatt, the architect, and, although it was originally proposed to set up three engines, only two were actually erected. The first engine started work on February 15, 1786,[1] and the second engine three years later in 1789 ;[2] but, although the engines had proved a technical success, the partners were dissatisfied. The cost of the erection was in excess of the estimate, and Watt in particular was worried about the prosperity of the concern. His anxieties were mainly about the commercial aspect of the undertaking, and he was afraid that the business would fail to make a profit unless capable management was forthcoming. He also found fault, and not unjustly, with the practice of making the mill a show place,[3]

[1] Rennie to Watt, 1786, Feb. 15. B. & W. Colln.
[2] Rennie to Watt, 1789, Jan. 27, *ibid.*
[3] Watt to Boulton, 1786, April 17. A.O. MSS.

and considered that the best advertisement would be to be " content with doing."

When the mill began to work its daily output was considerable ; and, as it was a large purchaser of corn,[1] the corn market was much disturbed and prices dropped to 35s. and 36s. per quarter. The concern, however, was far from being a commercial success notwithstanding its great productive capacity, which Boulton estimated to be sufficient flour per week for the consumption of 150,000 people. The mill was constantly making calls on the engine firm, and Boulton was from time to time very concerned about the bad state of the company's finance and organisation. It was doing well, however, towards the end of 1789,[2] but nine months after Boulton had been able to report that the sales per week had reached £6800,[3] the whole place was destroyed by fire. [March 2, 1791.] The suspicion that the fire was the work of incendiaries was maintained until recently,[4] but it appears that Rennie, at any rate, considered it an accident. It was very serious as far as Boulton & Watt were concerned ; for Boulton lost £6000 and Watt £3000 in the undertaking.

The general results of the Albion Mill were, nevertheless, beneficial in another respect ; for the high standard of performance obtained by Watt's engine served as a useful advertisement. Orders for engines became even more numerous than before, and the supply had to be restricted owing to the impossibility of meeting the whole demand with the organisation, the machines and above all the workmen at the firm's disposal. This 'rush of orders gave rise to an extremely im-

---

[1] Boulton to Watt, 1786, March 15. B. & W. Colln.
[2] Watt to Boulton, 1789, Oct. 1. A.O. MSS. " He (Wyatt) says the Mill sold £4000 of flour last week and is doing well."
[3] Boulton to Watt, 1790, June 26. B. & W. Colln.
[4] For a discussion of this, see Dickinson and Jenkins, op. cit., p. 167.

portant movement in the direction of standardisation ; and all the attempts at processing which we shall meet with later can be traced to these years, 1782-86. Boulton was apparently the first to realise the possibilities in this situation, and in a letter to Watt in 1782,[1] he suggests that the difficulty of building engines could be overcome by making a pattern card of them, and he thought that they should confine themselves to the standard sorts and sizes. Four years later we find Watt expressing a similar idea.[2] They would be obliged he thought to

> " methodize the rotative engines so as to get on with them at a great pace. Indeed that is already in some degree the case. But we must have more men, and these we can only have by the slow process of breeding them."

In the meantime other technical changes had been adopted. A few years before the expiration of Pickard's patent in 1794, the crank had been applied to engines, but the " Sun and Planet " gear motion continued to be used as well until 1802. The expansion of the new power in industry became greater and greater as more industries acquired a capitalist nature and were in a position to lay down capital for this expensive plant. Winding engines, too, had become more general, but the most important customers to Boulton & Watt, at the beginning of the new century, were the cotton mills.

The most significant reaction of the increased business and of the change in the nature of the market was that on the price policy of the firm. In essence Boulton & Watt still remained engineers, granting licences to work a patented contrivance erected according to their plans. In practice, however, the

---

[1] Boulton to Watt, 1782, Dec. 7. A.O. MSS.
[2] Watt to Boulton, 1786, Sept. 23, *ibid.*

number of the parts actually made at Soho increased considerably. The nature of the enterprise to which the new engine was applied rather than a change in the business of Boulton & Watt, whose status remained theoretically the same, was responsible for the change in the mode of payment adopted with the introduction of the rotative engine. The new type of customer was mainly interested in the power of the new engine, in the work which it could perform, as compared with his old sources of power, and this could no longer be measured in terms of savings of fuel nor could the premium be measured by them. The system to which recourse was then had was payment by horse-power unit. By calculations based on the load raised over a pulley by a mill-horse going at a certain pace, Watt was able to establish a standard measure of power for his engine and the customer was asked to pay on that basis. Already in 1786 we find Boulton writing that the firm now charged a premium on their engines of £5 per horse-power per annum,[1] and, some years later [1790], Watt informed the King, whom he visited at Windsor,[2] that Boulton & Watt now made engines principally for " brewers, distillers, cotton-spinners, iron men, etc." for which they were paid at the rate of £5 a year for each horse-power unit and that they made no engines under 4 h.p. He added that, although this mode of payment afforded sufficient profit on large engines, it did not do so on small ones. An interesting typical example of the way engines were sold at that time is the estimate for that supplied in 1791 to Samuel Oldknow for turning his winding machines[3] It was as follows :

[1] Boulton to Norris, 1786, Oct. 21. A.O. MSS.
[2] Watt to Boulton, 1790, June 27, *ibid.*
[3] Quoted in Unwin, G., *Samuel Oldknow and the Arkwrights* (1924), pp. 130, 131.

Estimate.	4 horses.	8 horses.
All the metal material except the boiler and the iron-work of the framing of the engine, about	£225 0 0	£320 0 0
Boiler, if of copper	40 0 0	90 0 0
Wood framing, including its iron-work, uncertain	50 0 0	77 0 0
Putting together, likewise uncertain, probably	40 0 0	53 0 0
	£355 0 0	£540 0 0

" This is exclusive of all brickwork and all timber of house and floors. Annual premium to Boulton & Watt till some time in 1800, ten horses £50—eight horses £40, but for six horses and under the premium is paid in one sum, viz. for six horses £210, and for four £140 in full."

The engine set up by Oldknow was one of 8 h.p. for which the premium was £40. From the last stipulation it will be seen that the firm had maintained their original policy of having premiums for small engines paid in one lump sum. This mode of payment was used more and more extensively, partly in consequence of the unfortunate experiences which the firm had had with their customers in Cornwall over the irritative payment of annuities, but more so because the expiration of the patent privilege was drawing nearer.

The prosperity of Soho increased greatly during the years 1782-95. Arrears of premiums from Cornwall were collected, and the income from that source alone for the years 1780-91 amounted to £76,000. Other evidence of the increasing ease of the financial situation is found in the fact that the terms of payment for engines were sometimes extended. This was the case in an agreement for a large engine with double rotary motion and spare parts which was supplied to Spain in 1791 [1] through the firm of Firmin Tastet & Co., London Merchants.

[1] Agreement with Firmin Tastet & Co., 1790, June 18. B. & W. Colln.

The total price amounted to £8412 at the works, and the engine was to be ready for shipment within twelve months. One-half of the purchase price was to be paid on delivery and the other half six months after the goods had been shipped ;[1] but more conclusive evidence for the great increase in the capital resources of the firm is to be found in the fact that in 1787 a credit of £4000 was opened for Watt's account with the London bankers, and another £1000 was paid for him to the Albion Mill.[2] There is in existence an accurate statement drawn up by the accountant Pearson in 1784,[3] which shows the accumulated profits up to that time and the balances in the partners' accounts, and is, therefore, worth quoting *in extenso* :

Statement of Profit of Boulton & Watt up to September 30, 1783, £17,681 6 6½ :

		£	s.	d.
Two-thirds to Mr. Boulton's credit		£11,787	11	0½
One-third to your credit	. .	5,893	15	6
		£17,681	6	6½

Partners' Account to :

					£	s.	d.
Watt	Cr. Balance	. . .			£4,014	13	4
Boulton	„ 1st A/c.	£9,573	11	8			
Deduct	2nd A/c.	2,610	0	6¼			
					6,963	11	1¾
Due by the company to both partners					£10,978	4	5¾

[1] There is an interesting provision regarding the workman who was to go out to erect the engine. He was to receive all travelling expenses, 25s. weekly wages and £30 gratuity on finishing the job. Furthermore, he was not to be employed on anything but this particular job, and was not to be detained longer than one year without his own and Boulton & Watt's express consent.

[2] Boulton to Matthews, 1787, Dec. 17. A.O. MSS.

[3] Pearson to Watt, 1784, March 10. B. & W. Colln.

Beginning with the financial year ending September 30, 1787, and for the fifteen years following, we possess a series of trading accounts for the Engine Manufactory [1] which, in addition to giving the realised gross profit or loss on manufacturing and figures for such important items as goods bought and sold, and wages, contain exact statements of the engines made during the respective years and of the number of men employed both in the engine yard and as engine erectors. It seems worth while to attempt an analysis of these important figures.

The composite table for the years ending 1787-94 [2] shows at first glance an almost continuous increase in all the figures exhibited, and the mere increase in the totals of the trading accounts from £6793 1s. 2¼d. in 1787 to £16,455 0s. 2d. in 1794 is an indication of the growth of the business. A real measure of the growth of business would be given by figures showing the production of engines and the number of men employed. The table for these [3] is, however, not very conclusive. During the period under review production was highest in 1792 with 26 engines and lowest in 1788 with 10 engines, the average annual production being about 16 or 17 engines. But the figures are hardly comparable year by year; for they not only include all the different types of engines manufactured, but they fail to take into account the horse-power of the different units. It is, in this connection, interesting to compare the figures for the years 1790, 1791, and 1792. In 1790, 14 engines were made, goods bought for manufacture during the year amounted to about £3340, and wages and petty cash came to £1468. During the next year the production was almost unchanged, 15 engines being made,

[1] " Order Book," *Muirhead Papers*, B. & W. Colln.
[2] See Appendix III.   [3] See Appendix II.

but the other two items had increased considerably, that for goods standing at £8400 (or more than double the previous figure) whilst wages had risen to £1914. During the next year the greatest increase of the whole period took place in the production, the number of engines made being 26. Workmen's wages rose, as would be expected, to £2600, but the figure for goods bought remained practically the same as before, i.e. £8400.

These figures become still more significant if we take into account the number of workmen employed during the respective years and the gross losses sustained. In 1790 between eighteen and twenty-four workmen had been employed in the engine yard. The next year the figure had risen to between twenty-five and thirty-eight ; and in 1792 between thirty-five and forty-two men were employed. Each of these three years shows a gross loss on manufacturing which from £762 in 1790 rose the next year to £1884 (the highest figure of the period for which records exist) and dropped again during the following year to £299, the lowest loss recorded. On the face of it, therefore, it would appear that the great rise in the value of materials bought from 1790 to 1791 was due to the fact that, although only one engine more was manufactured during the latter year, these fifteen engines must have been, on the whole, larger than those of the preceding year. This also explains the sharp rise in the number of workmen employed. During the next year [1792] production rose considerably as did the wages bill and the number of men employed, the rise of the latter not being quite so sharp ; but the fact that the materials bought amounted to practically the same sum would indicate that the 26 engines made were of smaller size.

This analysis thus demonstrates the fact that the figures

120

are not really comparable, and that we are only justified in concluding that, on the whole, there was a more or less regular rise in the amount of business done. The most striking point, however, about the accounts for these years [1787-94] is the fact that, with the exception of the year 1793 which showed a small profit, every year shows a more or less considerable loss. Here must be borne in mind the fact that these accounts exhibit merely the manufacturing losses and give no indication as to changes in the financial position of the firm. It must be remembered that the main source of income of the Soho firm lay in the royalties for engines, payable either according to horse-power or, for the older engines, according to savings of fuel. The explanation for these constant losses must, therefore, be sought in the peculiar status of the engine firm which persisted until about 1795. As Boulton & Watt were not manufacturers of steam engines they would, although many parts of engines had come to be made at Soho, pay little attention to the manufacturing side of the business. Premiums were the main thing that they were after, and it is safe to conjecture that the change in the character of the Soho business after 1795, which will be discussed later, and the attention to the organisation of a profitable " manufactory " were in large measure responsible for the change in the profit and loss figures after that date.

Again, the essential nature of the contract entered into with purchasers of engines had survived from an earlier date. Buyers were, in theory, still at liberty to have the constituent parts of engines made wherever they wished according to Watt's plans and with his licence for which the premium was paid, though in practice this liberty was seldom, if ever, exercised. One consequence, however, was that the fixing of prices for those parts which were made at Soho was not entirely under the control of Boulton & Watt. They had to pay due regard to the prices of competitors whose goods were, it is true, not of the same quality as those from Soho ; but the customer would not recognise this difference, while Boulton & Watt, anxious to secure the success of each engine, would have to lower their own prices for high quality goods which could not be manufactured elsewhere with the same precision. We have met examples of the greater expense of Soho goods even at a very early period, and it seems certain that the survival of an old price policy was responsible for the bad results of the manufactory.

The actual changes in the amounts of losses during these years are less capable of explanation. There is little if any correlation between the figures of production and the figures of losses except for the years 1792 and 1793 when production was highest, and in one of which the loss fell considerably while in the other a profit actually began to appear. On the whole, however, little can be deduced from the figures, for the loss was highest in 1791. It was in this year that the greatest rise occurred in the value of goods bought and in the number of men employed, a fact which may account for the great loss especially when we consider that, during 1793 when the first profit occurred, the number of men employed was considerably reduced.

A striking feature of these accounts is that no entries appear for engine erectors' charges. The first entry of this kind does not appear until later in 1796. The reason for this is to be found in the system of payment which prevailed. As mentioned previously, engine erectors were paid by the cus- tomers themselves, and although the practice of Boulton & Watt making the payment and getting it refunded later was more and more extended, it was not thought necessary until

1796 to pass the payments through the trading accounts. For the year ending 1795 we possess a detailed account of the wages of men erecting engines which was debited with the wages and expenses paid out by Boulton & Watt and credited with sums received on this account from the customers. It appears, however, that the rates charged to the customers were higher than those actually paid to the men, and although during that year such additional entries appear on the debit side as :

> John Varley
> Time and expenses going to Manchester,
> can be charged to nobody . . . £5 11 0

there is at the end of the year a total credit balance of £31 5s. 3d. It seems, therefore, that the firm actually gained on this particular item, and in the years following 1796, when the wages to engine erectors were passed through the trading accounts, the item on the credit side is, with one exception, always greater than that on the debit side.

The expenses for salaries did not vary very much during these eight years. They included salaries to clerks and draughtsmen, such as Southern, Pearson, Walker, Foreman, and others, the highest salary being that paid to John Southern, Watt's head draughtsman, which rose by regular increments of £10 per year from £122 10s. 0d. in 1787 to £222 10s. 0d. in 1797. Pearson's salary was about £60 per annum, and that of other draughtsmen, clerks, and juniors varied between £40 and £100 per annum.

Interesting light is thrown on the firm's method of book-keeping by the provision for interest at 5 per cent. per annum on the capital and for depreciation on buildings at the same rate. The latter item becomes very significant when it is re-called that even to-day the majority of up-to-date firms do not adopt a more scientific method of providing for depreciation. The one great shortcoming of these trading accounts rests in the fact that they do not give the actual yearly revenue or profit for the whole range of the firm's business. It has not been possible to find any evidence as to the actual amounts collected each year in premiums, and only rough guesses can be made on the basis of production figures and on that of the sums collected from Cornwall already given.[1] Only for one year do we possess an actual account of Premiums collected on Rotative Engines,[2] which may give some idea of the firm's yearly income. It is shown in full on opposite page, and includes only premiums on rotative engines and, furthermore, only those which were liquidated by a lump sum, so that those which were to be paid in annuities are not included.

The differences in the figures, which are based on £5 per h.p. per annum, can be explained by differences in the time during which the premium was computed to run according to the time of the various patents.

The information gleaned in this way on the actual financial position of the partnership is scanty beyond the clearly emerging facts that the firm's income, together with the range of business, had increased considerably during the years following the introduction of the new technical improvements, and that the firm had certainly been put on a very solid foundation by the end of our first period, the year 1795.

This is a convenient place to look back briefly on the history of the firm as it has so far been described. The fortunes of the partnership entered into in 1775 were closely bound up with changes on the technical side of the firm's product. In the capacity of consulting engineers Boulton & Watt had first

---

[1] See p. 84.
[2] " Order Book," *Muirhead Papers*, B. & W. Colln.

PREMIUM OF ROTATIVE ENGINES.

Dr.				1795.		Cr.		
To Balance	£2,060	10	3	Sept. 30 Randall & Suters, 10 horses . .	£265	10	8
				„ Yalleys, Groce & Johnson, 8 horses	245	6	8
				„ Benwell Colliery, 16 horses . .	204	13	6
				„ Jn. Taylor & Co., 4 horses . .	138	17	2
				„ Walker Colliery, 19 horses . .	227	18	3
				„ Grimshaw, Webster & Co., 16 horses .	381	2	10
				„ Roberts & Co., 20 horses . .	552	5	0
					£2,015	14	1
				By profit on Berkeley & Gloucester Canal . .	44	16	2
				N.B.—There remains a premium of £60 to be charged to Reciprocating engines for next year for this engine			
	£2,060	10	3		£2,060	10	3

supplied their pumping engines to mines and iron founders, and had found an extensive market in Cornwall. It has been shown how the penetration of the copper mining industry of that county by the steam engine led to the firm becoming involved in enterprises not essentially related to their own; and it has been ascertained how a somewhat rapid broadening in the range of business, in the face of slow returns and an initially weak financial foundation, had brought the firm into considerable monetary difficulties. More than once did ruin seem imminent and only very slowly was recovery effected, largely through the personal exertions of one of the partners. The firm's fortunes took an important turn for the better when the introduction of new technical appliances removed Cornwall from its place of pre-eminence and considerably widened the market open to their product, and when, through the nature of the system of payment adopted to suit the new inventions, the income was vastly increased and its collection put on a sound basis.

It was inevitable that sooner or later Boulton & Watt should begin the manufacture of steam engines as a whole ; and the number of articles made at Soho did actually increase during the period under review. Foundry parts, however, were still supplied from outside sources. Now, in 1795 the stage was set for the entry of the firm, in possession of abundant capital and with a firmly established reputation, upon the second phase in organisation and development.

CHAPTER FIVE.

GENERAL ACTIVITIES.

FROM 1795 a great change in the personnel of the partner-ship sets in. The two original partners begin to sever their connection with the steam engine business, and the consequences of the new administration which followed were of great importance in its future development. Before continuing the history of the manufacture of the steam engine at Soho, it is advisable to pause for a moment to consider certain aspects of the activities of the old partners which will complete the picture of them as men and of the undertaking which they had built up.

Soho was the site of a great variety of industrial enterprises which had developed from the old hardware business of Boulton & Fothergill and, to some extent, had grown through the influence of the new engine business and the new partner. If we allow ourselves to advance chronologically on our main theme, we shall find in the year 1800 a most impressive list of various styles of businesses concerned in the manufacture of various metal goods. These were all carried on at Soho, and were enterprises in which the ever active Boulton held an important share, even if they were not altogether actually his own creation. The following list, given by a contemporary writer,[1] is worth quoting in full :

[1] Shaw, *op. cit.*, vol. 2, p. 120.

" *Buttons in general*, gilt, plated, silvered, semilor, pinch-beck, platina, inlaid with steel, hard white metal, fancy compositions, mother-of-pearl, polished steel and jettina and steel tags, polished steel watch chains, patent cork screws &c. Boulton & Scale.

" *Patent latchets and buckles* : silver, strong-plated, pinch-beck and steel. Boulton & Smith.

" *Plated and silver wares* : in general for the dining table, tea table, sideboard vessels of various kinds, candlesticks, branches &c. Matthew Boulton & Plate Co.

" *Medals* in general and of various metals. By Matthew Boulton.

" *Rolled Metals* of all kinds and mixtures. By Matthew Boulton.

" *Iron Foundery* : Patent steam engines with rotative motions for mills of every kind or with reciprocating motions for pumps or mines, or for any other mechanical purposes, requiring different powers from 1-200 horses acting together. Pneumatical apparatus, large or portable for preparing medicinal airs. By Boulton & Watt & Sons.

" *Copying machines*—large for counting houses and port-able for travellers. By the sons of Messrs. Boulton & Watt under the firm of J. Watt & Co.

" *Mercantile trade* carried on in Birmingham to Europe and America. Matthew Boulton."

The firms on this list are, with two exceptions, original enterprises of Boulton. The most important is the first, which is the original hardware manufactory in which a change of partners had taken place. One undertaking, however, which must be mentioned in greater detail is the manufacture of copying machines. As the style of the partnership itself shows Watt's place in this particular enterprise was of greater pro-minence than that of Boulton, but the history of the setting up of this branch of manufacture shows again that Watt's success without any assistance from Boulton would have been doubtful.

Watt had been experimenting for some considerable time on a new method of copying letters. He himself was an indefatigable letter-writer, and in addition to his voluminous private correspondence that of the steam engine business was growing more and more difficult to manage. Enquiries were very numerous and, apart from answers to these and to customers, detailed instructions to suppliers and engineers had to be sent often several times a day. The incentive for a new invention was therefore present. In 1779 experiments were made, and at last Watt succeeded in inventing the wet copying press. By pressure writing made with mucilaginous ink was transferred on to transparent unsized copying paper which had first been moistened.

Boulton first heard of the invention in June, 1779, and soon afterwards Watt asked him to procure " a quire or two of the most evenly and whitest unsized cambric paper,"[1] which he required for his experiments. Boulton, then in London, took at once an interest in the new idea, and began to explore its commercial possibilities. He first approached the Directors of the Bank of England ; but they were afraid that the new invention would considerably facilitate forgery, and they were therefore inclined at first to use their power to suppress it. In Boulton's opinion they " behaved foolish and rude " about it, and he could not help adding : "Some of the Directors are Hogs."[2] He had, however, already evolved a plan for marketing the new machine. In his opinion the best way was to get subscribers, " Like unto a book, that is to be published,

---

[1] Watt to Boulton, 1779, June 28. A.O. MSS.
[2] Boulton to Watt, 1779, July 3. B. & W. Colln.

and then you don't expose the secret until you publish and furnish all the world at once."

He thought he could get a thousand subscribers at five guineas, a figure which he considered rather low. Watt, however, desired to have a patent first, and Boulton undertook to pay the expenses of it. He succeeded in a surprisingly short time, and on the 14th of February, 1780, the patent was granted. A partnership was formed to manufacture the patented machine, and the deed was drawn up on March 20 of the same year.[1]

The partners were Boulton, Watt and James Keir,[2] who had had a share in the silk reels contract for the East India Co. The shares were : James Watt one half, and Matthew Boulton and James Keir one quarter each, whilst the two last-named partners were to bear all the expenses of the patent. Boulton continued his efforts for obtaining a substantial number of subscribers, and although he had got a number of names, he demanded printed proposals and good specimens which he could show to prospective buyers. His handling of the whole affair in the face of the opposition and prejudice of the bankers shows once more his business genius. He proceeded to advertise the new invention by a variety of new means. He had a neat book made in which he affixed specimens of letters,

---

[1] Partnership agreement between Boulton, Watt and Keir, 1780, March 20. B. & W. Colln.

[2] James Keir was a glass manufacturer at Stourbridge. He was invited by Boulton to join the engine firm, and he went to Soho, giving up his own business. Boulton did not mention the proposed partnership again, and nothing came of it, a fact which seems to have annoyed Keir considerably. He denied Watt's statement that he had a general superintendence at Soho, and stated that he was only concerned with Rehe in the execution of the second order for silk reels for the East India Co. when Boulton was away in Cornwall. J. Keir to M. R. Boulton, 1809, Dec. 3. A.O. MSS.

drawings, and music. After having ascertained that the King was a great letter-writer, through his friend Lord Dartmouth, he had a machine shown at Court. Circulars were also issued to members of the Houses of Lords and Commons ; and Boulton demonstrated the machine at Westminster where he succeeded in arousing great interest among members of Parliament. " The Speaker," he wrote, ". . . was often obliged to send his proper officer to fetch away from me the members to vote and sometimes to make a House." [1]

Another method of advertising was to have specimens made of all conceivable kinds of writing and " to hang them up framed in the most capital coffee houses," [2] together with their copies. Several peers even, who had already subscribed, acted as advertisers for the machine : Lord Dartrie, for instance, took sixteen circulars with him to Ireland. The bankers and merchants were still opposed, but Boulton wrote :

> " I doubt not but they will subscribe, when we present at such places as Lloyd Coffee House a long catalogue of Royal, Noble, Honourable and respectable names, for all here goes by fashion." [3]

Adding, however,

> " To overcome the first prejudices, to obviate all the objections and to obtain a favourable introduction, will require considerable exertion."

It was in fact only through his own considerable exertions that the machine was successfully launched. His knowledge of the market resulted in valuable suggestions on the manufacturing side. Foreign orders for presses were coming in, and Boulton suggested that the springs should be made of

[1] Boulton to Watt, 1780, May 14. A.O. MSS.
[2] Boulton to Watt, 1780, April 18. B. & W. Colln.
[3] Boulton to Watt, 1780, April 19, *ibid.*

best steel so as to be able to bear the change of weather and climate, especially in the case of those wanted for India. He also suggested that the press could be made in the form of a table, for which he even gave sketches, and he desired Watt to contrive presses for the camp, the field, and the travellers.[1] His exertions bore fruit, and 150 machines were sold by the end of the first year while orders were still increasing. Soon the press had penetrated most counting houses; and few business offices were left without one. At Soho itself the press was adopted at once; and from 1780 onwards the letter books of the firm, in which the partners had from the very beginning made it a practice to copy all letters, contained only press copies.

Boulton's own enterprises, too, had blossomed out in a surprising manner, and, as the list shows, the number and variety of articles manufactured by him was truly remarkable. One example, not generally known, which illustrates his wide range of manufacture is that of Argand's lamps. Argand intended to commit to Boulton's care the manufacture of most parts of the lamp,[2] and it was in the Birmingham district that it was first made. But of all these manufactures, often taken up in quite a casual way and following rather the dictates of an active and restless mind than the immediate motive of a search for profit, the coining mill was the one which Boulton could call his very own and which, in fact, occupied all his time during the later years of his life. The importance of the new coinage process used at Soho is great and deserving

---

[1] Boulton to Watt, 1780, May 1. B. & W. Colln.
[2] Argand to Boulton, 1784, May 1. A.O. MSS. and correspondence from 1784 to 1786. Argand of Geneva had invented a burner of peculiar construction, which greatly increased the light and heat of the ordinary oil lamp.

of a detailed research which may be made at some future time. Some features of it at least must be mentioned here.

Boulton had from the very beginning envisaged the application of the new steam power to the stamping of money ; but the preoccupation with other business prevented him from pursuing this idea until the year 1786 when the engine business was on a fair way of becoming more and more one of routine. He then proceeded to erect a coining mill of his own design which at that time created a good deal of interest. This was done after he had executed his first order for over a hundred tons of copper coin for the East India Company. Illegal coining was at the time rampant, and Boulton conceived the idea of applying for the contract for the new Government copper coinage. Although he was not to succeed in obtaining such a contract until ten years later, he felt so confident that he began to set up the new coining mill. Erected in 1788, this mill worked in the beginning six machines, two more being added later. Each of these, in the words of a contemporary writer, " receives stamps and delivers and by the aid of only a little boy from seventy to ninety pieces of copper in one minute " ; [1] and another writer maintains that the degree of perfection is higher than that attained by " any other national money ever put into circulation." [2] All the operations were concentrated in one spot and were performed by machines which had been perfected to a very high degree. Among these operations were :

    1. Rolling the cakes of hot copper into sheets.
    2. Fine rolling the same cold in steel-polished rollers.

[1] *Birmingham Daily Post*, April 30, 1863, quoting from *Public Characters of* 1800-1801, by Sir Richard Phillips (1807).
[2] Shaw, *op. cit.*, vol. 2, p. 118.

3. Cutting out the blank pieces of coin, an operation which " could be done with greater ease and rapidity by girls than could possibly be done by strong men."

4. Operations such as shaking the coins in bags were also performed by the steam engine, and

5. The coining machines themselves, worked entirely by a few boys of 12 or 14 years of age.

There was little danger of accidents as the machine was entirely automatic. It laid the blanks upon the die and when struck displaced one piece and replaced another.

Remarkable though this early advance in the application of automatic machinery may seem, more amazing still is what can only be described as a very early anticipation of the modern organisation of manufacturing processes. In the words of the same contemporary writer : [1]

" Without any personal communication between the different classes of workmen &c. the blanks are conveyed to the rooms where they are shaken, and from thence to the coining room in boxes moving with immense velocity on an inclined plane and accompanied by a ticket of their weight." [2]

There can be no doubt that, technically, Boulton's mill had a very great productive capacity and was far superior to any other then in existence.

In anticipation of the Government contract, Boulton had also engaged Droz, a famous French die-sinker, at a high salary ; but the connection proved very troublesome and had to be dissolved.[3] The only contracts which were secured in the years following the establishment of the new mill were a

[1] *Birmingham Daily Post* quoted above.

[2] Boulton also tells us in a Memorandum in his handwriting that the mill is capable " of working night and day without fatigue to the boys, provided two sets of them work alternatively for 10 hours each." A.O. MSS.

[3] Watt's " Memorandum," *ibid.*

copper coinage for the East India Company and the Bermudas, and a silver coinage for Sierra Leone and the African Company. Later, the French revolutionary Government and the Madras Presidency were supplied, and Boulton also executed orders for a large number of provincial halfpenny tokens. At last in the year 1797 he was employed to execute a copper coinage for the British Government, which consisted of two-penny, penny, halfpenny and farthing pieces. Between 1797 and 1806 about 4200 tons of coins were issued from Soho. The new Royal Mint on Tower Hill was erected according to Boulton's plans, and the steam engines and coining machines used were made at Soho. This branch of the business occupied Boulton completely during the closing years of his life, and at a very advanced age he supplied Mints for the Russian, Spanish, Danish and Mexican Governments, and also for Bombay and Calcutta.

Notwithstanding the exacting nature of his business—it must be remembered that as far as steam engines were concerned the commercial side rested during the early years almost entirely on his shoulders—Boulton found sufficient time for a great number of activities in general commercial and industrial life, mainly, of course, connected with the Birmingham district. Even before his partnership with Watt he had assumed a leading place among Midland Industrialists ; and as early as 1773 he had earned the gratitude of the extensive silver plate trade by succeeding with his petition to Parliament for the establishment of an Assay Office in Birmingham. He was certainly not one of the many frugal, and even mean puritan industrialists usually taken as typical of the industrial revolution, and, although business interests were paramount, he was associated with many movements for a more liberal attitude towards the amusements of the workers, though usually justifying his support by these interests. Typical of the man is his support of the application for a licence for a playhouse made by Yates, the founder of the theatre in King's Street. Boulton was foremost in the endeavours to overcome the strong opposition, and one of his letters to the Earl of Dartmouth explaining his attitude is of considerable interest. After emphasising the necessity for indulging the people in amusements and the fact that these were of a far better kind than the diversions of the previous century, especially " the abominable drunkenness," he went on to give what might well be the argument of a progressive business man of to-day :

> " Of late years," he wrote, " Birmingham hath been visited much in the summer season by persons of fashion, and it is some inducement to prolong the stay when their evenings can be spent at a commodious airy theatre. This is a fact I mention from experience, and it is certainly our interest to bring company to Birmingham as it contributes much to public good, not only from the money they leave behind them, but from their explaining their wants to the manufacturers themselves, and from their correcting the taste and giving hints for various improvements, which nothing promotes so much as an intercourse with persons from different parts of the world." [1]

The petition was defeated, but when it was at last successful in 1807, two years before his death, Boulton headed the list of the five persons to whom the letters patent were granted.[2]

Of the greatest importance, however, were Boulton's activities in connection with the first attempts at association of manufacturers. When one of the earliest examples of

---

[1] Rhodes, R. C., *The Theatre Royal, Birmingham* (1924), p. 8, quoting from the Dartmouth MSS.

[2] Letters patent granted to Matthew Boulton and others for conducting a playhouse, 1807, Sept. 29. B. & W. Colln.

these, the Birmingham Standing General Commercial Committee, was formed in September, 1783, " for the purpose of watching over and conducting the public interest of this town and neighbourhood," [1] Boulton was, together with his friend Samuel Garbett, prominent in the new movement for concerted action among manufacturers. The incentive came from local interest in the proposed repeal of the embargo on the exportation of brass, but the committee soon came to concern itself with most questions affecting the common interests of Midland manufacturers, and as they considered these identical with the welfare not only of their own district but even of the whole country, they took steps to keep in touch with similar bodies formed elsewhere.

Much correspondence discussing such problems as commercial policy and labour difficulties passed between Boulton and Watt and the leading manufacturers in the new industries in the Midlands and the North, among whom Josiah Wedgwood was particularly active in his efforts to bring about the establishment of a national organisation of manufacturers. Emigration of workmen was one of the major problems with which they had to deal; and in 1784 Wedgwood in a letter to Boulton made the following interesting suggestion :

" With a little assistance from government in the alteration of some of our laws and a society formed out of the principal manufacturers in different parts of the island much of the evil of emigration might be prevented." [2]

The occasion for the formation of such a body arose under the premiership of the younger Pitt. The great increase in the Excise on dyed stuffs of cotton, the " fustian " tax as it

[1] Reports of Proceedings, etc., of the Birmingham Commercial Committee. A.O. MSS.
[2] Wedgwood to Boulton, 1784, Jan. 30. B. & W. Colln.

137

was called, roused the opposition of the cotton interests ; while fear of an extension of new Excise duties brought the other industrialists into line, especially the Midland iron-masters. Protest meetings were held all over the country and the movement received a still greater impetus by Pitt's Irish policy, which involved, with certain restrictions, equality between England and Ireland in colonial and foreign trade and, what was more important, a reduction of tariffs on manufactured goods between the two countries, to the level of that country where they were lower, which was Ireland.

Opposition to the Irish Resolutions were numerous and led at last to the formation of a united body of manufacturers. At a meeting held in the London Tavern on March 14, 1785, under the chairmanship of Sir Herbert Mackworth, it was resolved to form a " General Chamber of Manufacturers." [1] Provision was made for corresponding provincial chambers to be represented, and very detailed regulations regarding the constitution of the Chamber were drawn up.[2] The Chamber achieved a signal success with regard to the Irish Propositions. Pitt was obliged to change them to a considerable extent, and they were in the end rejected by the Irish themselves. The seeds of dissension, however, existed in the Chamber from its very beginning. The interests of the older London capitalists and those of the " new men " of the Midlands and North were bound to clash sooner or later. Very early in its history difficulties had arisen in the Chamber regarding the representation of trades and districts, and the conflict of interests is brought out in one of Wedgwood's letters to Watt. He was

[1] Report of the meeting signed by J. Wedgwood, A.O. MSS. ; for a detailed account of the Chamber, see Witt Bowden, *op. cit.*, p. 169 *sqq.*, supplemented by Ashton, *op. cit.*, p. 169 *sqq.*

[2] " Plan of the General Chamber of Manufacturers of Great Britain." A.O. MSS.

undecided as to the constitution of the Chamber, and added, " a man, who should get a delegation for the toothbrush makers of London would have a vote equal with a delegate sent from Birmingham or Manchester." [1]

The real cleavage came when the Chamber had to define its attitude to the new commercial treaty with France which was signed on September 26, 1786. A resolution passed by the Chamber on the 9th of December of that year, with Wedgwood in the chair, hailed the treaty's " liberal and equitable principles " as promising to be advantageous to their manufacturing and commercial interests ; but while the interests of Manchester, of the Potteries led by Wedgwood and of the Midlands led by Boulton & Watt,[2] were this time on the side of free trade hoping " our buttons will barter for pipes of Champaigne," [3] those of the older industries were strongly opposed and the result was that the national organisation was broken up.

It is not without a certain irony that Boulton & Watt should then have been advocating liberalism and freedom of trade, together with persons who some ten years before had on the same grounds opposed their patent. The connection of the two partners with these movements shows once more that their views, and indeed those of the early industrialists in general, were formed less by reference to any general theory of economic policy than by expediency and their own interests often naïvely or otherwise identified with the general interests of the country.

A further very interesting example of this and of some of the difficulties of the early engineering industry is to be found in Boulton & Watt's attitude towards the system of rating

---

[1] Wedgwood to Watt, 1787, March 20. B. & W. Colln.
[2] Watt to Wedgwood, 1787, Feb., *ibid.*
[3] Langford, *A Century of Birmingham Life* (1870), vol. I, p. 329.

for Poor Relief. The case of Boulton & Watt versus the Parish of Harborne belongs chronologically to a later period, for it concerns Soho Foundry. But the fact that the firm's appeal aroused a great deal of interest among manufacturers generally [1] makes it advisable to discuss it in connection with Boulton & Watt's place in general commercial life.

The inclusion of personal property, machinery and manufacturers' stock-in-trade in the property to be rated for Poor Relief had largely been in abeyance owing to the difficulty of assessment, and usually land and houses alone were rated. In 1798 the surveyors appointed by the Parish of Harborne to value the properties subject to the rates had estimated the rent of the shops at Soho Foundry at £150 and together with the various houses belonging to it at £215.[2] But when the assessment was made and other houses in the parish remained at the figure stated by the surveyors, some being even reduced, the rent of Soho Foundry alone deduced from the assessment appeared to be £620, i.e. more than four times the previous figure. Boulton & Watt first contested this excessive assessment and supplied a valuation made by Wyatt which stated the rent for rating purposes at £218 and, incidentally, gave interesting information regarding the value of the various buildings and plant.[3] Law and Southern, too, made a valuation of the engine and machinery at the foundry, and came to the conclusion that the value for the purpose of assessing the machinery to the Poor Rates should not be set higher than £44 6s. od. per annum.[4]

[1] J. Amphlett to Boulton, 1799, Jan. 3. A.O. MSS.
[2] " A reduced valuation of the Rents of buildings at the Soho Foundry." B. & W. Colln.
[3] See Appendix IV.
[4] Law and Southern's valuation of engine and machinery of Soho foundry, 1799, Jan. 11. B. & W. Colln.

But Boulton & Watt had other and more serious grounds of objection to the assessment than merely its excessive amount. Although they did not contest the legality of rating machinery according to its full cost, they reminded the Church-Wardens that the general practice in manufacturing parishes was against it, and they maintained that custom rather than the letter of the law ought to be adhered to. They also maintained that the provision that stock-in-trade of manufacturers and shop-keepers should be rated had generally been abandoned, and they adduced the evidence of the manufacturers of Leeds and Manchester in general and of the Low Moor Iron Works and the works of Messrs. Walker at Rotherham in particular.

" One of the largest establishments in Leeds," Boulton wrote, " where not less than £40,000 has been expended in Buildings and Machinery is only rated at the low rent of £140, while the land—15 acres—is stated at £17 10s. od. Rent." [1]

Not satisfied with his prospects of persuading the parish officers to change the assessment, Boulton proceeded to arouse public opinion in the district. A circular letter was sent to all manufacturers convening them to a meeting on January 14, 1799, to discuss the " Mode of assessment of manufactories to the Poor Rates." The resolution drawn up by Boulton is one of the most interesting documents among the records ; and its argumentation throws an exceedingly interesting light on the attitude of the new industrial capitalists to certain questions of public policy.[2] The grounds of opposition can be summarised under the following heads :

    1. The practice of rating " Stock profits and implements of Trade " would be highly prejudicial not only to the

[1] " Observations relating to the Harborne Poor Rates."   B. & W. Colln.
[2] See Appendix V.

district but to the whole country, by subjecting manufacturers to the caprice of parish officers and by disclosing their trade secrets.

2. Stock-in-trade is continually fluctuating and often bought on credit. It can therefore form no just criterion of the manufacturer's capital or ability to pay. The practice would also lead to an undesirable exposure of his books and accounts.

3. The development of the industries in the district would be arrested and enterprise driven to places where the practice has been discontinued.

4. Lastly such a tax would ultimately fall upon those employed by machinery. It would raise the price of manufactured articles and thereby deprive the manufacturers of this country of the competitive advantages enjoyed on account of the greater application of machinery.

This curious mixture of arguments, showing the first traces of " laisser faire " and in the frank admission on whom the incidence of the tax would fall, reminiscent of mercantilism, failed to convince the parish overseers, and much troublesome litigation followed. Boulton had tried to avoid this knowing that he had no case in law against the rating of machinery ; and so the mere size of the assessment became the only point of contention. The case dragged on for some considerable time, and in 1800 the dispute was submitted to arbitration. John Burr, a millwright of Halesowen, and Sam Wyatt were appointed to act for the parish officers and the Soho Foundry respectively, and John Bishton was appointed third arbitrator. The two last-named arbitrators made the following majority award on January 9, 1801 :

The Foundry was valued at an annual rental of £320, reduced in accordance with other rateable property in the neighbourhood to £160 which at 6d. in the £ amounted to £4 per rate.

The land valued at £36 per annum was reduced to £18, which at 6d. in the £ amounted to 9s. per rate.

It appears, however, from further voluminous correspondence in existence that this dispute continued for some years even after the arbitration award.

Watt, being concerned mainly with technical problems, had through lack of inclination, ability and time taken much less interest in questions of general commercial policy than his partner. But in the many instances of infringement of his patent and the attacks on patents in general, his attitude becomes naturally of the greatest importance. In the correspondence and other records of the firm there is no evidence to show that Boulton & Watt suffered from any competition of those engineers who continued to build engines of the old type, nor did the numerous improvements attempted by others appear to them as dangerous, and since Watt's patent was so complete—he held that it covered every feature of his engine whether used separately or together—there was little possibility of any improvement on the old engine which would not embody one or other of the principles of Watt's patent and would thereby infringe it. The only competition, if it can be so called, which the firm had to suffer was, therefore, that of pirates who undertook to supply engines on Watt's principles without a licence.

A great number of such infringements all over the country were discovered, sometimes through the information of friends such as Wedgwood. Watt was not at first decided how to deal with the pirates, and he was averse to actions at law. It was, however, necessary to put a stop to these practices, less with a view to protecting the patent which had not many more years to run, than with that of recovering unpaid royalties and ensuring future payments which had become endangered. The sons of the two partners, who had by that time entered the business, as well as some of the engine erectors, were sent out to find and report on any infringement ; and, often, the mere threat of an action was sufficient to bring the pirates to book. An example is furnished by the case of the Bowling Ironworks at Leeds. Young Watt succeeded in obtaining a settlement after first threatening to prosecute.[1] Sometimes recourse was had to arbitration. Lawson had discovered an engine erected by Thackeray of Manchester for a mill belonging to James Stockdale, Wilkinson's brother-in-law. Again the same procedure followed, and in the end both parties agreed to the arbitration award of £550 made by William Wilkinson.[2]

The largest number of piracies were, however, to be found in Cornwall where the engineers, Hornblower, Maberley and Bull had been erecting engines of an improved type which Watt considered a piracy on his own. Negotiations in these cases came to nothing, and since the arrears due from Cornwall amounted to a considerable sum, Watt at last decided to take the case to a Court of Law. Injunctions were issued in 1796 against Hornblower and Maberley ; and, finally, an action for infringement was brought. Even before that, in 1793, an action had been brought against Bull, but no decision was then arrived at as to the validity of the patent which had become the main issue. The action against Hornblower and Maberley was decided in the Court of Common Pleas in Boulton & Watt's favour. The case was however retried, and, at last, one year before the expiration of the patent, in January, 1799,

[1] J. Watt, jr., to M. R. Boulton, 1796, Feb. 24. A.O. MSS.
[2] Arbitration Award, 1797, Aug. 2. B. & W. Colln.

the patent was upheld unanimously by a decision of the Court of King's Bench.[1] Although Cornwall remained for years divided into two rival camps,[2] the patent was now definitely upheld and, what was more important, most of the Cornish mines paid their arrears.

It was thus not until the last decade of the century that the validity of the patent became an issue of practical importance. But the whole question of patent rights had been hotly debated for many years past in connection with Watt's monopoly. The patent law of England, the basis of which was at that time, and is still, largely the Statute of Monopolies of 1624, was of a peculiarly controversial character, and opinion on it was sharply divided. On the one hand, the old antagonism against all forms of monopoly was naturally extended to that granted to inventors of technical contrivances ; while on the other hand, those who championed the cause of the inventors were opposed to the strict and cumbersome regulations laid down by the Act regarding the granting of patents which included the requirement of very great exactness in the specifications. The opponents of patent rights maintained that a patentee could acquire a number of privileges and exercise a virtual monopoly,[3] and they talked of the " pernicious effect of patents." Watt was indignant at the many attacks against his patent, emanating mainly from its users.

> " The squire's land," he exclaimed, " has not been so much of his own making as the condensing engine has been of mine. He has only passively inherited his property, while this invention has been the product of my own labour and of God knows how much anguish of mind and body." [4]

[1] Watt to Boulton, 1799, Jan. 25. A.O. MSS.
[2] Hamilton Jenkin, A., op. cit., p. 160.
[3] Levy, H., op. cit., p. 19.
[4] Watt to Boulton, 1780, Oct. 31. A.O. MSS.

145

Attacks by some of the leading manufacturers continued until a climax was reached when the cotton interests of Manchester succeeded in 1785 in having Arkwright's patent annulled. Naturally Watt's anxiety was considerably increased, and probably from this year dates a very important document still in existence. In September, 1785, Wedgwood, announcing to Watt Arkwright's intended visit to Soho, wrote :

" I told him you were considering the subjects of patents and you two great geniuses may probably strike out some new lights together, which neither of you might think of separately." [1]

The " Heads of a Bill to explain and amend the laws relative to Letters Patent and grants of privileges for new Inventions " [2] can, therefore, be considered the result of this interchange of views and experiences of the two inventors. The preamble, after reciting part of the existing Act, explains the need for a new law, from the doubts caused by the possible difference in the interpretation of the words " any manner of new manufacture " as used in the Act and as used in the actual letters patent. The definition is then considerably extended and more strictly worded. Provisions are contained for the granting of patents to the " first introducers into this realm " of inventions from foreign countries and sections regarding facilitation of procedure in obtaining patents are included. Lastly, and as might well be expected from Watt, it is provided that the detailed specification shall no longer be accessible to the public,

[1] Wedgwood to Watt, 1785, Sept. 17. B. & W. Colln.
[2] B. & W. Colln., see Appendix VI. The manuscript is in Watt's handwriting, but contains corrections and additions in a different writing. With the kind assistance of Mr. Leonard Chubb of the Birmingham Public Reference Library, this writing has been compared with specimens of Arkwright's writing of a similar date, and there remains no doubt that the two are identical.

but only be produced on the express order of the Lord Chancellor in case of dispute. The Bill ends up with the provision that in all disputes the law shall be construed in the most beneficial sense for the patentee.

Prophetically, Watt had complained of the insecurity of the patentee from litigation at a time when he himself had not yet experienced it. For although the patent law was, as far as its principle was concerned, open to criticism on the ground of excessive monopoly grants, and although it did, as sometimes stated, foster inventions in this country, this was more through the mere fact that such a law did exist. Its detailed provisions, however, do not seem to have afforded the inventor much protection from long and harassing lawsuits.

PART TWO.

BOULTON, WATT & SONS

CHAPTER ONE.

SOHO FOUNDRY.

WHEN, in 1795, Boulton & Watt decided to build their own Foundry, they made a great step forward in the development of the Engineering industry, a fact far less surprising than that they had for twenty years been content to rely on others for the supply of the constituent engine parts. The reasons which had led to this peculiar organisation of production have already been discussed. Intent on the exploitation of the invention for improved engines rather than on their manufacture, Boulton & Watt took the line most convenient to themselves in ordering the engine parts from others.

Wilkinson had erected an extensive foundry plant, and with his improved boring machine, which was secured by patent, he was in a position to supply at once cylinders and condensers produced with just that exactness which was required. What was more natural than that he should, for the time being, have been entrusted with the manufacture of these parts; since the proprietors of the engine patent were anxious to avoid all possible delay in demonstrating the practical superiority of their machine.

The launching of the new invention was, moreover, a

difficult matter in spite of the need felt for it, and since difficulties of a commercial character absorbed most of the partners' time, they were naturally glad to be saved the additional attention and care which the actual production required. Apart from the delay, which the laying down of an extensive new foundry would have entailed, there was also the great outlay of capital to be considered. Confident though the partners were of the ultimate success of the new engine, the profitability of the project had yet to be proved. And although Boulton, the financier of the undertaking, was able to support the early experiments and meet the still small charges of the business, he would have found it exceedingly difficult to have raised sufficient capital for the building of a foundry.

Custom, too, had established a certain system in engine building. Engineers acted as designers and supervisors only ; and the mine-owners, the principal customers for fire engines, placed their own orders for the supply of parts. This system seemed, especially to Watt, to afford a very good basis for the introduction of the new engine. Approached from the inventor's point of view it seemed to be capable of supplying an excellent standard for measuring the superiority of the new engine. By it, any possible charges of exploitation of the monopoly would be eliminated though, as we have seen, expectations in this direction were not realised. At the time this system with the system of remuneration growing out of it seemed to be a very " just " one.

Once friendly connections with the many suppliers had been established, the expansion of the business together with natural *vis inertiae* would tend to preserve them as long as possible. The opening up of new markets on the one hand and the constant preoccupation with new technical improvements on the other, left the partners little time to think of extensions of plant as long as the technical basis of the business was unsettled and changing. They were content to continue in the once adopted way, and to increase only very gradually the range of production at Soho. Indeed the only parts that were regularly made there throughout the whole period were valves and nozzles.

The procedure for ordering various engine parts had become very elaborate. Printed forms dating from as early as 1778 are in existence, setting out in detail all the parts of the engine to be supplied by the iron-founders named, with blank spaces left for the insertion of dimensions and other instructions. In 1779, too, a booklet was printed giving "Directions for erecting and working the newly-invented steam engines, by Boulton & Watt,"[1] and a standard set of printed "Proposals to the adventurers in . . . By Boulton & Watt "[2] was also in use. The circle of iron-founders from whom castings were ordered was also considerably widened from time to time as conveniences of locality, transport, or technical preferences demanded.

A gradual change set in with the introduction of the rotative engine. The new customers in various industrial enterprises were unaccustomed to erecting their own engines. In most cases, they had not even used steam power before ; and the same reasons, which would have made them averse to the old system of calculating the premiums, made them also unwilling to have any further responsibility after having given the order for an engine. The consequence of this was that more and more engine parts were made at Soho. These, however, were still mostly parts of a more complicated technical character, such as working gears, parallel and rotative motions. The

[1] B. & W. Colln.   [2] *Ibid.*

151

main parts of the engine proper, the cylinder, condenser, piston, were still made at one or other of John Wilkinson's ironworks,[1] mostly at Bersham or Bradley, at Dearman's Eagle Foundry in Birmingham, and at other foundries.

The period was one of transition, and the most important changes were less on the production than on the fitting side, in some cases the entire engine being put together at Soho. At any rate it is apparent that the system was undergoing a change, and that departure from the old procedure was frequent.

> " I should wish to hear," wrote Southern, " by letter, whether you would have anything more than the cylinder and air pump cast at Bersham and whether we shall furnish from Soho the other castings . . . and likewise whether the Bersham goods shall come here to be fitted or be sent from Chester to London." [2]

During the years 1791-94, for which figures are available,[3] the proportion of the goods supplied by different founders to the total of goods sent out from Soho declined steadily. The total value of goods supplied from Bersham, the most important foundry, amounted to £4125 12s. 9d. in 1791 but had by 1794 declined to £1419 18s. 4d. The figures for the four principal suppliers fell from £6708 13s. 11d. in 1791 to £2493 10s. 4d. in 1794. Part of the decrease may be accounted for by the general fall in the value of goods sent out from Soho, which decreased from £11,895 6s. 9d. in 1791 to £6329 13s. 2d. in 1794. Trade in these years seems to have been bad, and

---

[1] John Wilkinson owned in addition to the original New Willey Company at Broseley in Shropshire, two other ironworks, one at Bradley near Bilston, Staffordshire, and the other at Bersham, near Wrexham, in Denbighshire.

[2] Southern to Watt, 1794, Feb. 15. B. & W. Colln.

[3] See Appendices VIII. and IX.

the production and profit figures [1] illustrate this fact. But the fall of the figures for outside suppliers was proportionately greater than the fall in the totals, and the proportion of the goods made at Soho actually rose, the figures for the years 1792 and 1793 forming over 50 per cent. of the respective totals, a fact which shows clearly that Soho was well on the way to becoming the actual production centre of the engine business.

There is little information among the records of the firm of the plant and machinery employed in this production before the building of Soho Foundry, and what there is seems to indicate that the plant was certainly not very extensive. The general abundance of records at all stages of the firm's history justifies the assumption that the lack of this particular information is simply due to the absence of any large plant or experiments in organisation worth recording. Obviously, as long as production remained confined to only a certain number of articles, which were not even always the same, the need for organising this production and for the laying down of extensive shops and the application of elaborate tools would not be felt.

The Soho building, which was originally used for the manufacture of silver and plated goods, was in the form of the letter E, the wings of which were used as dwellings for managers and foremen. Two yards lay behind it, the first a story lower than the ground at the front, the second still lower. All the additional industries which arose at Soho were carried on in buildings erected in these yards.[2] When the engine business under the style of " Soho Engine Manufactory " was started, a smith's shop with two hearths was erected in one of the yards, henceforth referred to as the " Engine Yard." There

[1] See Appendices II. and III.
[2] *Birmingham Weekly Post*, 1895, April 20.

153

is no exact indication as to the size of this shop, and although Boulton refers to it alternately as the " formidable " or the " great " smith's shop it is very unlikely that it was large at the time. At least one lathe, which is referred to in correspondence, was set up in it, and the shop served also for fitting· Another lathe was set up in April, 1777, for turning piston rods, but although a piston rod was actually made after a number of accidents and unsuccessful trials, the firm afterwards relied almost entirely on outside supplies of this part.

Pattern-makers are often referred to in the letters, those of Watt usually containing complaints of their drunkenness and lack of skill. Thus the firm from the beginning made its own patterns. Details of the processes and the places where they were carried on are, however, missing ; but it is certain that pattern-making was not a distinct craft, and engine erectors or fitters such as Murdock would sometimes be engaged on it.

For some years the firm contented itself with this equipment, especially as the production of many parts had to be restricted owing to the competitive prices prevailing in Cornwall. However, the expanding business in that county made some extensions necessary, and at one time the setting up in Cornwall of a foundry or at least a workshop was contemplated.[1] Instead of this a new engine shop, a two-story building, was erected in 1781 at a cost of £110.

Up to the year 1789 the value of the buildings appears in the trading accounts for the purposes of charging depreciation at about £550.[2] After that year additions were made : In 1790 to the value of £435 and in 1791, £525, but it is not apparent from the accounts for the next three years whether any further additions followed.

[1] Boulton to Watt, 1782, Dec. 5. B. & W. Colln.
[2] See Appendix III.

Machinery was equally limited by the nature and variety of the articles made, nozzles being the only important and regular product, and consequently the main attention was given to improvements in fitting the castings obtained from elsewhere. The nozzles were cast at Bradley, and it is worthy of notice that Boulton proposed to visit the ironworks in order to discuss improvements in the castings. Considerable expense was apparently entailed in the fitting of nozzles, through the necessity of chipping and filing " a great deal at the flanches and valve holes, etc.," and it was thought that this could be avoided by improvements of patterns or greater care in moulding.[1] Thus the fact that business relations were usually accompanied by personal friendships made it possible for Boulton & Watt to control to some extent the production of their suppliers.

Roughly speaking, there was then little division of labour at the Soho Engine Manufactory. Apart from general labourers and apprentices, the skilled workers were usually described as smiths and engineers and were employed on a great variety of jobs.[2] Watt had his own office at his house at Harper's Hill, where his drawings, calculations, and even correspondence were carried out. It is probable, judging from the bulk of the work which he performed, that he visited the works only at infrequent intervals. The drawing office remained at Harper's Hill until 1790, when it was removed to Soho. The assistants whom Watt eventually engaged, Playfair, Southern, Ponden, and others, worked at his private house ; and in some of the

[1] Boulton & Watt to John Threlkeld, 1782, June 13. Office Letter Books, vol. 3. B. & W. Colln.
[2] Practically all the agreements between the firm and the workmen of those years contain a provision for sending the men on outside business. In practice only a few, who were more skilled and reliable than the rest, were actually so employed.

trading accounts expenses of the drawing office, such as salaries of draughtsmen, materials, etc., are summarised under the heading " Harper's Hill."

Theoretically, Boulton & Watt had so far remained what they originally set out to be, consulting engineers. In practice, however, they had not been able to avoid being gradually drawn into the actual manufacturing business, and in a way, therefore, the building of Soho Foundry and the establishment of an engineering works was an historic growth. Yet it forms an important landmark both in the history of the firm as well as in general industrial history. Not only did it mean a complete and deliberate departure from the firm's previous business policy, but together with the change in managerial personnel it involved a thorough and systematic internal reorganisation of plant, machinery, production processes, remuneration of labour and costing. The combination in one concern of ironmaster and engineer [1] meant, moreover, the establishment of the first factory in the engineering industry of the world.

Apart from this general tendency, which had been growing for several years, there were several very important immediate reasons leading to the extensions in 1795.

The patent extended by the Act of 1775 had only a few more years to run, and with its expiration the firm's main source of income would cease. The infringements and the action against Bull in 1794, involving the validity of the patent, had made it clear that in 1800, when the new principles were thrown open for general use, a very fierce competition would set in. The

---

[1] These terms are not used in their present meaning. Engineers were primarily designers and supervisors like those mentioned in Cornwall, while iron-masters were those who like Wilkinson and the Darbys were concerned in the actual making of iron (see Ashton, *op. cit.*).

firm had so far, so it appears from the trading accounts, not concentrated on efficient and profitable production. The large and all-important royalties and the dependence on outside supplies would tend to the preservation of inefficient methods. It was obvious that if no change were made the firm, deprived of its monopoly in 1800, would be unable to compete and business would have to cease.

The lack of capital, the old difficulty in the way of erecting extensive plant and buildings, had disappeared. Apart from the substantial annual income large sums had been collected in arrears from Cornwall, and these were now available. Skilled workmen had been trained, and the many technical improvements, especially in boring mills, considerably decreased Wilkinson's supremacy. A further impetus was given by the infusion of new blood into the partnership. The sons of the older partners, Matthew Robinson Boulton and James and Gregory Watt, had reached the age when they could be entrusted with the management of business affairs. Both Boulton and Watt were considerably advanced in years, but while the former was still active—the coining mill now absorbed all his time and interest—the latter, financially secure at last, was settling down to enjoy a peaceful old age. The fact that the supply of the greater part of castings was jeopardised through internal dissension at the Bersham Ironworks of John Wilkinson was, however, of immediate importance. There, a disagreement had arisen between the two partners, John and his younger brother William. By 1794 the rupture had become definite, and the dispute was carried to the law courts early the next year. Boulton & Watt were first drawn into the quarrel through the close personal friendship with William Wilkinson, whose daughter afterwards married Matthew Robinson Boulton. They had offered to mediate, but when William Wilkinson took

Weston, Boulton & Watt's attorney, as his legal adviser, John Wilkinson suspected a conspiracy and, quick tempered as he was, broke off the friendship that had lasted for twenty years.[1] More serious for Boulton & Watt was the fact that the Bersham Ironworks had been closed by an injunction of the Court, and that orders for cylinders could not be executed.[2] Orders were, therefore, at once given to the Dale Company,[3] but the products of their boring mill were not of the accuracy required by the engine firm and long delays occurred.[4]

Arbitrators had been appointed in the dispute between the Wilkinsons ; and at an auction of the Bersham Works, John became the sole owner. William Wilkinson had in the meantime disclosed to Boulton & Watt the fact that his brother had since 1782 pirated their engine. Not only had he erected several engines for his own use, but he had also, unknown to the engine firm, supplied outside customers.[5] The two junior partners, not bound by ties of old friendship, like their fathers, proceeded to deal with Wilkinson in the same way in which they had dealt with the other cases of infringement. Wilkinson was asked to pay compensation for all unpaid premiums and, doubtless intimidated by the example of other pirates, he at once agreed.[6] Settlement was, however, not yet forthcoming since Wilkinson was anxiously awaiting the result of the many attacks on Watt's patent. In the end, no alternative was left but surrender and the final agreement was drawn up on August 5, 1796.[7]

[1] J. Watt, jr., to Weston, 1795, March 30.   B. & W. Colln.
[2] Watt to Wm. Wilkinson, 1795, March 8, *ibid.*
[3] Southern to J. Watt, jr., 1795, May 29, *ibid.*
[4] J. Watt, jr., to William Wilkinson, 1795, Dec. 30, *ibid.*
[5] J. Watt, jr., to Weston, 1795, Sept. 24, *ibid.*
[6] J. Watt, jr., to Weston, 1795, Dec. 10, *ibid.*
[7] Agreement between Boulton & Watt and John Wilkinson, 1796, Aug. 5. *ibid.*

The number of engines erected by Wilkinson for outside customers without a licence was nineteen ; and two more were being set up at his new works at Brymbo near Bersham. On the other hand, the balance of goods and cash between the parties stood at £3425 17s. 5d. in Wilkinson's favour. This sum was " mutually agreed and acknowledged to be liquidated by the premiums due to the said Boulton & Watt upon sundry engines erected by the said John Wilkinson upon their patent principles." In addition, John Wilkinson was to pay a further £1000 " as soon as the mine of Llynypandu upon which four of the said engines are erected shall have paid up the money expended on it." He promised to erect no more engines without Boulton & Watt's licence, and for the moment peace was restored. The agreement of August 5, 1796, marks, however, the final breach in the long connection between the ironmaster and the engineer. Wilkinson could never forget the humiliation he had suffered, and long afterwards, on the occasion of the Hornblower trial, he showed that he still bore them ill-will.[1]

On the other hand, the firm had now become more or less independent of the ironfounder. In 1793, a share in the Neath Abbey Ironworks had been offered to them, and in the following year the purchase of the furnaces and collieries at Madeley Wood was suggested.[2] But no more came of these schemes than of William Wilkinson's invitation to join the firm. The idea then arose of setting up a boring mill, and Peter Ewart, a Manchester millwright who acted as engine erector for the firm, was engaged to design and superintend the mill. Out of this scheme the Soho Foundry eventually originated. It was decided to enlarge the whole engine

---

[1] J. Wilkinson to Boulton & Watt, 1797, Jan. 16. B. & W. Colln.
[2] Ashton, op. cit., p. 78.

manufactory itself, and a site was selected on the bank of the canal at Smethwick, about a mile distant from the parent establishment.

The selection of the site showed considerable forethought. Soho had no communication by water ; and road transport of large engine parts, especially cylinders, would have been a difficult matter. Consequently, the canal site was chosen. The negotiations for the purchase of the land were quickly concluded, and on August 27, 1795, the purchase deed was drawn up. The land, an area of 18½ acres, was bought by James Watt from a Mr. Kennedy. An interesting provision is contained in the purchase deed. The purchaser covenants not to erect on the land

> " Any Brass works or other works which may be injurious to the vegetation of the remaining lands of the said George Kennedy, it being understood and agreed that Iron founderies and Steam Engines are not comprehended and meant or intended to be comprehended in this restriction and that it shall and may be lawful . . . to erect and build so many Iron founderies and Steam Engines and also such dwelling-houses, shops, buildings and other works as he or they, [the purchaser], &c. shall from time to time and at any time or times think fit. . . ." [1]

Building operations were soon started and, if from 1775 onwards the old building had grown in a more or less casual way, the planning of the new buildings was very thorough and systematic indeed. It was due to the energy of the sons, especially James Watt, jr., that the work on the buildings progressed so quickly. By October, two buildings had been roofed in and the Foundry building was well advanced.[2] In

---

[1] " Extract from the Purchase Deed of the land at Soho Foundry from Mr. Kennedy, August 27, 1795." B. & W. Colln.
[2] Peter Ewart to G. Lawson, 1795, Oct. 22, *ibid.*

December the roofing of the Foundry, which measured 100 ft. by 70 ft., was started. The Foundry department does not seem to have been ready before February of the next year ; for it is in that month that the first entry, under that heading, appears in the works' wages book. The smithy was the first shop completed, and was ready in October, 1795.[1] The formal opening did not take place until January 30, 1796, and was made the occasion of an elaborate ceremony. Much feasting took place, and Matthew Boulton solemnly declared the works open, naming them " Soho Foundry." [2]

This is how the historian of the district some years later described the origin of the Foundry :

" In order to obtain the desired degree of perfection in the manufactory of steam engines, Messrs. Boulton & Watt found it necessary to erect and establish an iron foundery for that purpose and they have accordingly in partnership with their sons (to whose activity, genius, and judgment it must be attributed, that this great work was begun and finished in the course of three winter months) erected at a convenient place and contiguous to the same stream at Smethwick a great and complete manufactory and foundery into which a branch from the Birmingham Canal enters and thereby the coals, pig iron, bricks, sand, &c. are brought and their engines or other heavy goods are transported to every part of the kingdom, there being wet dock within their walls for four boats to lie." [3]

Regarding the actual layout of the works, he goes on to say, " The place of this work being well digested and settled previous to laying the first stone, the whole is thereby rendered

---

[1] " Wages Book from the commencement of the works," Aug. 5, 1795, to March 31, 1797. B. & W. Colln.

[2] Report of the opening of Soho Foundry, *Aris's Birmingham Gazette*, 1796, Feb. 1.

[3] Shaw, *op. cit.*, vol. 2, p. 119.

more complete than such works as generally arise gradually from disjointed ideas."

Although this was written some years later, when important changes which form the subject-matter of the next three chapters had been made, there can be no doubt that the new establishment was very carefully planned. The experience of the old partners was combined with the progressive outlook of the new ones, and important help was available from the more experienced workmen, William Murdock, James Lawson, Peter Ewart, and John Southern. At the beginning of 1796, Boulton himself gave an account of the new business : " I and my partner, James Watt," he wrote to Captain Apsley, " have laid out £10,000 in erecting a Foundry on the bank of the Birmingham Canal, for the purpose of casting everything relating to our steam engines." [1] Quick to see the possibilities of this extension he offered the service of his firm to the Board of Ordnance as Cannon founders, and in case they should desire to build their own foundry at Woolwich, which had so far been impossible for want of water power, he drew the Board's attention to the fact that by the improvements in steam engines, " which may be erected anywhere and for any purpose," a revolution had been effected. He concluded, " If Lord Cornwallis and the Board think favourably of our plan, I offer my best services to establish the most complete Gun Foundry in the world." [2]

There can be no doubt however that, although carefully planned for continual extensions, Soho Foundry was in the beginning a small concern. The greatest difficulty in getting it into going order was experienced through the lack of suitable

[1] Boulton to Capt. Apsley, 1796, Jan. 26. A.O. MSS.
[2] Clapham, J. H., op. cit., p. 152 : " Long after 1830 the boring bar at Woolwich was still driven by a four-horse mill."

workmen. The closing of the Bersham works had thrown several of Wilkinson's skilled men out of work and efforts were made to secure some of them for Soho, a fact which naturally tended to make worse the already strained relations between the two firms. Gilbert Gilpin, the manager of Bersham, and Abraham Storey, Wilkinson's head caster, were engaged.[1] John Kendrick was another of Wilkinson's men for whom employment was found ; but the scruples of the older partners stopped for the time being the taking on of men discharged from Bersham. In March, 1796, a caster of the name of John Wells was engaged with a five years' agreement,[2] the first, incidentally, to mention an elaborate piece-rate. The scarcity of labour continued and Southern was sent to various parts of the country to try and find workmen.[3] In the end, however, the works were set going satisfactorily, and considerable extensions followed which will be discussed in detail later.

At this stage we may take leave of the original founders of the firm and briefly trace the personal changes. It has already been mentioned that the sons had entered the business. In October, 1794, the Soho Engine Manufactory was taken over by a new partnership formed under the style of " Boulton, Watt & Sons," which, in addition to the original partners, comprised Matthew Robinson Boulton, James Watt, junior, and Gregory Watt.[4] The old firm continued in existence but handed over to the new one the future business. Gregory Watt's connection with the concern was a short one.

[1] Southern to J. Watt, jr., 1796, March 27. B. & W. Colln.
[2] Agreement with John Wells, 1796, March, *ibid.*
[3] M. R. Boulton to G. Southern, 1798, July 6, *ibid.*
[4] Dickinson and Jenkins, quoting from the Doldowlod Papers, *op. cit.*, p. 345.

163

Of undoubted talent both in the exact sciences and in engineering, he was, however, in poor health and unable to give much attention to the business. He died on October 16, 1804, and his share in the partnership reverted to his brother.

On the formation of the new partnership, the shares were held in the proportion originally laid down. In 1800, on the dissolution of the old partnership, its shares were equally divided between the Boultons and the Watts, the style of the firm being at the same time changed to Boulton, Watt & Co., Soho. James Watt handed his share over to his son, thus definitely retiring from the business, and on Boulton's death in 1809, the two sons remained the sole partners in the Soho Engine Manufactory. The Soho Foundry, which was carried on as a separate concern, was owned, in partnership, by Boulton and his son and the two young Watts. James Watt himself, although he had purchased the land on which the Foundry was built, held no share in the new concern. The style of this partnership was " Boulton, Watt & Co., Soho Foundry," and the capital for laying down the plant was advanced by the old firm. This amounted to £21,624 16s. 6½d. in October, 1797, and interest was charged at the rate of 5 per cent. per annum.

From the correspondence of the years 1794-1800, it is evident that the old partners had begun to retire from the business in the former year although the partnership did not expire until the latter. In 1798 Watt informed Dr. Black, " I now take little part in it (the engine business) but it goes on successfully." [1] He continued to live a more or less leisurely life during his remaining years, enjoying the fruits of his labour and his fame which was by then definitely established. He

---

[1] Smiles, *op. cit.*, p. 395.

died at Heathfield Hall in Staffordshire on August 25, 1819.[1] Boulton continued to be active in business with undiminished vigour until his death on August 17, 1809, but the engine business did not interest him any more. To him business had become almost an end in itself, and the coinage occupied his sole time during his remaining years.

The great development which Soho made after 1795 is, therefore, bound up with the names of Matthew Robinson Boulton and James Watt, jr.; and it is to them that all credit must be ascribed. Combining a thorough education in the gentlemanly pursuit of the time with an early training as practical engineers in all stages of production, they brought to the task of organisation an entirely new outlook. Theirs was a rôle quite different from that of the early pioneers, and the details of the following chapters will show them much more akin to the generation to which the majority of modern business men belong than to that immediately preceding their own.

[1] Heathfield Hall was situated in the parish of Handsworth, and was demolished in 1925 when the site was incorporated in a new building estate. Watt's garret workshop was reproduced at the Science Museum, South Kensington.

CHAPTER TWO.

SCIENTIFIC ORGANISATION.

PROGRESS in organisation remained slow during the years 1795 to 1800, and a number of castings were still produced by outside firms. Even as late as 1801 we find evidence that a great variety of smaller engine parts was manufactured at Dearman's Eagle Foundry and at Izon's, another local foundry.[1] The quality of the work turned out by the new Soho Foundry was very poor for the first few years. Its greensand castings were considerably inferior to the work produced by the Lowmoor Ironworks, and remained so for some time, although the smith's work, equally poor at first, had considerably improved by 1799.[2] " The emulation of our men has now been awakened," M. R. Boulton was able to report, adding : " I am hopeful of turning out the working gear in such a manner as will render filing a superfluous operation." Various improved tools, some copied from Murray, the famous engineer, and others of Murdock's design, had apparently been introduced.

The question of greensand castings continued to present difficulties up to 1803. Methods adopted by the most prominent competitors were studied closely, and improvements initiated. The foundry of Murray, the great Leeds iron-

[1] " Articles proposed to be cast at Izon's," " Articles proposed to be cast at Dearman's," 1801. B. & W. Colln.

[2] M. R. Boulton to J. Watt, jr., 1799, Feb. 1, *ibid*.

founder and engineer, in particular seems to have served as a model during the early years of the Soho Foundry. Murray employed as drysand moulder one, Halligan, a former Soho employee; and through him, Boulton, jr., and Watt, jr., obtained all the desired information. The output at Murray's two foundries—the drysand and greensand foundries were housed in separate buildings—seems to have been about the same as that at Soho : between three and four tons a day. According to Halligan, the poor quality of the Soho castings was due to the mixing of the sand with too much coal dust.[1] He also informed the Soho firm of the proportion between castings made in drysand and those made in greensand at Murray's. Nozzles were made in drysand ; while cylinder bottoms, lids and pistons as well as rods, shafts and wheels were all made in greensand. Halligan was in the end induced to come back to Soho ; and his experience undoubtedly proved very valuable in the reorganisation of the Foundry.[2]

For some years information regarding the actual size of buildings and the extent of machinery is somewhat scanty. At the Foundry a cupola had been set up to assist the air furnaces and it seems to have worked very satisfactorily, melting down on an average about a ton during a day of twelve hours:[3] No further details are available until two years later when, during the dispute over the poor rates, elaborate lists of buildings and machinery were drawn up.

Some information is, however, in existence regarding the progress of the boring mill which has already been mentioned. The designs were prepared in 1795 by Ewart and Southern and submitted to Watt. They were both of the horizontal

---

[1] J. Watt, jr., to M. R. Boulton, 1802, June 12. B. & W. Colln.
[2] J. Watt, jr., to M. R. Boulton, 1802, June 15, *ibid.*
[3] J. Watt, jr., to M. R. Boulton, 1797, June 10, *ibid.*

and vertical types, and the former, it seems, was preferred by Watt. Towards the end of 1796, the boring mill was actually set to work,[1] but although Boulton wrote to Watt, jr., that "boreing goes on well," the machine did not work satisfactorily, probably through defects in the boring-bar. An improved machine was later designed by Murdock, and the bar for this mill was supplied by the Lowmoor Ironworks. The first large cylinder, one with a 64-in. diameter, took twenty-seven and a half days on this machine,[2] whose novelty lay in the use of a worm gear—or "endless screw" as it is referred to in Murdock's patent of 1799—for turning the bar. This method was later generally adopted for all the larger lathes,[3] the first to answer satisfactorily being the air-pump lathe.

As already mentioned, it is in the year 1799 that we find the first detailed lists of the several shops. Samuel Wyatt's valuation of the Foundry of 1799 has been referred to.[4] It enumerates :

Foundry stoves and furnaces ; a boring mill ; turning, fitting, carpenters', smiths' and pattern shops ; a boiling-house ; magazine ; a shed for sand ; a drying kiln and, in addition, thirteen workmen's houses.

We have, too, a list of the machinery that had been installed by that year (also made for the purpose of establishing the rateable value) drawn up by James Law and John Southern. The following are included :

Wharf ; foundry cranes ; moveable triangular crane ; engine ; blowing apparatus ; piston lathe ; shaft lathe ; wharf drill ; two drills in the fitting shop, two lathes in

---

[1] M. R. Boulton to J. Watt, jr., 1796, Dec. 1. B. & W. Colln.

[2] "Abstract account of cylinders bored from Dec. 31, 1796, to Jan. 11, 1800," *ibid.*

[3] M. R. Boulton to J. Watt, jr., 1799, Feb. 1, *ibid.*

[4] See Appendix IV.

the same, wood lathe and grind shop, two lathes in the parallel motion shop, the nozzle crane, together with all their connecting machinery.[1]

Although this list is not very detailed it gives an idea of the extent to which machinery had been applied. The best contemporaneous account of Soho goes so far as to say : " And from the great experience of the proprietors, they have applied the power of steam to the boring of cylinders, pumps, etc., to drilling, to turning, to blowing their smelting furnaces and whatever tends to abridge human labour and obtain accuracy, for by a superiority of their tools they are enabled to obtain expedition and perfection in a higher degree than heretofore." [2]

It is a significant fact that the expiration of the original partnership in the year 1800 should coincide with a great extension of plant and buildings. The years 1800 and 1801 mark not only a turning-point in the planning of extensions at Soho, but appear to provide also the earliest records in existence of systematic factory planning. It is, without a doubt, to the sons of the original partners that the alterations commencing in those years are due. The " spirit of emulation " in their workmen, to which one of them had referred, seems to have been awakened in them too ; and, aware of the superiority of their competitors' work, they found that it was high time to reform.[3]

Consequently, schemes of extensions of the " Soho Manufactory" were taken in hand, and papers are in existence showing the details of new buildings and machinery required, such as " Memoranda of sundry articles wanted for the completion of

[1] " Valuation of Engine and Machinery of Soho Foundry," by J. Law and J. Southern, Jan. 11, 1799. B. & W. Colln.

[2] Shaw, op. cit., vol. 11, p. 119.

[3] J. Watt, jr., to M. R. Boulton, 1802, June 15. B. & W. Colln.

the new and alteration of the old machinery at Soho, 1801." [1]
The most important entry on this paper relates to the power
supply. This had been discussed some time before, and an
estimate of various methods had been drawn up. In the end
it was decided to set up three engines, namely, " one six-horse,
to drive the small lathes ; one four-horse to drive the drilling
machine and nozzle lathe ; one three-horse to turn the large
lathe." [2] This was estimated to involve an initial cost of
£1057 3s. 0d. after deducting the sale value of the old engine
which was put at £136.

Extensions of both concerns continued well into 1803 ; and
in that year James Watt, jr., reporting the building of a new
shop at the Soho Foundry which was to be 134 feet long,
writes as follows :

" It is intended for the fitting of the little engines, and
I hope will enable us to get on with at least one per week,
which will scarcely enable us to meet the present demand.
Some other alterations of minor importance are going on there,
which I hope will be finished in the course of the summer ;
and if it should afterwards be found expedient to add a shed
for making boilers and a counting house, that establishment
will have reached what I should vote to be its ne plus ultra." [3]

So far there is nothing exceptional in this natural expansion
of a progressive business. The careful lists of tools wanted
may show greater forethought on the part of the management
than was perhaps common in other industrial enterprises of
the time ; but, otherwise, expansion on these lines still remains

[1] B. & W. Colln.

[2] This paper, entitled, " Estimate of the different proposed methods of
communicating motion to the machinery at Soho Engine Manufactory,
Dec. 15, 1800 " enumerates in addition to the method adopted, two others,
viz. by one ten-horse engine, and by several smaller engines. The cost of
all three was approximately the same.

[3] J. Watt, jr., to Gregory Watt, 1803, June 8. B. & W. Colln.

quite within contemporary ideas of business practice. What distinguishes Soho from all other factories of the time—and there were at the beginning of the new century many industrial enterprises which could be called factories—was the fact that these lists were the result of a definite systematic and preconceived plan of what the Soho Engine Manufactory should be.

A number of documents are in existence which show that the methods of planning and works designing were by no means different from those stipulated to-day by Industrial Works Designers, Scientific Managers, or Efficiency Engineers. The limitations were only those imposed by the degree of technical knowledge or rather by the degree of its application. " More can be attributed to the quiet, pervasive influence of the engineers who rose to executive positions in industry," writes a foremost authority on this new modern science,[1] in discussing the new spirit in American industry in the present century, and this factor will certainly have to be included when we come to discuss later the probable incentives for this " new spirit " at Soho in 1800.

The basic document in the series mentioned deals with the layout proper and is entitled " Arrangement of the Engine Manufactory, Soho, December, 1801." [2] The memorandum consists of two parts. The first gives a list of the shops, mostly already in existence, but partly still to be erected, together with their machinery, the operations performed in each and, most important of all, their relative situation and communications. The second part contains a list of all the machines required in the production process already in use at Soho, together with their respective uses.

The first part of this document evidently served as the

[1] Jones, E. D., *The Administration of Industrial Enterprises* (1926), p. 6.
[2] B. & W. Colln. See plates.

basis for all the arrangements that were made later. In the first column it enumerates ten different shops, designated from A to K, by which letters they were afterwards referred to. These shops were :

A. The drilling shop, or rather the heavy drilling shop in which the boring and drilling of such heavy articles as condensers, air and hot and cold water pumps, steam pipes, &c., was done. A large and a small drill were used in this shop, and it was provided with a hearth, a convenience for holding grinding and mending tools, and other minor appliances.

B. The heavy turning shop, provided with the great lathe and a second special lathe for turning piston rods, in addition to the usual conveniences. Worthy of mention, among these, is a " tackle for lifting heavy weights into lathe." This shop was used for all turning work, such as for pistons, cylinder lids, gudgeons, shafts, piston rods, rotative wheels, &c.

C. The heavy fitting shop, which, in addition to the usual benches and grinding stone, was to have a lapping machine and a small drill. Here the heavier articles were fitted, such as plumber blocks, pistons, glands, &c.

D. The nozzle shop, used exclusively for the fitting of nozzles.

E. A general fitting shop which was intended to be provided with a separate drill, and, apart from the usual conveniences, with a " small portable furnace for heating pins " as well as with " a crane for lifting heavy weights." Here, steam cases, inner and outer bottoms and pipes were fitted and the fitting of air pumps was completed.

F. This was a special shop for the fitting of parallel motions and working gears and governors, and had two lathes as well as another smaller lathe for turning pins.

172

G. This was the next and was called the light fitting shop. Here all the lighter parts—safety, throttle and stop pipes, &c., were fitted.

H. Was the pattern-makers' shop and had the usual benches, grind stone, and a lathe.

I. Was the casters' shop, and for this no particulars are given.

K. The last on the list was the smiths' shop, and was stated to contain a hearth and a vice-bench.

It seems that some of the machinery considered necessary and enumerated in this list had not yet been set up. At any rate the second part dealing with machinery mentions the following as already in use : A large and a small drill, both vertical and with gear control and sliding ; the large turning lathe with both " centres " and " chucks," also special lathes for piston rods, nozzles, parallel motions, a lathe in the light fitting shop, one other small lathe, and the pattern-makers' lathe. A lapping machine used for " lapping all brasses and plummer blocks, &c.," and, lastly, there was installed a steam case drill in the fitting shed.

As far as the technical side of the machinery is concerned, it is of interest to note that both " centre-lathe working " and " face-lathe working " were used. The latter method is, of course, the most widely used to-day, and has given rise to a very great increase in the application of automatic and semi-automatic machines. There is no evidence to show which of the two methods was more extensively employed at Soho ; but we know, at any rate, that they both were available.

Soho also did not depart from old practice in the use of hand tools by the turners. The most important factor diminishing the degree of skill required at the present time of the turners is the almost complete disappearance of the hand tool. From the references in the lists of machinery to " conveniences for holding tools " and " tool cupboards," it is obvious that hand tools were still largely in use at Soho. The now usual special grinding and cutting department did not exist, and each bench was provided with a grindstone. It is usually supposed that, as regards the provision of new tools, the almost universal practice in the early days of the nineteenth century was for workmen not only to bear the expense of repairs, but also that of new tools. In this respect the following provision for borers—it was probably applied generally—shows Soho in advance of the time : " Current repairs of tools and grinding them to be borne by the borer and new tools to be provided at our expense." [1]

The most surprising advance, however, is the fact that the list of machines contains, together with statements of their present speeds, proposed new speeds which were evidently calculated to serve as standards. Generally, the proposed speed showed an increase over the existing speed. The small drill was to be speeded up from 50 revolutions per minute to 75 ; the pattern-makers' lathe was to have a speed of between 200 and 300 revolutions per minute, and for most other machines three or four standard speeds were established, such as for the parallel motion lathe which, from a speed of 65 revolutions per minute, was to run at 18, 50, 70 and 100 per minute. " Forty or even thirty years ago," remarks a recent writer,[2] " the turner would have to decide for himself what ' speed ' and ' feed ' he required : to-day, tables are worked out for nearly all machines. . . ." According to this statement, Soho would correspond more nearly to what is described as the practice of " to-day " than to that of thirty or forty years ago. Specula-

---

[1] " Calculations of piece prices of articles bored under the great drill, Nov. 1801, General Observations." B. & W. Colln.
[2] Rowe, J. W. F., *Wages in Practice and Theory* (1928), p. 264.

tions on the reasons for the introduction of such methods are very interesting; but they will be deferred for the moment until more of them have been discussed.

An interesting difference between modern and older practice is shown in the firm's use of boring machines. According to the writer above quoted, the introduction of specialised boring machines did not begin until about thirty-five years ago, all boring previously being done by a turner on an ordinary lathe. Again, vertical boring mills came only into existence comparatively recently. Unfortunately, on this point no information is available in the Soho documents. It has been stated that Watt preferred the horizontal boring mill, but it is not known which type was actually introduced. The large drill mentioned in the list of machinery was an upright one, and certainly served for boring purposes so that, in this respect too, Boulton & Watt were probably very quick in recognising technical advantages. For drilling, present practice tends to an almost exclusive use of the " radial " drill which has given rise to highly specialised automatic machines. The " pillar " drill, in which the work had to be moved on the table until it was in the desired position, was used before; and there is no indication to show that Soho was in this respect an exception from contemporary practice. Nor were the planing or milling machines that are common to-day used at Soho, all chipping and filing having to be done by hand.

So far, the most exceptional qualities of this new plan of Soho lay in the fact that a list of all required shops had been drawn up, the machinery to be included, and the operations to be performed in each explicitly stated, and definite specialised uses assigned to each machine and their speed standardised. A more remarkable sign of " modernity," however, is to be found in the fourth column of the Memorandum dealing

with the arrangement of the shops which is entitled :
" Relative Situation and Communications," for this, although
in primitive form, definitely shows that the persons responsible
for the design had a very clear idea of what is now termed
" routing."

The first two shops are for drilling and turning respectively.
The next three are for fitting in general. These five shops are
concerned, on the one hand, with the production of the engine
proper, that is, its power generating parts, and on the other
hand, with those parts producing the rotative motion ; and
they form, therefore, the centre of the whole plant, with the
drilling shop a centre within it.

The actual positions are given as follows : The drilling
shop, where boring in general and drilling of the heavy parts
took place, was to have direct communication with the heavy
turning shop on the one hand, and with the three fitting shops
on the other—" the principal heavy articles being carried from
hence to those shops."   Again, this central shop, A, was to be
directly accessible from the yard " for the convenience of
bringing in the goods." The heavy turning shop, B, too,
was to be entered from the yard and was to have direct communication with A, and C, the heavy fitting shop. It was
also to be near the original power. This provision for the
shop in which the principal lathes were situated can be easily
understood ; for if it had been at a great distance from the
source of power, much inconvenience would have been experienced in the transmission. The heavy fitting shop, C,
was to be contiguous both to the drilling machine and the two
large lathes. D, the nozzle shop, needed direct communication with the drilling shop only ; while the position of E,
the fitting shed for steam cases and air pumps, depended on
whether it was provided with a separate drill or not. In the

former case its communications were of less importance, but in the latter it was necessary that it should have easy access to the drilling shop where the steam case panels could be drilled.

The position of the next five shops is not so clearly stated, and was obviously considered less important. The parallel motion shop was to be on the ground floor preferably ; but, most of the articles worked in it being portable, it was not imperative that it should be contiguous to the drilling machine. The shop was to be provided with three lathes, and the communications with the engine were, therefore, important. It was not necessary that the light fitting shop should be on the ground floor or immediately accessible to the great turning lathe and great drill as the articles to be fitted in it were also portable. The position of the pattern-makers' shop was not material, except in so far as the convenience of transmitting power for turning the lathe was concerned ; while the situation of the last two, the casters' and smiths' shops, is stated to be immaterial.

Unfortunately, the earliest plan of Soho in existence dates from nearly half a century later than the Memorandum outlined above. It is, therefore, impossible to compare the arrangement of the shops on the actual site with the positions here stipulated. According to these, there would be a more or less radial arrangement of the workshops : A would occupy a central position. Communicating with it and each other would be, on the one side, shops B and C and on the other, shop D. The position of E, which depended on the installation of another drilling machine, is not certain. According to the machinery list it was proposed to install a steam case drill in the fitting shed, and if that was done, the latter would not necessarily have had any direct communication with A. Shop F was probably at some distance from the first five, although not too far from the engine house. Shop G was on a second floor, the lathe in it being referred to as " lathe in upper fitting shop." The other three shops would be more or less separate buildings.

From this we gain some idea of the layout of the Soho factory, and we can also see the considerations that dictated it. A certain sequence of production processes was definitely contemplated as the basis of the layout. Some castings would be brought from the yard into shop, A, to be bored and drilled, and others into the heavy turning shop. The two would also have to be communicating ; for most castings would have to be turned first and drilled afterwards. From these two shops the articles would then go to their respective fitting shops. One was reserved for heavy articles—pistons, plumber blocks, rotative wheels and shafts, and the other for steam cases, air pumps, inner and outer bottoms, that is, those articles which would probably demand less alterations in the fitting. Here also the fitting together of most of the articles already finished would be completed. Lastly, there was a special shop in which the all-important nozzle was fitted. Two special fitting shops were in existence—one for the parallel motions and working gears and one in which all the smaller and lighter articles, mainly boiler furniture such as injection cocks, steam gauges, reverse valves, etc., were fitted.

Two other papers approach the same matter from a different angle. The first of these, with the same date as that already discussed, is entitled " Specification of the Fitting of Engine Materials and the Shops where it is to be done. December 3, 1801." [1] This gives in one column a complete

---

[1] B. & W. Colln. This very elaborate document has been considered of sufficient interest to be included *in extenso* as Appendix XI.

list of all the constituent parts of the steam engine, with their subdivisions, and sets out in very great detail all the operations to be performed on each article in their proper sequence. In the second column, the shops and the machines on which each particular job is to be done are stated. This paper provides a complete list of all the production processes and fixes a definite standard regulation on the part of the management, thus relieving the workmen of the larger part of their independence and individual responsibility.

The details of jobs are remarkable. The cylinder heads the list and the other articles follow in practically the same order in which they are dealt with in the shops. First, all the articles belonging to the cylinder—pistons, piston rods, steam cases ; then the several pumps—air, hot and cold water, followed by the nozzles and the various gudgeons. The rotative motion or crank is next dealt with, together with the connecting rod and, lastly, the condenser. A very detailed list of boiler furniture follows ; and the rest is made up of such additional articles as fly-wheel, governor, parallel motion and working gear. The last two items are : General Fitting and Labour, the latter including the weighing, blacking, and packing of goods. For each article or part thereof, the operations are given in their temporal sequence and are, therefore, of considerable technico-historical interest. From our point of view their main importance lies in the fact that at Soho the production processes had, for each particular article, already been broken up into a long series of various minor operations, showing thus a very high degree of the application of division of labour to factory routine.

One example of this subdivision is the following for the :

179

Condenser.

Fitting Condenser, viz. :

Drilling.	Drilling Machine.
Chipping.	Heavy Fitting Shop (C) or
Fitting Plate to Bottom.	Yard.

Fitting Blow Pipe, viz. :

Drilling Blow Pipe and Valve	Drilling Machine.
Seat.	Light Fitting Shop (G)
Chipping.	Lathes, Nos. 8 and 9.
Fitting Valve and Seat.	

Fitting Injection Cock, viz. :

Drilling.	Drilling Machine.
Fitting Pipe and Valve.	Light Fitting Shop (G),
Fitting Rod and Handle, and	Lathes, Nos. 8 and 9.
Pipe and Valve to Cock.	

The directions regarding the shops in which the operations were to be performed are also surprisingly systematic. For the completed cylinder is given : " Goes to Steam Case Fitting Shed (E) and is then finished ready to be sent away." General fitting, we read, is done in that shed, and from other entries it appears that there and in the yard the fitting of the engine was completed. The general labour, i.e. the work connected with the despatching of goods, was carried on in the magazine and in the yard.

The statement that division of labour and subdivision of jobs had been developed to a high degree, is borne out by the last paper in this series which is of a somewhat earlier date than the one preceding. Entitled " Arrangement of Work-men and Distribution of Work at Soho Foundry, September 14,

1801," [1] it gives a detailed list of the jobs assigned to each work-man or small group of workmen. The total number of work-people enumerated on this list is forty-one men and seven boys ; but a note at the end informs us that, to make up that complement, eight men and four boys were required. There can be no doubt that this list was intended to supply a fixed standard job for each worker. The first item states that Wells, two assistant men and one lad were " to be employed constantly in fitting nozzles." The word " constantly," though not ex-plicitly repeated in the following entries, applied, no doubt, to them all. We are thus afforded an interesting view of the classes of skill into which machine production in the early engineering industry had divided the workers.

The first important group are the fitters. In this class, which to-day still preserves the old generic name, the new industrial revolution, as it is sometimes called, has brought an important change. To-day there exist a large number of " fitters " whose degree of skill is by no means equal. Whilst the engine erector proper still remains a highly-skilled crafts-man whose efficiency will be measured by his experience and personal touch, the skill of the others is certainly lower than that required forty or fifty years ago. The great advance in the quality of the castings and the superiority of the work performed on them in the subsequent stages of production, such as turning, boring and drilling, owing to the introduction of improved machinery, have minimised the adjustments to which they have to be subjected by the fitter ; further, where these are necessary, they are no longer done by hand. Plan-ing and milling machines are used extensively. Automatic machinery with its mass production has divided the fitters

[1] B. & W. Colln.   See Appendix X.

into a number of classes, each performing a small job that has become almost as much one of routine as that of the other semi-skilled workers.

In the early days of the nineteenth century the fitter was still a very highly-skilled craftsman, with an experience acquired only after many years of apprenticeship and work as an assistant. Soho formed no exception. All filing and chipping was still done by hand, and the fitter had to combine manual skill with a certain degree of empirical technical knowledge demanded by the undeveloped state of both the product and the machinery which produced it. In one way, however, the beginnings of modern practice can. be seen. Fitting did not remain a general unregulated job. A subdivision had already taken place, and the varieties of fitting work were strictly systematised. To each fitter or group of fitters only one article or group of similar articles was assigned. The nozzles, which demanded a very high degree of skill were, as we have seen, dealt with separately. Similarly all the different valves were fitted by one man and two assistants ; and the following are some of the other groups of engine parts fitted separately : parallel motions ; governors and throttle valves ; working gears ; steam cases ; the various pumps and so on.

The grouping of these parts was done in the same logical way in which they appeared on the Memoranda previously discussed. The basis was technological and the articles which each group of workmen (consisting, sometimes, of a foreman with several assistants, sometimes, of only one or two men with one boy) was asked to work, were all more or less of a similar type. The principle of division of labour had in this way obtained a strong foothold in the engineering industry— the least suited to an early introduction of it—and it is undoubtedly the desire to increase each man's efficiency in the performance of a particular job, though probably decreasing his general skill, which accounts for it.

The next important class is that of the turners. They, too, had long been general workmen of whom a high degree of skill was expected. Most of the boring work also was usually done by them on an ordinary lathe. To-day greater subdivisions have been introduced, and with the improvements in lathes, such as the automatic lathe, " the province of the turner has been lessened more and more. . . . The natural result is that he has ceased to be the all-round workman that he used to be." [1] At Soho, although he was a skilled craftsman, the turner was by no means the general workman taken as typical even of the later part of the last century. We find that a number of different classes had been set up and that different work was assigned to each. So the turning, draw-filing and finishing of pistons and air-pump rods was to be done by William Buxton and John Mincham, while John Allport and John Hunt were detailed for the turning of the heavier parts—cylinders, pistons, rotative shafts, etc. Another man and his assistant did the turning of smaller parts, such as gudgeons for engines below 16 horse-power ; but here a certain mixing of functions seems to have existed, for they were also to fit the " Sun and Planet " wheels and certain other parts.

Boring was done by two other men specially employed for this job, and the large and small drills were worked by Samuel Eales and Francis Evans respectively.

Little information is given regarding pattern-making, but it is safe to conclude from the existence of a special patternmakers' shop that this operation, too, had, to some extent,

[1] Rowe, J. W. F., *op. cit.*, p. 98.

become a specialised craft. Lastly, six general labourers were employed in weighing, packing, loading and unloading.

It would appear, however, from other papers of the same date that the above specialised assignment of jobs was a plan for the future and that it was as yet not quite strictly adhered to. There are in existence several abstracts of the time and cost of the fitting of engines which show in one instance that, out of eight workmen mentioned, four were employed on one job only while the other four were employed on two or more jobs. In the latter case, however, the time spent on one operation greatly exceeded that spent on the others. For a 2 horse-power engine for Liverpool Waterworks, we find that William Harrison was employed seven days in turning and thirty-one days in fitting; Simeon Allport three and one-half days in turning, one day in boring and thirty-nine and three-quarter days in fitting; John Johnson one day in turning and forty-four and one-half days in fitting, and lastly John Allport, who was employed in all stages, five days in turning, five days in boring, one-quarter day in drilling, and three and one-quarter days in fitting. Thus some overlapping was still usual; but from a comparison of the times spent by each man on the operations he performed, it will be seen that this was not serious. Essentially each man did specialised work; and it is safe to assume that the division established in September, 1801, would be carried out more and more strictly as the manufacturing side of the business developed.

Now, after this detailed study of the four papers dealing with the layout of shops and machinery, routing of processes and division of work, some general idea can, perhaps, be formed of the organisation of production at Soho and the principles underlying these plans. The first thing to note is the fact that plans were drawn up at all; and the methods of planning adopted can, without any exaggeration, be described as scientific. In essence they follow the steps laid down as scientifically correct by modern theories. What is the main principle of this new science ? For the best and shortest definition of it we must look to the economist rather than to the professional expert. " Scientific Management," writes Marshall, " is in the main a method of redistributing and reorganising the functions and the mutual relations of the personnel of a great business, with the purpose of increasing aggregate efficiency by narrowing the range of responsibility of its employees and bringing careful studies to bear on the instructions given in regard to the simplest manual operations." [1]

This simple, yet fundamental, definition is certainly applicable to the Soho firm. One authority quoted before describes the scientific method as mainly consisting of the analysis of the problems into their elements, the collection of elaborate statistical data concerning these problems and the drawing of inferences from the records so collected.[2] It is exactly in this way that Matthew Robinson Boulton and James Watt, jr., proceeded once they had reached the decision to extend and reorganise the existing plant. For some time previous to the drawing up of the plans, elaborate statistical records had been kept and these continued for some years after the establishment of the new *régime*. From the tables showing the value of goods sent out from Soho, together with the proportions of those made outside for the years 1791 to 1794, it is clear that some thought had been bestowed on the problem of estimating the prospective production. Details of the technical side of processes were also recorded. One of these, a " Specification of articles bored under the large drill for ye

[1] Marshall, A., *Industry and Trade* (1923), p. 368.
[2] Jones, E. D., *op. cit.*, pp. 15 and 16.

purpose of fixing a ratio for ye firm," [1] gives such items as the number, diameter, length and thickness of all bored parts for the various sizes of engines.

Thus, after some idea of the desired productive capacity of the plant had been reached, the problem of organising the production processes was tackled from the technical point of view. The requirements in the way of machinery were ascertained, together with the shops in which it was to be housed, and the men who would be required to work it. In deciding the situation of the shops and the sequence of processes the state of development of engineering was the determining factor. Already, in 1779, Watt had written and printed for private circulation a small booklet entitled " Directions for erecting and working the newly invented steam engines by Boulton & Watt." [2] It was intended to be used by clients of the firm and, above all, by their engine erectors ; and it deals at great length with every step in the erection of an engine. By 1800 the booklet was to some extent out of date ; but it undoubtedly helped considerably in the drawing up of the order of operations to be performed at Soho.

How does the layout compare with what is now considered the " optimum " ? It is usual to contrast the modern " flow-of-work " structure with the old workshop structure. In the latter the arrangement is on the basis of shops in each of which only one particular operation is performed, e.g. drilling, boring, turning, or fitting. Historically this system arose as a result of manual production being superseded by the new machine technique which shifted the centre of interest from the whole product to a part process. Shops became separated in space. The new industrial revolution, however, established the doc-

[1] B. & W. Colln. [2] *Ibid.*

trine of cheaper production through mass production. This could only be achieved through the avoidance of wasteful intervals (one of the causes of which is the retrograde movement of articles necessitated by the shop structure) in which the raw material would be brought from the stores into the first shop where it would travel to and fro between the various benches, and so on through the different shops, causing lack of work in one place and congestion in another.

The shop structure is by modern authorities considered a "historical rather than a logical category." It forms "a transition between handicraft production and modern mass production."[1] The writer here quoted qualifies himself, however, by admitting that the workshop structure may be quite a good system provided the situation of the workshops follows the sequence of the production process. This would be similar, to some extent, to the flow of work structure according to which there is only one gigantic shop in which the benches follow each other in space in the same order as the operations in time. The compromise between the two systems corresponds actually to the method employed at Soho. It is evident from the arrangement that this easy flow of the castings from one shop to the next was kept in mind. As far as the technical achievements of the time permitted, this was the best plan that could have been adopted. It was suited both to the size of the demand which, though considerable for the time, was certainly not large enough to call for mass production as well as to the degree to which the application of machinery had been carried. In this respect there can be no doubt that all that the time could offer was adopted ; and that amounted to considerably more than was customary. It brought with it

---

[1] Ermanski, J., *Theorie und Praxis der Rationalisierung* (1928), p. 362.

an extension in the division and specialisation of labour, and, although manual work still remained in use for finer operations, it can, nevertheless, be stated that Soho was a scientifically planned factory, manufacturing steam engines by machines driven in their turn by steam power.

To-day the adoption of scientific methods in the designing of plant is expected to lead to the all-round employment of the same methods : in solving problems of wage payment, book-keeping, costing, etc. ; and since a high degree of scientific planning is claimed for Soho, further proof for this contention will be forthcoming in the discussion of those records that deal with the other factors mentioned.

CHAPTER THREE.

WAGES AND LABOUR CONDITIONS.

THE problem of labour remuneration occupies an important place in all modern systems of industrial organisation. At Soho changes in the methods of wage payment were closely associated with changes in the organisation of production. Some of the rates of wages prevailing during the earlier years of the steam engine business have already been mentioned.[1] The system of production then in force demanded little specialisation of functions, and this fact was reflected in the wage rates. Comparatively few men were employed in the engine yard, while until as late as 1795 the number of engine erectors did not rise above eighteen, the figure usually being much lower, Among these workmen little specialisation had taken place. Roughly speaking, apart from the salaried clerks and draughtsmen, they can be divided into engine smiths and general labourers who were all paid a fixed wage, the former between 12s. 6d. and 15s. and the latter about 10s. per week. Some of the engine smiths who were exceptionally capable and reliable were trained as engine erectors and then received a slightly higher wage, usually between one and two guineas. in addition to travelling expenses.

It is difficult to form a correct idea of how these wages compare with the general level of industrial wages at the time. The great scarcity of skilled workers tended to raise the level

[1] See p. 64.

of wages in the new industries, which were in this way able to absorb much labour previously employed in agriculture. The variations in the level of wages from one place to another depended in fact on the existence or absence of flourishing new industries. On the whole, it would seem that wages at Soho compared favourably with those in other parts of the country, at any rate until the late eighties. Many of the millwrights engaged there came from Scotland and obtained a wage of between 12s. 6d. and 15s. a week. As early as 1779, Boulton mentions that Wilkinson was offering the Scottish millwrights 8s. or 9s. per week, " but they can do better in this neighbourhood." [1]

For the later years, however, the evidence is rather conflicting. A recent research maintains that wages at Soho were kept down to a low level; [2] but this observation is based exclusively on a comparison with the Manchester district where the flourishing cotton industry created a somewhat exceptional state of affairs. Compared with Manchester, wages at Soho were indeed low ; and when, in 1792, Peter Ewart was asked to engage eight or ten workmen in Manchester, he could only report that there 57s. or 58s. a week was the minimum paid to skilled workers. Even as late as 1803, James Lawson reported from Manchester : " Workmen here are getting very great wages—common labourers from 16s. to 18s. per week, and hardly to be got." [3]

On the other hand, we have evidence that, in comparison with Cornwall, the Soho wages were high. Well-tried erectors were scarce, and when, in 1794, one was wanted for Cornwall Foreman, the head clerk, reported that the only man available

---

[1] Boulton to Watt, 1779, Oct. 4. B. & W. Colln.
[2] Dickinson and Jenkins, *op. cit.*, p. 267.
[3] J. Lawson to Boulton, 1803, Feb. 27. A.O. MSS.

was James Price who received 18s. a week ; but since people in Cornwall were " unwilling to pay even a good hand high wages," he did not venture to send him.[1] Thus conditions varied considerably throughout the country, although it would appear that wages at Soho compared less favourably with the general level of industrial wages during the later years in the firm's history, probably on account of the diminishing scarcity of suitable labour.

During the earlier years the workers at Soho were quite well off. Their wages were high, and as production, consisting of a minimum of smaller and more elaborate engine parts, was carried on in a more or less unregulated way, the pressure of the new factory routine was little felt. Moreover, since the erection of the engine depended on the timely supply of the main parts, the Soho workmen had not as a rule to work to any too exacting a time-table. The engine erectors, too, could work in their own time ; and often spells of work would alternate with spells of drunkenness. Their wages were, perhaps, not as high as the superiority of their skill over that of the other workmen would have warranted ; but their expenses were paid in addition to other allowances—mainly for drink—and the firm's dependence on them placed them in a privileged position.

It has been stated that weekly wages were paid at Soho during the earlier years ; and this is, on the whole, true. The comparative advantages of piece-rates over a set wage, however, received some attention. Boulton first raised the question in 1778. " Query," he wrote to Watt, " if it would not be better to persuade Joseph Horton to undertake the work by the pound." [2] And in the same letter he reported that he was

[1] Foreman to Watt, 1794, March 26. B. & W. Colln.
[2] Boulton to Watt, 1778, Feb. 3, *ibid.*

negotiating a new piece-rate with another workman named Hall. He desired him to agree to a rate of 28s. per valve for all nozzles of cylinders with a diameter of over 50 ins., and a guinea per valve for all nozzles of cylinders below 50 ins. ". . . 'Tis nearer," he added, " what they should be than day work will make ' em." It has been impossible to ascertain whether this rate was actually agreed upon ; but the interest which this question aroused would probably justify the conjecture that to some extent piece-rates were in operation at that time.

The engine erectors' wages, too, seem to have been subject to some experiment. One of the erectors proposed to charge by the piece in 1778, and when Boulton reported this to Watt, the latter doubted how it could be done.[1] The time basis necessary for the fixing of a piece-rate would be difficult to ascertain since the time of erection varied so much, and such variations were largely caused by external factors. In Watt's opinion, however, the workman referred to ought to charge his own price, whether by the piece or by day ; and if this should be too high, then Boulton & Watt would have to bear a part of it. This indifference is easily explained by the fact that the engine erectors' charges were borne by the firm's customers and not by the firm itself. For many years afterwards this question of piece-rates for erectors seems to have remained in the background, no further discussion on the point appearing in the firm's correspondence or other records.

In 1797, Lawson writing to Boulton about the efficiency of one of the workmen, Benjamin Frith, states :

" . . . he will by no means be fit to be left to himself, except he has piecework—for I know he has made very long hours—generally nine or ten days per week—when the work might have been done without overtime." [2]

[1] Watt to Boulton, 1778, Aug. 6. A.O. MSS.
[2] Lawson to Boulton, 1797, Dec. 14, *ibid.*

Some years before that date, definite piece-rates appear in the firm's agreements with their men. In 1792 J. Cooper was engaged on a three years' contract as labourer at a wage of 10s. per week,[1] although apparently he was, later, employed as a founder ; for this rate was altered to 10s. per cwt. of brass, iron, or other metal cast. A more elaborate piece-rate appears in 1796, when John Wells was engaged as a caster for a period of three years.[2] He was to receive :

" . . . for every cwt. of brass, iron or other metal cast or molten by him, the said John Wells, and according to patterns to be furnished by the said Matthew Boulton and James Watt into the following articles, viz.,

	Per Cwt.	
	s.	d.
Mixing metals and running the same into ingots .	10	0
Engine brasses	6	6
Large brass cocks	14	0
Small rolls for copying machines . .	14	0
12- and 15-in. rolls for copying machines . .	8	0

and so on in proportion for any other articles not included in the above."

For any articles that could not be included in the above list he was to be paid a weekly wage, the amount of which was not stated in the agreement.

The application of a piece-rate was then, as now, restricted to those articles which had reached a certain degree of standardisation and which were easily classified into various groups. Founders and casters were usually paid according to output, and this custom was adhered to at Soho when the Foundry was built. From 1795 onwards, therefore, the percentage of workers

---

[1] Agreement with J. Cooper, 1792, March 10. B. & W. Colln.
[2] Agreement with J. Wells, 1796, March, *ibid*.

on a piece-rate increased. As far as smiths and engineers were concerned, we could only expect an increase in the range of operations to which piecework was applied with an increase in the number of articles manufactured.

With the introduction of technical improvements, notably that of the rotative engine, and the increase in the output of steam engines, the various engine parts became more capable of gradation and standardisation. The power of the new engines measured in horse-power units depended on the various dimensions of the cylinder ; and either these or the horse-power itself would form a good basis for a piece-rate. Furthermore, the taking over by the Soho Manufactory of the production of practically all the engine parts led to a greater use of machinery. One consequence of this was that it became much easier to measure and standardise the time taken for various operations ; and, since this is an indispensable preliminary to the fixing of a piece-rate, the introduction of a system of payment by result became possible. In addition, the new organisation at Soho brought about a greater specialisation of labour and a breaking up of the different classes of workmen into many groups of varying degrees of skill. This, too, would lead to the adoption of more elaborate methods of wage payment.

Altogether, then, the same forces which led to the organisation of efficient methods of production brought about a greater concern with the problem of labour remuneration ; and, from 1795 onwards, a series of documents exist which illustrate this concern, and the fact that both at the Soho Foundry and the Soho Engine Manufactory payment by result was used more and more extensively. The majority of these tables, memoranda, and calculations date from the same period as the papers discussed in the last chapter—1800-01, and it would, therefore, be correct to state that technical and economic innovations and improvements went hand in hand.

The first document in this series gives a detailed list for the Soho Engine Manufactory of all operations paid by time and piece. The full title of this paper is : " Account of the Work done by the Day and by the Piece in the Engine Yard," and it is dated : " Soho, June, 1800." [1] The operations paid at day rates are far more numerous than those paid by the piece. All the operations on the cylinder, the piston, the steam case, the crank, rotative wheels, the fly-wheel, the connecting rod and a number of pipes—in short, the majority of the most important engine parts—were paid for on a day rate basis. These operations included, for each part, turning, boring, drilling, and fitting ; and the name of the workman employed on each of these is also stated on the list. The second column enumerates the operations done by the piece, the rate and the names of the workmen concerned. It is worthy of notice that, according to this list, no one article was produced entirely by the piece, but only one operation—the fitting of certain engine parts—was paid in that way. The rate was not based on a uniform system throughout, but three different systems were applied :

1. There was a flat piece-rate, i.e. a certain sum for each article fitted. Examples of this type were :

The fitting of blowing valves to the blow pipes, which was paid at the rate of 2s. 6d. per valve. The fitting of safety and socket pipes, for which James Wright received 8s. and 12s. each respectively. He also fitted throttle pipes at the rate of 10s. 6d. each and, together with another workman, he fitted feeding and reverse valves for 2s. each. Lastly, the governor was fitted at the rate of 18s. per piece.

[1] B. & W. Colln. See Appendix XII.

2. A piece-rate varying according to the size of the diameter :

The fitting of air pumps and buckets with valves was paid at the rate of 3s. per inch of diameter. The fitting of nozzles with valves, one of the most important and difficult operations, was done by one foreman, assisted by two men and one lad. The rate for this operation was 22s. per inch of diameter for double and 18s. for single sets of valves, while that for parallel motions was again 3s. per inch of diameter.

3. Lastly, there was a rate varying with the horse-power of the engine, and this was applied to the fitting of working gears only. The rates given in the list are :

£2 18s. 6d. for 4 h.p.
£3 3s. od. ,, 6-12 h.p.
£3 13s. 6d. ,, 14-20 h.p.

Dating from the same year we possess a similar list for the Foundry endorsed " Particulars of the work done by the Piece at Soho Foundry, 1800." [1] This, however, gives, as the title shows, only those operations which were paid for by the piece, and it shows some interesting differences from the previous list. First of all a much greater variety of operations is included in this list, and several which were paid for by the day at the Engine Manufactory were paid for by the piece at the Foundry. These included all operations on the cylinder glands, the fitting of pistons with covers, the turning and filing of the piston rods and the turning and filing of air-pump bucket rods. In addition, all the work paid by the piece at the Engine Manufactory is also included. Apart from this difference, there appears also an additional system of varying the piece-rate, namely by weight of output. For the boring and turning of cylinder glands, one man was paid 5s. per cwt.

[1] B. & W. Colln. See Appendix XIII.

for all sizes. The same man also turned piston rods for which he was paid at the rate of 1¼d. per lb. net weight.

The two lists reveal several other differences. A comparison shows that a somewhat greater specialisation of labour had taken place at the Engine Manufactory than at the Foundry. At the former, the men were not only employed on producing fewer engine parts ; but, on the whole, each man was throughout engaged in one particular operation only. At the Foundry one man, Bunting, was employed on the following variety of operations—he bored and turned cylinder glands, turned and filed piston rods and air-pump bucket rods, and he fitted parallel motions.

On balance, however, the two documents discussed support the statement that a high degree of subdivision of functions had been attained. Although few men were, according to these lists, concerned in the production of one article only, the majority of them performed only one operation on them. Within one year the remarkable development discussed in the previous chapter had taken place. The lists of the piece-rates at Soho Foundry of 1800 when compared with the distribution of workmen in 1801,[1] shows how the pace of improvement had been increased. The specialisation of labour had, within that one year, been carried out to a surprising degree as a careful comparison of these documents shows, one particularly striking example being that of the aforementioned Bunting whose jobs, from the variety enumerated, were reduced to that of fitting parallel motions only.

As regards the actual wage-rates, there is ample evidence to show that, even before the drawing up of the above papers, experiments had taken place. Since the fitting of various parts

[1] See Appendix X.

197

was the main operation to which piecework rates were applied, this was the operation which received the greatest attention before 1800. The best example is that of the fitting of nozzles, stated to be done by the piece by " Joseph Turner & Co." A detailed record is preserved of the total work done for the two years ending September 30, 1799, by this group which consisted in the beginning of John Turner, W. Smallwood, and Joseph Turner, jr., an apprentice. This paper is entitled " Profit made by the men in fitting nozzles by the Piece at Soho, September 30, 1797, to September 30, 1799." [1] and it throws an interesting light on the firm's experiments with labour remuneration. It is a detailed record for each individual job, and gives particulars of the time taken, the wage-rate, and the total earnings. It is drawn up in the following form :

No.		Days.		£	s.	d.
1	Drinkwater valve, 3¼ ins.					
	John Turner & Smallwood . . .	18½	16s.	2	9	4
	Joseph Turner, jr.	10	4s.	0	6	8
				2	16	0
	Valve, 3¼ ins. . . . . . —		22s.	3	11	6
	Profit			£0	15	6

Men's profit—10d. per day.
Wages—2s. 8d. = 3s. 6d. per day each, Turner & Smallwood.

According to this example, a curious system seems to have been in operation. The table shows on the one hand. a time-rate (in the case of the two senior workmen, 2s. 3d. a day or 16s. a week, and in that of the apprentice, 4s. a week), and on the other hand, the same piece-rate as is stated to have been in force in June, 1800, namely 22s. per inch of diameter for each valve fitted. The obvious conclusion from a study of the

[1] B. & W. Colln.

list is that the workmen were originally engaged on a weekly wage as stated. Afterwards, however, the firm appears to have decided to pay this particular job by the piece, and the only motive that could have induced them to do this must have been the desire to speed up the work. In almost all the instances recorded on this list, the price per job by the piece is higher than that by the time. In one case only does the piece-rate fall below the time wage. Then the difference was 5s. 7d. and the men were paid their agreed time-rate.

The total profit, as it was called, on the job was ascertained and divided by the time taken by the two workmen, when it gave a daily profit which was added to each man's daily wage. The wage of the apprentice was not increased in the same way ; but the time taken by him on each job was also included in the total time wage which was deducted from the piece price. In this way the system would operate exactly like a piece-rate with a guaranteed minimum time wage, and would, therefore, act as an incentive to a speeding up of production. The daily earning of each man was thus invariably increased above the guaranteed daily wage, in some cases considerably. In one case it reached 6s. 9d. per day, which meant an addition to the daily wage of about 150 per cent., and never, under this system, did the earnings fall below 3s. 3d. per day.

The piece-rate was, however, not always the same. For single valves, as has already been stated, it was 18s. per inch of diameter ; but in one instance, at least, the rate is stated at a very much lower figure without any indication of the grounds on which it was reduced. This item refers to a $9\frac{1}{2}$-in. valve which is stated at 11s. per inch of diameter. It may have been an isolated attempt at rate cutting (in this instance the daily earnings were increased by $1\frac{1}{4}$d. only), for the next item again returns to the 22s. rate.

Of great interest is the apportionment of the total earnings per article worked over the three people concerned in its production. Soho was, in every way, a factory; and the journeyman system, an extension of the sub-letting by the merchants which was almost universal at the time in Birmingham district, did not exist. Each worker was employed by the firm, with which he entered into agreements and which was accountable to each man for his earnings. Yet the payment of wages to the men employed in the fitting of nozzles with valves (other examples will be mentioned later) indicates a certain survival of the journeyman system. First, in the case of the two workmen, although each was paid individually, the total time taken by them together over the job was taken into account when computing the piece-rate addition. Furthermore, the time taken by the apprentice who worked under them was also included.

A still more striking example, however, is revealed from the later entries on this record which show that the method had changed to approximate even more closely to the journeyman system. At a later stage the constitution of this group of workmen was changed, and Joseph Turner, sen., was also engaged in the fitting of nozzles. As the later designation " Joseph Turner & Co." shows, he became the foreman of this group, consisting then of the two other men and one apprentice. The first entry concerning the work done by this new group is as follows :

No. 23 Jesson valve, 7¼ ins.	Days.		£	s.	d.
Turner & Smallwood	24¼	16s.	3	4	8
J. Turner, sen.	6	18s.	0	18	0
J. Turner, jr.	12¾	4s.	0	8	6
			4	11	2
Valve, 7¼ ins.	—	18s.	6	10	6
		Profit .	£1	19	4

J. Turner—6 days is equal to 9s. 6½d. per day wages and profit.

200

Thus, as soon as this particular operation had been put under the supervision of a foreman, he alone was given the gain resulting from the difference between piecework earnings and time wages, the method used being the computation of the cost of the job on a day-work basis and the subtraction of the result from the piecework price of the operation. This difference was given to the foreman as an addition to his daily wage which was itself higher than that of the other men.

Although no specific agreement between the firm and the men engaged in fitting valves to the nozzles has been preserved, it is easy to form some idea from this record of the form which it might have taken. The firm would engage the men at a certain weekly wage—18s. for the foreman, 16s. for the two fitters, and 4s. for the apprentice—and would then enter into an additional agreement with the foreman of the group to perform a certain job, with the men working under him at a set rate. Provided the time taken over the job could be reduced, piecework would be more profitable than day-work; and, since the foreman was the only one to profit, it would be to his interest to speed up the work as much as possible.

This is, then, to some extent a survival (in a firm which had, to all intents and purposes, become a factory) of the journeyman system. Under the latter the journeyman would contract to supply a specified article or perform a certain job by the piece; and would himself engage all the men required, paying them a daily wage. The system was naturally conducive to sweating; but of this there was less danger at Soho, for all the workmen were employed directly by Boulton & Watt.

The only result of such a system at Soho would be an excessive desire on the part of the foreman to speed up the work in order to reap the exclusive benefit of what amounted, virtually, to a bonus. The foreman's function may, therefore, in some instances, have approximated to that of the notorious speed boss ; and in most cases the earnings of Joseph Turner, sen., far exceeded his wages. In one instance, when this particular group of men was engaged on the fitting of fifty safety and socket pipes, the gain resulting from the difference between time- and piece-rates amounted to £20 5s. 0d., which was paid to the foreman only. Since he himself worked only four days on this particular job, it meant an increase in his earnings from a wage of 3s. to one of 32s. 10d. per day.

The conclusions drawn from this paper are borne out by the more numerous records in existence for a different operation—the general fitting of small engines. Apart from affording a further example of this curious mixture of an old and a new system, these records illustrate the great interest and attention bestowed upon problems of wage payment.

The fitting of the 2, 3 and 4 h.p. engines was done by William Harrison, an experienced engine-fitter, who had between six and fourteen men working under him. Harrison was given an agreement with Boulton & Watt on January 1,[1] 1800, for four years at a weekly wage of 25s. This agreement further stipulated that every year Boulton & Watt were to make him a donation or present " as shall make his gains equal to 30s. weekly," or they would employ him in " piecework whereby he shall gain that amount."

The latter alternative was later adopted in practice, as is shown from some records for the year 1801. Before definitely fixing a standard system of payment for this particular operation the firm drew up detailed job records and made careful calculations from them. Tables were compiled for three 2 h.p.,

---

[1] Agreement with W. Harrison, 1800, Jan. 1. B. & W. Colln.

one 3 h.p. and one 4 h.p. engines in order to obtain information on the average cost of fitting these sizes. The average cost
for the fitting of the three 2 h.p. engines (exclusive of boilers,
blowing apparatus, fly-wheels and rotative shafts) was found
to be £19 8s. 11⅛d., while the cost of the 3 h.p. and the 4 h.p.
engines was £21 3s. 11d. and £23 9s. 5d. respectively.[1]

After these figures had been ascertained James Watt, jr.,
succeeded in inducing W. Harrison to enter into an additional
agreement, the following main provisions of which are enumerated in a letter addressed to M. R. Boulton, then in London : [2]

> " He will undertake, with the present hands working
> under him and others that are to be got, to fit 2, 3 and 4
> horse engines complete in a workmanlike manner to be
> judged of by Messrs. Boulton & Watt, put them up, try them,
> take them down, black and put them in the magazine ready
> for packing up and keep all his tools in good repair for £20,
> providing he has a constant supply of castings and forged
> work.
>
> " The great and small drills to be used by Wm. Harrison
> at over hours, and when J. Allport's is used by Wm. Harrison,
> J. Allport shall be employed on Wm. Harrison's account for
> a whole day together, the tumbling bar lathe in the Mill
> to be at his disposal at all convenient opportunities. If,
> after any of the castings are begun to be turned or bored,
> should prove wasters, the wages of the men for the time
> employed in turning or boring of such wasters, to be divided
> between both parties.
>
> " If the engines are not put up and tried, three pounds
> to be deducted from the aforementioned price. This
> Agreement to be good for five-and-twenty engines."

---

[1] " Abstract of Fitting of three 2 H. Engines " ; " Abstract of Fitting
3 H. Engine, Mr. Clarke of Bath " ; " Fitting of 4 Horse, Leith Harbour."
B. & W. Colln.

[2] Copy of agreement with W. Harrison for fitting the small engines,
March, 1801, *ibid.*

In this way the firm succeeded in making an exceedingly profitable bargain. The cost of fitting certain sizes of engines was reduced to a permanent standard, a very important preliminary for a sound system of costing. In the second place this standard was in all probability lower than the average cost hitherto of fitting these engines. The average for the five engines chosen is over £21, and there is every reason to suppose that the firm exercised its bargaining power to fix the figure as low as possible.

Above all they had in this way introduced what was, from their point of view, an excellent incentive for speeding-up the work. The foreman would be willing to agree to a somewhat low figure because he had in any case a certain daily wage and was, under the new system, enabled to earn more since he would pocket all the gains obtained through speedier work. The other workmen were not consulted but were left to receive their usual wage which varied between 1s. 8d. and 2s. 10d. a day. They would realise only later that through this new system, although their money wages remained the same, the speed, intensity, and regularity of their work was considerably affected. Then, as to-day, their only safeguard against any excessive speeding up were the limitations imposed by purely technical considerations ; and it is to be assumed that the strictness of the irksome factory routine would increase in proportion to the decrease in the number of manual operations required. As long as castings remained faulty, as long as turners, drillers, and borers turned out work which had to undergo a number of adjustments at the hands of the fitters, and, above all, as long as most of these adjustments could not be done by the aid of machinery, the skilled fitter being at the same time very scarce, the obstacles in the way of speeding-up production by a mere intensification of labour were very formidable indeed. Variations in the time taken over different jobs were not easily subjected to control, and although, in the case of the fitting of one particular part, the foreman was able to increase his earnings considerably, it is likely that in the case of the more complex task of the fitting of the entire engine his power in this direction was limited.

Some information is available for another kind of fitting —that of steam cases. The remuneration for this operation seems to have been subjected to a great deal of experimenting. The following explanatory note attached to a tabulated record of the time taken and the labour cost for the fitting of various sizes of steam cases [1] may be quoted *in extenso* as an illustration of the care bestowed on these experiments and of the considerations guiding the firm in arriving at the ultimate price lists.

" The anomalies in the series of time arise from several causes :

" More or less perfect castings, particularly in regard to the position of the holes which are frequently obliged to be drilled from the negligence of the moulder in placing them erroneously.

" The ratio of the price is neither in the proportion of the diameter nor length of strokes, first because the number of holes into which the pipes of the top and bottom flanks are fitted are the same for several diameters, and secondly, because the holes in the side joints which are principally influenced by the length of stroke, are drilled or cast in the foundry and not by the steam case fitters.

" The ratio of the price will, however, be nearer in proportion to the diameter than to the lengths of the strokes.

" The weights of the pieces and number of pannels are also considerations which increase not only with the diameter, but also with the length of stroke. Besides, in large pannels

---

[1] " Fitting of Steam Cases, Nov. 1801." B. & W. Colln.

the risk of warping and of course the difficulty of fitting the
pannels is increased—for which reason it appears that the
times of fitting large cylinders are longer in proportion to
their diameter than for small cylinders. It appears from
the actual times of fitting, as stated in the annexed tables,
that in 564 days, sixteen Steam Cases have been fitted and
the medium diameter about 33 ins. The medium of the
time being 35 days, or a little more than a day per inch of
diameter for the medium sizes, but in the smaller sizes a
less proportion of days, and in the large a greater appears
to be required. The following theorem will coincide nearly
with the results of the table :

$$d \times 1\text{·}2\text{-}5 = \text{time in days.}$$

but it has been found that the cylinders which, from the
tables, appear to require twelve days, or £1 17s. od. for
fitting, may be fitted per piece for £1 1s. od., and the 21″
and 24″ amount, by the tables to £2 14s. od. were fitted by
the piece for £2 os. od., so that the amount per theorem
must be reduced in the same proportion."

Apparently the firm had decided to introduce piece-rates
for this operation, and in order to arrive at the average time
taken—the necessary basis for the computation of a piece-rate
—the records were studied for a considerable period. After
it had been ascertained that the time taken over different sizes
varied more nearly in proportion to the diameter than to any
other factor a formula was drawn up which expressed, roughly,
the time necessary for the fitting of a certain size of steam case.
Since the obvious motive for introducing a price-rate was,
however, the desire to effect a saving in the labour cost, it was
decided to reduce the price per fitting arrived at on the basis
of the time by the formula. Two examples of fittings which
had been done by the piece were taken as a standard, and
reductions in the prices were effected all round in the same

proportion. In this way it was possible to draw up a new price list [1] which, apart from lumping together several dimensions of steam cases according to the number of panels on each, showed considerable reductions from the prices computed on the basis of the " theorem." An additional list of " proposed prices " [2] shows rates still further reduced, and these, according to the title, were to be enforced. However, it is not clear whether these were intended entirely to supersede the old time-rates. The fitting of steam cases was, like that of nozzles, entire engines and indeed any kind of fitting, gangwork ; and it is, therefore, quite possible that the piece prices for steam-case fitting were also intended for the foreman only, who alone would reap the benefit of the difference between the piece-price and the total time-cost. No explicit statement on this point is available.

These attempts at a radical introduction of payment by results were not confined to the fitting of engines and engine parts only, but experiments were also made with other operations, such as boring, drilling, and turning. In some of these operations the application of machinery had reached a higher degree, and they were, therefore, more suited to the introduction of direct incentives than fitting where they had to be introduced indirectly.

The boring of cylinders and air pumps was one of the most important operations to receive greater attention. This part of the production process had, throughout the development of the steam engine, been of the utmost importance ; and on the exactness and speed with which cylinders were bored depended to a large extent the technical and commercial success of the engine. When the manufacture of steam engines

---

[1] See Appendix XIV.   [2] See Appendix XV.

was taken over entirely by the Soho firm, boring became even more important than it had been before ; and, since technical and economic considerations were constantly applied in practice to all stages of production, in this branch, too, improvements were soon introduced.

Technically, all that was available at the time had been applied and the progress of the Soho boring mill has already been mentioned.

Improvements of an economic nature followed quickly and incentives for speeding-up, to be included in the remuneration for this particular operation, were considered. The system ultimately adopted for the borers differs considerably from those already mentioned, and demonstrates once more how peculiarly " modern " were the methods at Soho.

The difficulties in the way of introducing direct payment by results for borers were still considerable. In spite of the introduction of improved machines the time taken over each job seems, from a detailed record in existence,[1] to have varied considerably and not always in proportion to any of the dimensions of the articles bored. It would, therefore, have been very difficult to establish the time which each particular size of cylinder and air pump ought to take in boring on the basis of which a piece-rate could have been calculated. It is probable that any attempt to introduce a piece-rate on such unsound foundations would have met with considerable opposition on the part of the workmen. At all events there is no evidence that it was ever attempted.

But, although day-work rates had to be left in force for the borers, a certain measure of incentive was introduced by the granting of a bonus addition for cylinders and air pumps

[1] " Abstract account of cylinders bored from 1796, Dec. 31, to 1800, Jan. 11." B. & W. Colln.

bored, varying according to their sizes. In the computation of these " gratuities," as they were called, the firm employed the methods which might lead to the establishment of a piece-rate ; and three tables illustrate each step in the procedure.[1]

In order to compute a bonus it was first necessary to find the average time taken for the different sizes, and, here, the difficulties were great. There was, first of all, the average time calculated from the actual time records by dividing the total time taken for each size by the number of cylinders of that size bored. The times arrived at in this way are set out in column four of the table for cylinders. This method was unsatisfactory for obvious reasons. The times were not necessarily the same for each cylinder of the same size owing to differences of a technical nature ; nor did they vary in direct proportion to the different sizes. In order to bring the figures more nearly in proportion to the real times an attempt was made to combine the two dimensions of the cylinders, the diameter and the length. These two, the first in inches and the second in feet, were multiplied and the result was called " surface " ; but this new factor was, of course, only a figure which would vary in direct proportion to the surface. It was then possible to arrive at a new set of average times for each size on the basis of this new factor ; but this, as an explanatory note to the table states, was also found to be unsatisfactory since : " the times of facing the cylinders and some other parts of the operation are not in the ratio of their diameter and length."

A new theorem was therefore substituted. To the " surface " was added 72 and the total thus obtained, when divided

---

[1] See Appendices Nos. XVI., XVII., and XVIII. It will be observed that in the tables a number of items show minor deviations from the rule set out above. This may be explained by clerical errors or, in some cases, by the introduction of additional factors which are not explicitly stated.

by 30, gave the number of days which the job ought to take. By multiplying the number of days by 5 the gratuity in pence is found for each particular size of cylinder. The same method was used for calculating the bonus for air pumps, but here the rate was only 3d. per day instead of 5d.

It can hardly be said that the method ultimately adopted was scientifically satisfactory or that it overcame all the difficulties in the way of finding a correct measure for the time each job ought to take. To-day, the industrial psychologist and the scientific manager maintain that they can, by the aid of careful study of time and motion, ascertain scientifically the time necessary for any particular operation. The method adopted at Soho was limited by many technical imperfections ; but its motives and the calculations which led to it are surprisingly in advance of the age, for it must be remembered that machine production was then in its infancy. It cannot, therefore, be called a rough and ready one ; and the firm was apparently satisfied with it, for a final table was drawn up,[1] setting out the gratuities varying for each size from 9d. to 4s. 1d. for air pumps and from 1s. 8d. to 11s. 4d. for cylinders.

It is very difficult to estimate how far these premiums provided an effective incentive. The decrease in subsequent years in the time required for boring is so largely bound up with improvements in the machines that speculations on the part played by these economic measures would be useless. Their potential strength can be judged by a comparison of the gratuity with the average daily wage for borers of 2s. 6d. Since the gratuities were calculated on a time basis, the percentage addition to the wages would not vary for the different sizes of cylinders or air pumps. For cylinders a gratuity of

[1] See Appendix XVIII.

5d. per day meant an addition of a little over 16 per cent. on the daily wage, and for air pumps, the addition was 10 per cent. Thus a man, boring a small cylinder of 4 ft. in length and with a diameter of $12\frac{1}{4}$ ins., might earn about 10s. as his wages for four days, with an additional " gratuity " of 1s. 8d. On a very large cylinder of 11 ft. in length and with a 5 ft. 4 in. diameter he would work about twenty-seven days and get £3 7s. 6d., plus a bonus of 11s. 4d.

How strong an incentive a 10 per cent. or 16 per cent. output bonus was it is difficult to say. That the system was intended as an incentive to increase the output there can be no doubt. It can certainly be described as one of the systems of payment by results [1] all of which are primarily intended to act as incentives. The system had, at any rate, the advantage of being straightforward, and was one which could easily be understood by the workmen who were given their usual time wages plus an additional bonus per unit of output which would, in however small a measure, have induced a certain intensification of production. Even to-day, when an enormous number of bonus, premium-bonus and efficiency systems are used in the engineering industry, a recent writer with great practical experience seems to favour this simple method and quotes another authority in support, mentioning the extremely successful results of " a scheme which gave to the actual producers a bonus on output, superimposed on plain time-rates " [2] introduced at the National Factory, Cardoland.

The next important operation to be considered is drilling.

---

[1] See Spicer, R. S., *British Engineering Wages* (1928), p. 22. The classification of " Systems of Payment by Result " includes : " Time-rate plus price per article."

[2] Watson, W. F., " Wages Differentia," in *Realist*, Nov. 1929, quoting from an article by F. S. Button, entitled " Payment by Results."

The general practice at Soho, until the end of 1801, seems to have been to pay time wages to the drillers. Two drills were generally used. The first, the large drill, was the more important one and served for boring nozzles, pumps, and pipes, etc., while the small drill was used only for drilling of holes in lids and similar work. The workers operating the large drills received, as a rule, 2s. 8d. per day, and their work shows less specialisation than that of some of the other operatives ; generally, they bored a great variety of articles though mostly groups of articles of a similar nature.

In 1801, a year, as we have already seen, of great importance in the organisation of the firm, it was apparently decided to reduce the labour cost of the various articles bored under the large drill ; and, with this aim in view, a record of all the articles bored by one of the men was drawn up. Francis Evans, one of the skilled workers, was chosen, and his work record for the period May 2 to October 24, 1801, was tabulated under various headings, such as nozzles, safety pipes, forcing pumps, stop pipes, etc.[1] This is the form which the record took :

CONNECTING RODS.

Power.	Number of Days.	Price per Day.	Amount of Wages upon each Article.
H.P.		s. d.	s. d.
8	$\frac{1}{2}$	2 8	1 4
20	$\frac{1}{4}$	2 8	1 4
6	$\frac{1}{2}$	2 8	1 4
8	$\frac{1}{4}$	2 8	0 8
14	$\frac{1}{2}$	2 8	1 4

[1] " Goods Bored under the Large Drill by Francis Evans, from May 2 to Oct. 24, 1801." B. & W. Colln.

STOP PIPES.

Power.	Number of Days.	Price per Day.		Amount of Wages upon each Article.	
H.P.		s.	d.	s.	d.
40L	½	2	8	1	4
8H	½	2	8	1	4
40L	1¼	2	8	3	4
248	¼	2	8	0	8
32	¾	2	8	2	0
T.W.	¾	2	8	2	0
36	½	2	8	1	4

In the same way the labour costs of all articles bored by this particular workman were ascertained and recorded. A study of the table shows that variations in the time taken over each job, and consequently in its cost, did not correspond directly to variations in the power of the engine to which the article belonged. This is evident from the two examples given above; but one particularly striking instance is that of three hot-water pumps bored by Francis Evans; two for 8 h.p. engines and one for a 20 h.p. engine. The two former jobs took 1¼ and ¾ days respectively, and their cost was 3s. 4d. and 2s.; the latter took only half a day at a cost of 1s. 4d. Here, again, variations must be explained by technical considerations, by faulty casting and delays caused by machinery which was not very exact.

The job record of this one man was, however, taken as the basis for the introduction of piece-work rates for this particular operation. In this instance, the choice of the worker above did not "enable the capitalist all the more easily to increase the normal degree of intensity of labour."[1] Francis Evans does not appear to have been an exceptionally efficient

[1] Marx, K., *Capital* (Everyman edition, 1930), vol. 2, p. 605.

workman ; and other time-sheets show that the time taken by him over different jobs was by no means lower than the average.

On the other hand, it cannot be said that any benevolent considerations guided the firm in choosing the performance of this worker as the basis for study. The list of piece-prices,[1] drawn up after the job record of Francis Evans, contains a series of very drastic changes. In practically all instances the new piece-rate shows a considerable reduction on the time-work cost. One example of this is to be found in the new rates for throttle pipes which are stated to be as follows :

> " 1s. 6d. to 2-in. thickness inclusive.
> 2s. 0d. to 2½-in.   „   „
> 2s. 6d.   all above."

On Francis Evans' list there appears for this article a far greater variety, ranging from a cost of 1s. 4d. to 5s. 4d. per job.

Still more striking is the reduction in safety pipes. Evans had, during the period recorded, bored five at 8d. each, five at 1s. 4d., one at 2s. 0d. and one at 2s. 8d. The new list stipulates a uniform rate, " safety pipes to be 6d. each." Connecting rods were reduced to two rates only :

> " 1s. 0d. to 4-in. diameter of hole.
> 1s. 2d. above,"

and in almost all other instances the new piece-rate is considerably reduced and smaller variations are allowed. It will be noticed from the examples quoted above that, on the new list, the piece-rate varies according to the dimension of the article bored. Sometimes this variation was, as exampled by the boring of cold-water pumps, paid at 7d. per inch of diameter. Since the dimensions are not stated on Francis Evans' record,

---

[1] " Calculations of piece prices of articles bored under the Great Drill, Nov., 1801." B. & W. Colln.

it is impossible to compare the cost on time-work and piece-work of any particular item, although the great reductions in the range of rates is apparent.

Unfortunately, it is impossible to state in exactly what way the new rates were applied, i.e. whether or not they were to supersede entirely the old system of time-work for this operation. Most of the old agreements with the men employed in the Soho engine yard lapsed in the years 1800 and 1801 ; and although for several classes of workmen—mostly fitters—new agreements stipulating a weekly wage were made from those years onwards, not one such agreement—if ever made—is in existence for the men employed in drilling and boring. One may, therefore, be justified in assuming that after November, 1801, it was intended to pay these men by the piece. More-over, it seems difficult to believe, in view of the comparatively low figures at which these new rates were stated, that they were intended to remain in existence side by side with the high time-rates, which would then have taken the place of a guaranteed minimum.

On the other hand, there exists a list of the labour cost of the turning of some articles drawn up in 1802 on the basis of day wages, which includes also a list for the boring of several nozzles. These seem to have taken considerably longer in boring than the items on Evans' list ; and, although the daily wage was only 2s. 6d., their average cost was 6s. 7¼d. each as compared with 3s. 4d. in 1801. One explanation might be that these were nozzles of a new construction which were just being introduced ; and this would account both for the longer time taken and for the fact that, during the experimental stage, time-rates were paid, but it is also possible that the firm was forced to return to time-work for this operation which was very difficult to standardise. Or, in view of the disproportionate variations in the time taken, the narrow range of piece-prices adopted might have appeared to the workers as a very high-handed measure ; and it is quite likely that they brought strong pressure to bear on the management to return to the old system.

In connection with the piece-rates there is also the question of the standard of quality to be considered. On this point the piece-price list contains the following :

" *General Observations.*

" When articles are defective in the casting and the borer is obliged to go through twice from this cause, he is to be paid one half more. When wasters occur from his own negligence, or he is obliged to bore articles a second time to remedy defects caused by his inattention, the borer is to suffer the loss of his time. When the articles prove wasters from the defects of the casting, the borer is to be paid wages for the time employed, before the defect is discovered. . . ."

This is the only (and very vague) provision on a point of great importance under a system of payment by results. The borers would be largely at the mercy of their employers ; " for," as Marx says, " the work must be of an average goodness if the piece-price is to be paid in full. From this point of view, piece-wages become a fruitful source of deductions from wages and of capitalist cheating." [1]

Whether this was actually so at Soho would depend very largely on the benevolence of the employer ; and, in the absence of any definite evidence, it can only be assumed that under the new *régime*, which aimed scientifically at efficient production, strictness in the enforcement of different rules would increase.

[1] Marx, K., *op. cit.*, vol. 2, p. 603.

The last instance in this series of wage experiments is that concerning the remuneration of the turners. This class of workmen was of great importance in view of the comparatively high degree of exactness attained by the improved lathes at Soho, and also in view of the fact that practically every article had to pass through the turning process. It was, moreover, as is seen from the distribution of the workmen, the most specialised operation, each turner being generally employed on a small range of jobs only. In one case alone was the then rather uncommon practice of complete separation between turning and boring broken, a note on the time record of the turning of various engine parts informing us that " the large pistons are bored in the lathe. The times of this operation are therefore, in such cases, included under the turning." [1]

It may be assumed that a standardisation of the times required for this operation would have been easier than for the others. From the time-sheet it would seem that the times required for turning articles remained fairly constant for each size and varied only in proportion to variations in the size. Thus the system of payment ultimately chosen for this operation is of great importance, for it would, in all probability, be the one which the firm preferred on purely economic grounds, technical considerations being of less consequence.

The system adopted was the same as that for the boring of cylinders—a time wage plus a piece bonus. The procedure was also similar. A time record of the turning of all pistons, covers, shafts, gudgeons, etc., was first made and the average time for several units of each size of the article or power of the engine was calculated. A " Proposed Standard Time "

[1] " Time of turning sundry articles, in order to ascertain the times employed by the turner, 1800." B. & W. Colln.

was then fixed and all the figures were tabulated in the following way :

PISTONS AND COVERS.

Sizes or Power.	Turning.		Whole Time.	Average Time.	Proposed Standard Time.
	Centring.	Turning.			
64D.	—	—	12	—	11
60d.	—	—	9	—	10
50H.	½	6½	7	—	7
etc.	etc.	etc.	etc.	etc.	etc.

In the case of this operation, however, unlike in that of boring cylinders, the standard times were not based on any complicated calculation or theorem. As a matter of fact, they show little variation from the average times actually taken. In the majority of instances these were slightly reduced ; but in one or two cases they were increased. Since the times taken varied more or less in proportion to the dimensions of the article turned, it was probably thought that the averages corresponded more closely to the times the jobs ought to take than would otherwise have been the case. The premium was then calculated for each size of the articles concerned, or power of the engine, on the basis of 2s. 6d. per week of the proposed standard time ; and the premium list ultimately drawn up is in the following form :

PISTONS AND COVERS.

Sizes or Power.	Average of Times.	Premium at rate of 2s. 6d. per Week.
	hours.	s.　d.
64D. to 60D.	10½	4　0
etc.	etc.	etc.

It will be noticed that in the above table a number of sizes were taken together. The "average of times" in this table is, however, not the same as the "average time" in the preceding table, but is an average of the standard times for the sizes concerned. The premium was the same as that for boring cylinders, and since the wages of the turners were approximately the same as those of the borers, that is, at the rate of 2s. 6d. per day, the piece premium would mean the same percentage addition to the turners, namely, 16 per cent., but would probably result in a greater speeding-up since the technical obstacles were not so great.

A summary of the different methods of wage payment outlined above shows that all important operations were made a subject for experiment. The following is a list of the operations included :

    1. Fitting—of small engine parts (nozzles) ;
              of steam cases ;
              of entire engines.
    2. Drilling in general and some boring.
    3. Boring of cylinders and air pumps.
    4. Turning in general and some boring.

The general tendency at Soho was to introduce payment by results for all regular labour (apart from salaried employees and general labourers, who were always paid by the time). The three operations under the heading "Fitting" were done by gangs or groups of men. It is, therefore, in these operations—certainly in the first and third and, in all probability, also in the second—that a certain measure of sub-contracting survived. The "contractor" or "piece-master" has disappeared in the same measure as organised labour, which always considered him an enemy, grew stronger. Even to-day the intermediate system between out-and-out sub-contracting and individual piecework, which played so prominent a part at Soho, is in existence in some coal-fields, shipyards, and engineering works.[1]

At Soho, the economic exigencies of factory organisation, rather than any resistance on the part of labour still unorganised, led to its adoption in spite of the traditional local popularity of sub-letting. To the workers it was certainly more advantageous ; although, by providing a strong stimulus to the self-interest of the foreman, it subjected them to a certain pressure on his part. His power was, however, considerably limited, and his very high gains in the fitting of nozzles may be due to the piece-rate being fixed excessively high rather than to any considerable speeding-up of the work.

The reasons for the apparent adoption of an out-and-out piece-rate for drilling, an operation largely not one of routine, are not clear ; and there has been mentioned some indication that this particular method was abandoned in favour of the old-time wage.

Probably the most successful of all methods was the one adopted for operations 3 and 4—boring and turning. In the case of the latter piece-rates could have been more easily introduced than in the former, or indeed in any other operation ; but the fact that the firm adopted the same system of time wages plus a bonus on output for turning as for boring indicates that this method must have worked very satisfactorily.

The mere fact that new and more elaborate methods of wage payment were being devised shows that, with all the other changes at Soho, had come also a gradual but complete change in the attitude to labour and, consequently, in labour

[1] Cole, G. D. H., *The Payment of Wages* (1918), p. 33.

conditions. During the earlier years of the steam engine business the type of labour required and its scarcity were such as to impose certain limits to the wage-fixing power of the management even if it had desired to pay as little as possible. Custom in the case of scarce and highly-skilled engine men would be as strong a wage-fixing factor as the strongest trade-union action of to-day; and although Boulton & Watt, as good and individualist business men, would certainly endeavour to strike as hard a bargain as possible in taking on workmen, they would nevertheless submit to customary figures. It has been shown that the nature and degree of the development of business organisation attained during the years of the older management were not favourable to the organisation of a pro-duction both technically and economically efficient. Wages were, therefore, more or less left to find their own level in a haphazard way.

This indifference to modern management problems is often taken as a sign of the greater benevolence towards the workers where there is a " good " individualist master. Boulton cer-tainly deserved that attribute in the light of the views and practices of his period, and during the time that the Soho business was under his personal care, the conditions of the workers were certainly more favourable than were those obtaining in many of the industries of the " industrial revolu-tion " and in Soho after 1800 ; but it is at least doubtful whether this was due to a more benevolent master or to a less developed business organisation. Boulton's own attitude to-wards the workers, so typical of " paternalism," is well expressed in his speech at the opening of Soho Foundry :

" As the Smith," he said, " cannot do without his Striker, so neither can the Master do without his Workmen. Let each perform his part well and do their duty in that state

221

which it hath pleased God to call them, and this they will find to be the true rational ground of equality."[1]

This indeed was the secret of whatever industrial peace there was until the age of modern industrialism. Boulton acted up to his own dicta ; and, although there is little evidence from his letters that he was less impatient of excessive demands on the part of his workers than his partner, there is ample evidence to prove that he was at least more diplomatic in his personal intercourse with them. He endeavoured to instil a certain *esprit de corps* into all the workers connected with Soho and, among other things, he would often make special events the occasion for giving his workmen an entertainment.[2]

The close personal contact between master and men and, much more so, a factory discipline which was still lax, seems to have resulted in fairly smooth relations between the firm and the workmen. At any rate, no evidence of any disputes appears during the early years of the steam engine business. Whatever unpleasantness there was, arose on grounds such as drunkenness, inefficiency, and bad workmanship.

The first serious dispute was in 1791 when the engine smiths struck. The strike seems to have arisen out of difficulties over the settlement of certain piecework rates caused by the fact that Roberts, a clerk of the engine firm, had left and his account book could not be found. Boulton settled the strike, which seems to have lasted but one or two days, very quickly,[3] and for some years nothing in the nature of a dispute is mentioned.

---

[1] *Aris's Birmingham Gazette*, 1796, Feb. 1.

[2] In honour of his son's coming of age Boulton gave an entertainment, at which over 700 people were present, to all his workmen, their wives and children, *Birmingham Daily Post*, 1863, April 30.

[3] Boulton to Watt, 1791, March 23. B. & W. Colln.

In 1794 Foreman, the new head clerk and book-keeper, was assaulted by some of the men on the pretence that he caused the enlistment in the army of some of the apprentices. A memorandum by Southern [1] shows that there were other reasons too. Foreman seems to have been much stricter than the other clerks in the matter of wage payment, and in some cases appears to have reduced certain piecework rates. He also supervised more closely the contributions to the Soho Sick Club (which will be discussed presently), and lastly, there was also some dissatisfaction among the men over their contributions towards the cost of an additional watchman at Soho during the riots of 1791. When the extra watch was dispensed with the extra pay went, for some time, to the usual watch; but, later, the firm cut this off while continuing to receive the men's contributions, thus making a profit.

Another dispute which affected the firm indirectly is mentioned in 1795 by Lawson who was at work for the firm at Chelsea Waterworks. "We have got on very well at Chelsea," he wrote to Boulton,[2] "till Monday last when all the millwrights struck and are likely to continue for some time." He also mentions an extraordinary degree of solidarity among these unorganised men. "At several places they have left work, tho' the proprietors would give them their own terms, but they will not work till every master accedes to their proposals; they are already better paid than any other class of workman, having a guinea per week and allowance of 6d. per day for beer, and they always make seven days a week."

As regards hours of work there is, strangely enough, no information at all. That there was a definitely fixed number of hours per day and that, when these were exceeded, overtime

---

[1] B. & W. Colln.
[2] Lawson to Boulton, 1795, July 22. A.O. MSS.

EARLY INDUSTRIAL ORGANISATION

was paid, is proved by Lawson's reference to one workman, who " has made very long hours—generally nine or ten days per week—when the work might have been done without overtime." [1]   In the absence of anything else we must assume that the hours were those customary in this kind of employment at the time ; and we can take the Coalbrookdale practice of 10½ hours per day [2] as the best example.   Not until 1828 do we find any statement of hours at Soho.   From that year date a number of regulations dealing with the drawing office which contain a provision for singularly long hours—from 9 a.m. till 1 p.m. ; from 2 p.m. to 5 p.m., and from 5.30 p.m. " until Bellringing in the evening."

In many ways Matthew Boulton took an interest in questions affecting the welfare of his workmen.   Soho itself was well planned and, according to contemporary descriptions, a fairly pleasant workplace.   His interest in this direction is also evidenced by the fact that when the Albion Mill was being built he insisted on the whitewashing of the walls in order to counteract the darkness and dirtiness inside the mill.[3]   He was also averse to the truck system which he thought should not be allowed " lest oppressions should fall upon the weak by overcharges." [4]   In spite of his attitude, however, it remained a general practice at Soho, throughout the firm's history, to pay in rent part of the wages of those men who lived in the houses built for them.

When Boulton delivered his speech at the opening of the Foundry in 1796, the new management by the sons of the old partners had already started, and the seeds of a new organisa-

---

[1] Lawson to Boulton, 1797, Dec. 14.   A.O. MSS.
[2] See Ashton, T. S., *op. cit.*, p. 194.
[3] Boulton to Watt, 1786, March 15.   B. & W. Colln.
[4] Capper to Boulton, 1784, June 11.   A.O. MSS.

tion, with a more detached attitude towards labour, were already there. As the wage memoranda, price lists and calculations show, labour was already well on the way of becoming, as it is to-day, nothing more than one of the factors to be calculated in the costs of production and to be used in the manner most satisfactory to the employer.

To some extent, however, the old spirit of paternalism survived. The factory was still, in all its branches, under the direct supervision of the owners and personal contact was, therefore, not lost. This is illustrated by the survival of such customs as the giving of Christmas presents to all employees. For 1799 a very long list is in existence with presents ranging from 5s., 7s. 6d., and 10s. 6d. in clothing, books or other articles for apprentices, to 10 guineas for clerks, journeymen, fitters, and moulders. The average workman's wages were usually raised at Christmas by 1s. per week.

The most important of all welfare experiments at Soho was, however, the establishment of a mutual insurance society for the benefit of the employees. The organisation of this friendly society is sufficiently exceptional for that time to justify a more lengthy description.

The date of the founding of the "Insurance Society belonging to the Soho Manufactory" is not known. The earliest edition of the rules of the society [1] in existence was printed in 1792, whilst Shaw, in his *History of Staffordshire*, printed between 1798 and 1801, refers to it as "a long-established society for the sick and lame." [2] The motives for its establishment are also not clear. Smiles, with more sympathy

---

[1] " Rules for conducting the Insurance Society belonging to the Soho Manufactory. Printed by Thomas Pearson, 1792." Birmingham Public Reference Library. See Frontispiece.

[2] Shaw, *op. cit.*, vol. 2, p. 120.

than direct evidence or critical judgment, expresses them in
the following terms: " Still further to increase the attach-
ment of the workmen to Soho and keep together his school
of skilled industry as he called it, Boulton instituted a Mutual
Assurance Society in connection with the works." [1]

The same reason is put forward by a more recent and
usually more critical writer who quotes the establishment of
the Insurance Society in support of the statement that " the
paternal side of mastership had not wholly disappeared." [2]

The contemporary view appears, however, more accept-
able. ". . . every precaution has been always taken," writes
Shaw, " and in the most judicious manner, by the proprietors,
to diminish the poor's levies and keep their numerous workmen from becoming troublesome to the parish." [3] The establishment of the Soho Insurance Society is given as an instance.
This view finds some support in the fact that another important employer of that time openly admitted this reason for his
desire to found an insurance society for his men. The journal
of the House of Commons of February 4, 1788, mentions a
petition by John Wilkinson in which he complains of the fact
that, with every expansion of his works, his contribution to
the poor rates increased, together with the hostility of the
overseers. He proposed, therefore, to establish a sickness club
for his workmen and petitioned Parliament to be exempted
from the poor rates after its foundation. [4] The authority
quoting this petition concludes that: ". . . All endeavours
of the English upper classes towards relieving the lower classes,
originated from purely selfish motives. The rise in the burden

---

[1] Smiles, S., *op. cit.*, p. 436.   [2] Lord, J., *op. cit.*, p. 204.
[3] Shaw, *op. cit.*, vol. 2, p. 120.
[4] Hasbach, W., *Das englische Arbeiterversicherungswesen* (1883), p. 49,

of poor relief is, for the Englishman, a symptom of a social disease which he endeavours to remove at all costs—in order to save his own contribution." [1] While another economic historian states that already in the eighteenth century employers founded works insurance clubs ". . . in order to increase their power over their workmen." [2] He does not, however, mention any specific instance (unless he bases his statement on Wilkinson's petition or on the societies at Soho and at the Crowley Ironworks discussed below, neither of which he mentions), and it has been impossible to find any evidence in the contemporary literature for this general assertion.

The eighteenth century marks an epoch favourable to the development of friendly societies ; and a very great number sprang up, with different origins and different organisations. The majority of these lodges, boxes, clubs and funds, were, apart from freemasonry, which was of distinctly aristocratic origin, lower middle-class in character. It is not until this century that we meet any friendly societies catering for workmen, and the now commonly accepted view that they were direct descendants of the medieval gilds,[3] is supported by the fact that the vast majority of them were organised on a craft basis. Those organised on a different basis were exceptional. In 1776 the actors of Drury Lane and, later in the same year, those of Covent Garden, petitioned the House of Commons for the granting of a Charter for a Friendly Society ; and in 1788 the skippers and keelmen on the River Tyne were granted a Charter for their society which, however, did not include self-administration.

---

[1] Hasbach, W., *op. cit.*, p. 49.
[2] Brentano, L., *op. cit.*, vol. 3, p. 337.
[3] See Hasbach, *op. cit.*, pp. 23-29, and Ludlow, J. M. : " Gilds and Friendly Societies " in the *Contemporary Review*, March-April, 1873.

The only friendly society organised on the basis of all workers engaged in the same undertaking mentioned by contemporary writers, is a club established by Lord Harcourt on his estate in Nuneham, Oxfordshire. Such of his labourers as were approved by him paid 1d. each week to which he added a similar sum. " This forms a fund to which they may have recourse upon any exigency." [1]

It is very surprising that the Soho society is not mentioned in contemporary literature, especially in Sir Frederick Eden's elaborate survey ; [2] because it is one of the first examples of an insurance society founded by a manufacturer for all the workmen employed in his works.

There has been found only one earlier instance of such a society which exhibited, however, a very primitive organisation. Early in the eighteenth century the Crowleys had established at their Ironworks at Swalwell and Winlaton, a system of compulsory contributory insurance against death, sickness, and old age, the weekly contribution being 2d. [3]

The Soho scheme was much more ambitious. Its introduction may have been a survival of paternalism ; it may have been dictated by such selfish motives as a desire to reduce the contributions to the poor rates, or—most fascinating of all conjectures—it may have been a welfare move necessitated by such economic exigencies of a large and well-organised works as are stipulated by the enlightened self-interest of to-day.

The regulations of the society were exceptionally elaborate and show some features not found in any other contemporary friendly society. Three different editions of the rules are in

---

[1] Eden, F. M., *The State of the Poor* (1797), vol. 1, p. 614.

[2] None are mentioned in Hasbach, *op. cit.* ; Eden, *op. cit.*, or in Walford's voluminous *Insurance Cyclopædia*, 1876.

[3] Ashton, T. S., *op. cit.*, p. 196.

existence,[1] of which only the one already mentioned is dated. It was, however, possible, from a comparison of the printers of these different editions, to place them in their correct chronological order. Originally, the society was intended to include all persons employed at the Soho Manufactory who earned a minimum of 2s. 6d. and a maximum of 20s. per week. None below or above these limits were admitted. In the two subsequent editions, both printed after 1796, the employees of the Soho Foundry were included and the same limits of earnings kept. In the last edition of the rules, printed after 1804, certain other clauses regarding membership were included. Every prospective member had to be approved by the " elders " of whom more will be stated presently. Furthermore, new employees over 45 years of age, although they had the option of joining the society, were not under any circumstances to receive out of the funds more than four times the total amount of their contributions ; and in case the fund fell below £100 or below £50, their benefits were not to exceed three times or twice, respectively, the money paid in by them.

The society was, to a certain extent, self-administered, and there were two governing bodies, both being required to meet once a week. First, there was a committee of six members of the society who were to serve for three months and who were to choose, on retiring, another six to succeed them. This was later altered, three members retiring every quarter and the whole committee electing three new members in place of the retiring ones. In addition to the committee there were six

[1] In addition to the copy in the Birmingham Public Reference Library, printed by Thomas Pearson in 1792, there is one copy among the Assay Office Manuscripts, printed by Knott & Lloyd, who were Pearson's successors, and several copies both in the B. & W. Colln. and the A.O. MSS. of an edition printed by Thomas Knott, jr., the successor of Knott & Lloyd.

elders appointed by Boulton each quarter, who could be re-moved by him in case of non-performance of duty. These elders supervised the conduct of the committee and acted as arbitrators in cases of dispute, Boulton himself retaining the final control over the affairs of the society, together with the power of making new regulations and abolishing old ones.

Every new member had to pay an entrance fee of 1s. for men, 8d. for boys between 14 and 18, and 6d. for all under that age, for which he received a copy of the society's regula-tions. The scale of contributions varied according to the earnings of each member—an entirely new departure in the regulations of friendly societies—and was as follows :

Each member earning	2s. 6d. per week to pay	½d. per week
,,	,,	5s. 0d.	,,	,,	1d.	,,
,,	,,	7s. 6d.	,,	,,	1½d.	,,
,,	,,	10s. 0d.	,,	,,	2d.	,,
,,	,,	12s. 6d.	,,	,,	2½d.	,,
,,	,,	15s. 0d.	,,	,,	3d.	,,
,,	,,	17s. 6d.	,,	,,	3½d.	,,
,,	,,	20s. 0d.	,,	,,	4d.	,,

The committee had power to fix each member's average earnings for the purposes of this table, and any member setting himself down for more or less than he earned on an average was fined 5s. The names of the members were entered in a register in which all payments were also noted. Contributions were to be handed in every Saturday night—later changed to every Monday morning—and any member who was more than a fortnight behind in his payments was to pay a fine of as much as he owed. The members of the committee in turn had to attend for the purpose of receiving and entering the contri-butions ; and it was later made compulsory, probably on account of inaccuracies that had arisen, for such committee members to " be assisted by an accomptant appointed by the elders and committee, who shall pay such accomptant for his trouble out of the funds of the society." The account books kept by the treasurer were always open to the inspection of the committee.

. The scale of benefits varied according to the contributions, i.e. according to the earnings of the members. The following was the table of benefits payable to any member who was " sick, lame or incapable of work . . . during his illness," as stated in the original rules :

Members earning	2s. 6d.	per week to receive	2s. per week.
,, ,,	5s. 0d.	,, ,,	4s. ,,
,, ,,	7s. 6d.	,, ,,	6s. ,,
,, ,,	10s. 0d.	,, ,,	8s. ,,
,, ,,	12s. 6d.	,, ,,	10s. ,,
,, ,,	15s. 0d.	,, ,,	12s. ,,
,, ,,	17s. 6d.	,, ,,	14s. ,,
,, ,,	20s. 0d.	,, ,,	16s. ,,

These rates were to be valid only as long as the funds of the society were upwards of £100. When they were below that figure the benefits were at the rate of ninepence for every farthing paid in ; and if the fund fell below £50, the rate was reduced to sixpence for every farthing paid in. Members falling ill were also required to give notice to the committee, and the benefits became due three days after such notice had been given. The committee was entitled to allow an extra sum if the benefit was found insufficient ; and it had also the power to allow gratuities in case of illness or distress to workmen earning less than 2s. 6d. per week who were, therefore, not eligible for membership. The benefits for members who continued ill for over three months could, after that period, be reduced by the committee—this was later changed to six months—and any members sent from an hospital with an incurable disease could be expelled from the society upon payment to him of all the money he had contributed.

This scale of benefits seems very liberal in view of the fairly low contributions, and it is significant that, under the new management, they were considerably reduced. The following was the scale of benefits in force at a later date :

for 2s. 6d. .	.	.	.	1s.
„ 5s. 0d. .	.	.	.	2s.
„ 7s. 6d. .	.	.	.	3s.
„ 10s. 0d. .	.	.	.	4s.

and so on in the same proportion, which shows a reduction of 50 per cent., although the new scale left out the provisions regarding a decrease in the funds below £100 or below £50.

Another very important change was embodied in the following provision :

"Each person becoming a member of this society not to be entitled to receive pay unless from an accident met with in his employ, until he has been in the club three months."

On the other hand, only one clear day's notice of illness was then required for the benefit to become payable.

A fine of 5s. was imposed on any member malingering, and, later, members " not declaring themselves off the box immediately on returning to work," were to be fined one shilling. An attempt was made to counteract the evil of drunkenness by a stipulation that any member whose illness proceeded from " drunkenness, debauchery, quarrelling or fighting " was not to be entitled to benefit until ten days after giving notice.

Fines were imposed for neglect on the part of the committee or elders, and the retiring committee was also made responsible for all arrears of contributions.

The scale of funeral benefits was also changed in the new scheme. Originally it was fixed at 20s. for a weekly contribution of ½d., rising by increments of 5s. to 55s. for a contribution of 4d. per week. This benefit was raised later, and ranged from 30s. for ½d. to 100s. for 4d. It was also stipulated that in case of the death of a member every member of the club was to pay, if necessary, an extra week's contribution.

There are a number of other interesting provisions among the rules of the society. One makes it incumbent on every man who employs hands under him to give an account of them to the committee. This is illustrative of the nature of the new growing organisation at Soho which made increasing use of supervision by deputies and foremen. Another provision states that all members leaving Soho were to cease to be members of the society and were not to withdraw any money paid in. This rule was in accordance with usual insurance practice ; but it has also been taken as an illustration of the scarcity of labour and as a possible attempt to tie the men to Soho.[1] If this rule was really inspired by the employers' fear of a shortage of labour, then the fact that it was later changed throws an interesting light on the diminishing scarcity of labour. In the edition printed after 1804, the following new rule, which is curiously contrary to all contemporary insurance practice, was introduced :

> " When any member goes away, or is not employed at, or for this manufactory, it shall be optional for him to continue a member subject to all the laws and regulations of the society, provided he has been employed in this manu-

[1] Lord, J., *op. cit.*, p. 205.

factory seven years altogether and has not been discharged by his employers for misconduct. The subscriptions of absent members to be paid monthly, and if at any time his arrears amount to more than three months' subscriptions, he shall no longer continue a member. The absent member must produce a satisfactory proof of his illness from a surgeon and minister or church-warden of the parish, and that it does not proceed from any of the causes specified as exemptions in Article 9 (drunkenness, etc.), the date of his relief to commence from the date of the above-mentioned certificate."

Another interesting change is the mention in the later edition of the " club rooms of Soho and Soho Foundry," where annual statements of the funds of the society were to be posted up. It appears also that the society concerned itself with certain other questions besides those of sickness benefit, for Article XXIV. states :

" As it is for the health, interest, and credit of the men, as well as masters, to keep this Manufactory clean and decent, it shall be deemed a forfeit of one shilling to the box for any one found guilty of any indecencies, or keeping dirty shops, which indecency, etc., shall be judged by the committee. . . ."

Obviously the committee, in time, would assume all the functions included in modern welfare work ; and it can only be surmised that it may also have had some effect on the general relations between the men and the management.

Only one other fact in connection with this insurance society remains to be mentioned. Originally, men and women were included—one of the articles provided that gratuities from visitors to the works were to be put in the box and divided between men and women in proportion to their payments. Later, however, we find that all such gratuities were to be divided at the discretion of the elders " betwixt this society and that of the women." Thus it would appear that two societies had come into existence, one for male and one for female employees. As regards the reasons for this change or the details of the women's society, it has been impossible to find any record.

The actual working of the society in practice is also not referred to in the firm's records except for occasional letters by workmen formerly employed at Soho asking for assistance out of the society's funds. One wonders, therefore, how Smiles obtained the evidence for the following somewhat extravagant statement :

> " The effects of the Society were most salutary—it cultivated habits of providence and thoughtfulness among the men ; bound them together by ties of common interest, and it was only in cases of irreclaimable drunkenness that any members of the Soho Friendly Society ever came upon the parish." [1]

Even the contemporary historian is more sparing in his eulogy on this point :

> " The rules of this manufactory have certainly been productive of the most laudable and salutary effects, and besides the great attention paid to cleanliness and wholesome air, etc., this manufactory has always been distinguished for its order and good behaviour and particularly during the great riots at Birmingham." [2]

These last two assertions are certainly supported by many contemporary accounts of Soho ; but whether, or how far, these welfare experiments were productive of good feeling between master and man it is impossible to state. The changes

[1] Smiles, *op. cit.*, p. 436.
[2] Shaw, *op. cit.*, vol. 2, p. 121.

which the rules of this society underwent (alongside with those of a more important nature already discussed) under the management of the younger partners show, however, a considerable difference in the whole attitude towards labour in general, and in particular towards its remuneration.

CHAPTER FOUR.

BUSINESS POLICY.

AMONG the causes which led to the introduction of new methods of organisation, the expiration of Watt's patent in 1800 (and the consequent abrupt transformation of a state of monopoly into one of keen competition) has been assigned an important place. The business policy of the firm was equally profoundly affected ; for the disappearance of the legal basis of the royalty system raised the problem of a new price policy. The change in this respect was, however, less sudden than might be expected. For some years previous to the lapse of the patent it had become quite frequent to compound the premium payments into one lump sum, a practice which was both caused and facilitated by the small number of years which remained of the patent privilege and by the fact that the premiums amounted now to a fixed sum, determined beforehand on the basis of horse-power. The capitalist enterprises, such as the cotton mills, which were now the principal buyers of the Boulton & Watt engines, were quite willing to agree to this procedure since the compounded premium for five or six years did not amount to a very large sum. On the other hand, the firm, finding the call on its capital resources increasing as a result of the development of the manufacturing side at Soho, would prefer to have their revenue in the form of single payments rather than in small annual premiums. The fact that this practice became frequent at the time of the entry of the two sons into the business may, also, show their anxiety to obtain greater resources for their ambitious schemes of re-organisation and capital expansion.

Thus we find that about the year 1795 the comparative advantages of the lump-sum royalty system and of a flat percentage addition to the material cost of the various sizes of engines were carefully studied. Towards the middle of that year the prices of the most common sizes of engines were ascertained by the two methods and tabulated for purposes of comparison. This table [1] marks an interesting departure by the fact that a certain degree of standardisation in the products of the firm appears to have been effected, there being fourteen sizes of engines, rising from 4 h.p. to 50 h.p. Some such scale is constantly met with from 1795 onwards ; and, although a very small number of engines of intermediate horse-power were made, the fourteen sizes seem to have been intended as a standard, and certainly the general change in the methods of production which followed could not have been carried out without some degree of standardisation first having been introduced. A further cause was the custom of giving binding estimates to the customers, a practice which had begun when, through the introduction of the rotative engine, the supply of all engine parts and the manufacture of most of them was put in the charge of the Soho firm.

To Boulton, jr., and Watt, jr., it was evident that their position after 1800 would no longer be different from that of other manufacturers. They, too, would have to fix sale prices to include the manufacturing profit, and since, in most cases,

---

[1] See Appendix XIX.

the buyers of engines already paid a certain sum in addition to the cost of materials, it became merely a question of changing the method of computing this sum ; and, as a matter of prudent business policy, this change was introduced before it had become an absolute necessity. The prices shown on the table mentioned (which seems to refer to engines for sale abroad) are calculated in one column as a premium of about £3 17s. od. per h.p. for five years, and in the other as an addition of 50 per cent. on the cost of the materials. The premium, it will be seen, had been reduced from the previous figure of £5 per h.p. ; but the choice in the other case of the percentage would seem to have been quite arbitrary except for the fact that the results by the two methods do not show considerable differences. In all cases but one, the premium worked out at a little more than the percentage addition, the difference increasing with the power of the engine. Notwithstanding this, the second method was adopted as is evidenced by the fact that the last column, showing the total charges inclusive of the freight to Hull, is based on the new calculation. A second table of the same date entitled " Table of the Prices of Foreign Engines, August 1795," [1] is drawn up in the same way ; but it is of some significance that, in the case of this table of engines destined for abroad, the cost of duplicates for certain parts was included in the standard scale of prices.

It is impossible to state when this system was definitely adopted to the exclusion of the other. For foreign engines it seems to have been in existence in the elaborate form from 1795 onwards, and it was naturally adopted first in the case of these engines, since the royalty system would have had no

---

[1] B. & W. Colln.

239

legal basis abroad. It is also worthy of notice that the usual condition for the supply of engines abroad, namely the grant of a patent, had been abandoned. Boulton, Watt & Sons, were still endeavouring to obtain patents in various foreign countries ; but, from answers to enquiries, it would appear that they had ceased to make this a " conditio sine qua non." It may also be mentioned that, although enquiries from abroad continued very frequent, no engines beyond those already enumerated were exported.[1] From 1797 dates the first definite enquiry from America, the history of which it has not been possible to trace. At the beginning of that year, a Mr. William Tatham enquired from Chippendale, Boulton & Watt's London agent, about the possibility of exporting engines to America,[2] asking for answers to the following questions :

1. The price of one 10 h.p. engine and the possibility of shipping it to America.
2. Could Boulton & Watt ship two or three more engines to America in the course of twelve months, the terms of payment being one-half with the order and the rest spread over three years, interest to be paid annually ?
3. Should a large number of engines be wanted so as to make it inconvenient to send funds with the order, on what terms would they undertake to supply them ?

As regards engines for the home market the new price policy was certainly in existence in 1798 ; and the following prices of engines are given by M. R. Boulton in a letter to his partner : [3]

[1] I.e. three for France, two for Spain, and one must also include three for Ireland.
[2] W. Tatham to Chippendale, 1797, Feb. 7. B. & W. Colln.
[3] M. R. Boulton to J. Watt, jr., 1798, Dec. 18, *ibid.*

H.	L.	C.
	£	£
4	354	338
6	383	366
8	479	458
10	529	505
12	567	542
16	736	703
20	810	774
24	1053	1006
30	1134	1083
32	1170	1118

The first column shows the horse-power and the second and third the prices for London and the country respectively. The explanation for the two sets of prices is given in the letter itself :

"I send you herewith," writes Boulton, jr., "the prices referred to in my letter of this morning and we propose those for the ensuing month to be stated at one per cent. less, or at 34 and 28 per cent. upon Metal Materials and a similar reduction to take place monthly till we arrive at the permanent standard. . . . Perhaps it may be judged expedient to make a larger reduction from the London prices in order to bring them sooner to the same standard as the country . . . you will be enabled to judge whether the distinction has or is likely to create any dissatisfaction."

The letter "of this morning" referred to further elucidates this point :

"We find that considerable embarrassment will ensue unless the reduction of our estimates is made very gradually, the whole reduction proposed to take place before March 21, 1799, viz. from 45 per cent. to 33 on London, and from 33 to 25 per cent. on country, we think should be effected by monthly reductions."

241

Price discrimination was thus practised and three sets of prices were in force :

					Per Cent.
1.	Engines for abroad :	" Metal Materials " plus 50			
2.	„	London :	„	„	„ 45
3.	„	Country :	„	„	„ 33

it being proposed to reduce the last two figures to 33 per cent. and 25 per cent. respectively.

The reasons for this policy are not clearly stated ; but they are probably to be found in the monopoly which the firm enjoyed. It was no more than a " what the traffic will bear " policy and the gradation of prices which it brought about was a natural outcome. As far as the higher prices for London are concerned, it must be borne in mind that, even during the early years when premiums were measured by fuel consumption, London would have to pay higher prices since the strong organisation existing in its coal trade would tend to raise the price of coal. Although saving of fuel was no longer a criterion, this fact may have been taken into account when the firm fixed the prices for London at a higher level.

The monopolist price policy was bound to cease with the monopoly itself, and it is noteworthy that reductions in the percentages started some time before the critical date and that it was intended to reach the proposed standard nearly a year sooner. At the same time the effect of price discrimination on the market was taken into account, and, in general, the letter quoted above indicates the thorough preparation for countering competition.

As regards conditions of payment the usual practice at the time was three months from the date of delivery ; [1] while an

---

[1] M. R. Boulton to Frazer, 1798, May 28.   B. & W. Colln.

idea of the increased business may be gathered from the following statement :

> " The current sizes of 8, 10, 12, 16, and 20 may be completed where great dispatch is of moment, in two months, but I think in general we should not say less than ten weeks or three months." [1]

The new standard prices came into force in 1799 at the appointed date, but shortly afterwards another important change was introduced. According to estimates of the year 1801, a uniform addition of 25 per cent. was in force without any local discrimination. This estimate [2] gives the prices for a number of engines of different powers, ranging from 4 h.p. to 45 h.p. Several engines were taken of each category, an average being computed from the single items. The figure arrived at was rounded off, usually by a slight increase, to make allowance for variations. This was especially the case with small engines, e.g. for 4 h.p. engines the figure was £337 17s. od. " but as a greater proportionate profit should be laid on these small engines to compensate for the trouble of drawings, etc., it may stand . . . at £350."

This price system remained in force for at least twenty years from 1801 onwards. In some cases the percentage was raised slightly, or slightly reduced, but it never varied by more than 2 per cent. in either direction. At the same time as the prices of engines those of castings in general from the Soho Foundry were fixed and set out in a detailed list compiled in 1801. [3] This list shows the prices per cwt. of castings such as cylinders, pistons, etc., in two columns—" Foundry " and " Fitted." The variation in the prices is remarkably

[1] M. R. Boulton to J. Watt, jr., 1798, Dec. 18.   B. & W. Colln.
[2] " Table and calculations for new estimates, June 4, 1801," *ibid.*
[3] " Prices of Castings as charged by Soho Foundry up to 1801," *ibid.*

small and, in a list enumerating well over fifty different articles, only five sets of prices appear both in the foundry column and in that for fitted articles. The addition for fitting was not always the same, e.g. cylinders being stated at 20s. per cwt. from the foundry and 32s. fitted, while nozzles were 20s. and 21s. respectively.

The method of price fixing naturally reacted on the costing and book-keeping system; and in this respect, too, Soho appears to have been far in advance of the time. The books had always been kept in a very thorough manner. There were the usual goods accounts and personal ledgers, and we have seen that the trading accounts drawn up annually, although they do not convey all the information desired, can compare quite favourably with modern practice. The change in the organisation following on the taking over of the manufacture of steam engines, which brought about a splitting up into departments, tended to raise the standard in the methods of accounting. To cope with the changed conditions, a great number of new books of a statistical character had to be started, and this, it seems, was a very uncommon thing in contemporary business practice.

A letter from Z. Walker, the cashier of the hardware firm who often acted in that capacity for all the undertakings at Soho, throws an interesting sidelight on this point. Giving an account of a conversation with a new clerk of the engine firm, he writes:

"... but some part of your business appeared so difficult to him that hitherto he had his doubts of rendering you satisfaction. I could not learn what part of the employ appeared so difficult to him, as he informed me that he had learned the common method of keeping accounts, unless it is from your finding it necessary to keep several little books,

independent of the General books, for the purpose of receiving and delivering materials, etc., the reason whereof
he may not yet properly conceive." [1]

A list of the books kept at Soho has been found,[2] thus
making it unnecessary to undertake the difficult task of reconstructing the firm's accounting system from the voluminous
account books which have been preserved. This list does not
deal with the personal ledgers but with those books which
served for ascertaining the costs of production. Taking as
the basis for this purpose the formula :

> Material cost, plus direct wages, plus indirect wages, plus
> general charges,

the following books of a list of twenty-two may be mentioned
as specially important :

> " *Forgers' and Fitters' Book*, containing amount of Iron, etc.,
> given out in an unmanufactured state, and on the other
> hand credited when brought in."

> " *Fitting Book* :
> First the fitting is taken from the Time Book.
> Secondly, from what is called the fitting book, it is to
> be copied upon a sheet of paper and arranged in such
> a manner as to correspond with Mr. Foreman's Engine
> Book. Thirdly, it is again entered into a book somewhat
> different from Mr. Foreman's list, to ascertain more
> accurately the time that is taken in fitting separate parts
> of engines, as well as the sum calculated to be charged
> with the usual profit thereon."

> " *Book*—containing accounts with Soho Foundry and the
> different departments at Soho."

[1] Z. Walker to Boulton & Watt, jr., 1797, Aug. 15. B. & W. Colln.
[2] " Note of books kept by Mr. Foreman and Mr. Lodge, Dec., 1800,"
ibid.

245

" *Abstract Book*, wherein is charged to the different departments the sums paid ; also to Forgers, Fitters, etc., the monies paid."

" *Engine Book*, containing amount of Engines sent from Soho and Foundry."

These examples of books, together with the explanatory notes on their use, show, on the one hand, the remarkably elaborate procedure adopted, and on the other, help us to form an idea of the methods of costing. The purpose of keeping elaborate records of costs is twofold. In the first place, they provide a basis for the drawing up of estimates for future contracts, and in the second place, they enable a firm to ascertain accurately the profit realised on each completed contract.

As far as the first of these is concerned the method at Soho can be easily reconstructed. We have seen that in the estimates two items appear—one called " metal materials " and the other " premium " or " percentage " addition on metal materials. We are not at the moment concerned with the firm's profits ; but as regards the item " metal materials," it is important to understand that this included the estimated cost of all engine parts ; that is, both the cost of material and of labour, as well as the charges for putting the engine together. When, however, an enquiry for an engine was received, the firm would quote a certain figure which would be split up into material and labour costs of all engine parts, and an additional sum for the fitting of the entire engine, including the putting up and testing. To this total the percentage would then be added. As regards the material and labour costs for each part these were easily ascertained from the books mentioned, supplemented by various other records.

The ascertainment of these costs was invariably by contract. The " Forgers' and Fitters' Book " showed the material cost of each job ; the wages for time-work would be ascertained from the " Fitting Book " and those for piecework would be entered in a " Forgers' and Piece-Workers' Book."

In the method of charging for the fitting of the whole engine the old practice had, to some extent, survived. The fitters, whose functions had for many years been separated from those of the engine erectors, were no longer paid by the customers, but received their wages from the firm, the latter, however, being reimbursed separately on this head. But although a separate item for " putting the whole together " appears on the firm's invoices, the charges for fitting had been standardised, as far as the buyer was concerned, for various sizes of engines.

The method adopted for arriving at the standard is of considerable interest, the best example being that for the small 2, 3 and 4 h.p. engines. For these the firm had, as we have seen, contracted with W. Harrison for a piece-price of £20 per engine. The customer was, however, charged a different price which was calculated from one particular engine, the fitting of which had been paid for by the time. The following is a slightly abridged abstract of a paper entitled " Calculations of the Cost of Fitting, Oct. 9, 1801."

" *The following taken from Cooper & Anderson's Engine :*

	£	s.	d.
Total number of days : 170.			
Charge for Men's time	20	15	11
„ „ use of tools	3	16	10
„ „ use of machinery . . .	8	16	3
Total amount, exclusive of percentage . .	£33	9	0

Inferences :

Total time—170 days : Amount of charge for do. £20 15 11
= 2s. 5d. per day.

Amount for use of tools for 170 days . . £3 16 10
= 5½d. per day, or 18½ per cent. on amount of men's time.

Amount for use of machinery for 170 days . £8 16 3
= 1s. per day, or 43 per cent. on amount of men's time.

Application :	£	s.	d.
Wm. Harrison's charge for the total fitting, turning, boring and labour, exclusive of packing	20	o	o
£20 = 400s. 2s. 6d. = 160 days			
Charge for use of tools, say 6d. per day on 160	4	o	o
Charge for use of machinery, say 1s. per day .	8	o	o
Charge for weighing and loading . .	1	10	o
	£33	10	o
Plus 40 per cent. . .	15	o	o
	£48	o	o

or say £45 os. od." [1]

Except for one item the above calculation explains itself. It shows that for the particular sizes of engines mentioned a standard round-figure charge had been reached which included the new piece-price for the job, percentage additions for the use of tools and machinery, and a charge for weighing and loading. The 40 per cent. added to the total requires further explanation which is given in M. R. Boulton's letter to his partner, accompanying a copy of the agreement with W. Harrison. He states :

[1] B. & W. Colln.

" An allowance is made in the fitting, for hemp, tallow, oil, candles, coals, and interest of capital expended in the shed and machinery and for trying the engines."

Thus the total figure of £45 included a liberal allowance for indirect material and labour costs as well as for all other overhead charges. The final price for which the firm undertook the supply of an engine would be composed of the cost of materials and labour (the latter item including indirect and overhead charges), and, lastly, the estimated profit on the contract.

There were a number of very elaborate records for the purpose of calculating the actual profit realised on each engine. The books mentioned give the cost of materials and the direct labour cost ; while for recording the other indirect charge, such as fuel and lighting, other books were kept. Indirect labour costs were entered under such headings as " wheeling sand," " carting lime," and " errands." No information is available concerning the way in which they were apportioned for each job ; but it can be assumed that, if they were taken into account at all in the calculation of the profit on individual contracts, they would be charged up to each department for a certain period and then divided by the output of that department during that period.

Some of the overhead charges were also tabulated in a similar way, and statements covering a period of years were usually prepared for the future guidance of the firm. One very elaborate example is that of the consumption of oil and candles which, from a certain date onwards, was tabulated for each week under twenty-three different headings.[1]

[1] " Statement of the Oil and Candles consumed at Soho Foundry from Oct. 1, 1799, to Oct. 1, 1806, and from April, 1808, to Feb., 1809." B. & W. Colln.

The Wages Book of the Soho Foundry was kept in a similar manner from the commencement of the works. It contained, in tabulated form, statements of the weekly wages both for direct and indirect labour with cross references to the various ledger accounts. The columns under each heading were totalled, the result showing the wages bill for each week.[1]

The real significance of this system of costing lies, however, less in the immediate objects achieved by it than in the fact that it also served for supplying a basis for future charges. In the same way as in any well-organised factory of to-day, the purpose of keeping statistical records at Soho was mainly for the detection of waste and of lack of efficiency. When new methods of wage payment were being devised, recourse was had to the elaborate time-sheets for different shops. Thus these time-sheets fulfilled four objects—they supplied a basis for ascertaining the workers' wages for the job ; they were used in the calculation of the costs of engines ; they could serve as the starting-point for changes in the methods of production, such as speeding-up and greater application of machinery ; and, lastly, they were used, as already mentioned, in the computation of new wage-rates. In a similar way, most of the other departmental records of indirect charges, wages bills, etc., were used for maintaining a standard of efficiency.

In general, it may be stated that all the different aspects of the great changes at Soho were strictly co-ordinated and were, consciously or unconsciously, parts of a general and very elaborate plan of the new business organisation. In many ways the statistical tables, the calculations and the account books which have been preserved seem to exceed the limits of reasonableness in this respect for the time and for a business

[1] See Appendix XX.

of the size to which they refer. It is generally and justly assumed that the usefulness of elaborate methods of cost-accounting diminishes proportionately as the size of the business to which it is applied diminishes, and that the benefit of comprehensive and expensive schemes of this kind to small concerns is extremely doubtful.

The objection of great expense could not have weighed heavily at Soho. Two book-keepers, one cashier, who sometimes acted for the other Soho businesses as well, and a limited number of clerks were employed. Their salaries were not very high, and since regular hours for the office staff do not seem to have existed, the expense of keeping up the new system must have been negligible compared with its results. In this connection the amount of the work performed by this office staff (and also, of course, by the partners in the business) as it appears from the firm's records, is amazing when the absence of modern equipment and of labour-saving devices is borne in mind.

The actual motives, however, for the introduction of the new system are not quite so clear. It would not be too safe to assume that it was adopted deliberately or that it even formed a necessary corollary of such changes as the new design of the shops, the new machinery and the greater division of labour. But if such an assumption were correct, then the simultaneous adoption of the new methods and the change in managerial personnel again becomes of significance. It could be stated that not only did the changed organisation of production demand other changes, the necessity for which did not appear during the time of limited production, but also that these changes in book-keeping methods were to some extent bound up with the change in the partnership. The previously restricted business had grown in a spectacular way ; and one consequence of this growth was the greater use of the delegation of certain functions of management to supervisors, foremen, and clerks. As long as the old partners were in charge, their close personal contact with the production as well as with the commercial sides of the business, and their technical knowledge, superior even as regards details to that of most of their employees, insured a speedy prevention and detection of waste. Boulton & Watt would have a very accurate idea of the fair performance of each operative and of the quantity of raw material necessary for each article. They would be enabled " with but little effort or outlay to exercise so effective a check on sluggishness and waste that a large business conducted on traditional lines cannot attain to it even by lavish expenditure." [1]

With the entry into the business of the younger generations, things changed. Not only did the growing business prevent its owners from having " their eyes everywhere," but even had that been possible, their experience and knowledge would have been insufficient for the purpose. Many aspects of the new business were, moreover, such as to make any check but that of written records impossible. Thus the statistical methods employed seemed then, at least, as natural as they would to-day. In retrospect, however, they present a somewhat surprising contrast to what we believe to have been, and what in the vast majority of instances actually was, the organisation of business enterprises at the beginning of the nineteenth century.

Turning to the actual trading results and financial position of the firm from 1795 to the first years of the new century, we are again confronted with the difficulty of interpreting

---

[1] Marshall, *op. cit.*, p. 366.

existing records or reconstructing those which, if they were ever made, have not been preserved. The series of trading accounts discussed at an earlier stage continued for the years 1795 to 1801 ;[1] but conclusions drawn from them must of necessity again be very guarded. The upward trend of the yearly totals continued in an even greater measure than before, but the fact that the year 1795 was an important turning-point in the firm's fortunes is clearly borne out by the figures. Compared with the previous year, the trading account total shows a sharp fall accompanied by an even more striking decrease in the number of engines produced. This number amounts to nine and is the lowest during the period for which definite records exist. The fall, however, is only natural for a transition year which saw the breaking up of the connection with Wilkinson and the starting of the reorganisation of the methods of production. The figures of purchases and sales during the year show a similar diminution ; but the annual wages bill rose as a result of an increase in the number of employed, due, probably, to a preparation for the introduction of the new organisation. As a result of the restricted production, however, the gross loss on manufacturing for the year 1795 was reduced to about £880, a much smaller figure than that of the previous year.

The year 1796 presents another very sharp and even more significant contrast, since that year may be regarded as the first

[1] See Appendix XXIV. It will be noticed that items entitled "Pneumatic Apparatus" appear on this table. This demands a word of explanation. In conjunction with, and at the instigation of his friend, Dr. Thomas Beddoes, the founder of the Pneumatic Institution, Watt had designed an apparatus for the production of "factitious air" for medicinal uses. His interest in this matter was probably aroused by the many cases of consumption in his family. In a letter dated July 14, reprinted in a booklet describing the apparatus, Watt states : " Boulton & Watt have agreed to manufacture these machines for the Public."

under the new system of joint production at the Soho Foundry and the Soho Engine Manufactory. Although the accounts are actually for the latter concern only, the effect of the new establishment can be seen in the figures. The total production of the two enterprises reaches, with thirty engines, a new maximum in 1796 ; the number of men employed " in the yard " rises to fifty-five, and there is a rise of 50 per cent. in the wages bill ; the amount of goods bought is four times greater and the value of sales well over three times the figures of the preceding year, and, lastly, the first substantial profit, which amounted to £1500 is disclosed. In this year, too, the practice of charging interest on capital invested in the business, which had, for some unknown reason, been dropped the year before, was resumed. On the other hand, the charge of interest on stock, which had appeared in the accounts for 1795, is not met with in those for any of the other years. In 1796 the wages of engine erectors were, for the first time, passed through the trading account, and, since the customers were charged separately for this particular item, corresponding entries were made on the debit and credit sides. That year the debit entry was slightly higher than the credit entry ; for all the following years, however, the latter was always the higher.

In 1797 a small loss was again sustained, the reasons for which are not quite clear. The output remained at the same figure, and almost equally so the charges for wages. The amount of purchases, however, fell, but that of sales remained the same. On the other hand, a number of interest charges increased, while the amount of stock to be carried forward was considerably diminished, so that the total value of the raw materials used in the manufacture was larger than that of the previous year, this fact, in the face of an unchanged sales figure, accounting for the slight loss sustained.

From 1798 onwards each year shows a profit which reaches its maximum in 1801, the last year of the period under review, when the figure stood at over £4000. The output, too, increased from twenty-five engines in 1798 to fifty-two in 1801 ; but in spite of that the figure for wages was smaller in 1798, 1799, and 1800, reaching its previous level of over £3000 only in 1801. The somewhat striking decrease in salaries is accounted for by an apparent splitting up of the expenses under this heading for the two establishments, since the draughtsmen, clerks, and book-keepers were employed for both ; and this assumption is also borne out by the fact that, as the salaried employees began to work for Soho Foundry too, only one-half of their salaries began to be charged in the Engine Manufactory's accounts. Interest charges during those four years increased, as one would expect ; and for one year the interest charge on capital was analysed into its different constituents. In many other ways the entries became more thorough, and items such as repairs and provision for depreciation of machinery began to make their appearance.

The year 1801 must be considered apart from the rest, since it marks yet another epoch characterised by the absence of the patent monopoly and by the changed price policy. For the first time the item " goods bought " is separated into several items—" materials," " goods manufactured," " tools " and " boilers." On the other hand, the analysis of the various overhead expenses no longer appears in the trading account, but only a summary item entitled " General Expenses " which represents the total of an account now kept separately. The fact that this year was also the first in which the new efficient methods would show their earliest results encourages a conjecture about the possible relation between the increased output and the increased profit.

For the years 1800 and 1801 analyses of the profit according to departments are appended to the trading accounts. It is impossible in the absence of any explicit statement or other evidence to say on what basis they could have been drawn up. Owing to the methods of departmental book-keeping the consumption of raw materials and the outlay on wages and general charges for each department could have been ascertained quite easily. The output of each department was also recorded, and although it is open to doubt whether the apportioning of the profit over the various departments was scientifically correct, the methods of ascertaining the portions cannot be said to differ fundamentally from those employed to-day. Since the statements for the two years are of some interest, they may be given in full :

STATEMENT OF THE PROFIT AND LOSS UPON THE SUNDRY SUBDIVISIONS OF MANUFACTURING ACCOUNT, YEAR ENDING 1800.

	Loss.				Profit.		
	£	s.	d.		£	s.	d.
Brass Foundry .	130	6	11½	Pattern Manufactory.	451	4	1
Wrought Iron, Raw .	2	6	4	Smithy . . .	112	7	8½
Copper, Brass, etc.	0	0	4	Boilers . . .	300	7	9½
Pneumatic Apparatus	64	10	0	Fitting Department .	983	19	7½
				Engine Erectors .	69	19	5½
				Commission on Foundry			
				Engines . .	208	18	9
					£2126	17	5
	£197	3	7½		197	3	7½
				Balance in favour of			
				profit . . .	£1929	13	9½

In 1801 there was a profit in every department, and the statement therefore takes the following form :

THE PROFIT ARISES AS UNDER :

	£	s.	d.
Pattern Manufactory . . .	294	19	3½
Smithy	289	14	10½
Brass Foundry	476	15	2½
Boiler Account . . .	504	6	0
Pneumatic	38	14	9
Fitting Department . .	2005	1	0
Engine Erectors . . .	127	5	2
Commission on Foundry Engines .	293	5	8½
	£4030	2	0

The output of fifty-two engines in 1801 was repeated the following year, but for many years afterwards this figure was not attained again. This high-water mark in the production is naturally accompanied by high figures in the various expense items ; and it is interesting to notice that of these, two widely different ones—namely the figures for the consumption of oil and candles and those for the weekly wages bills at Soho Foundry, reach their maximum in the years 1801 and 1802. From 1801 to 1802 the consumption of oil and candles rose to £104 9s. 6d. as compared with £60 7s. 8½d. the following year, and the wages paid at the Soho Foundry during the week ending July 4, 1801, amounted to £216 16s. 0½d., which shows an increase of nearly 100 per cent. over the average for the preceding and following weeks.

The series of trading accounts so far discussed ceases with the year 1801 ; but from that year onwards a number of statements are in existence [1] which illustrate, to some extent, the growing revenue of the firm. As a survival of the old regime a difference between the manufacturing result and what was still termed " premium " continued to be made. The

[1] " Statements of engines made and amount of Premium, 1801-1820." B. & W. Colln.

statements which were extracts from the premium account—
the latter included the balance of the Manufacturing account
and was therefore a comprehensive trading account—give
particulars of each engine manufactured, the agreed sale prices,
the cost of the " Metal Materials " ; and what is termed
" Premium " being the difference between the former and
the latter. A further column gives the estimated premium
on the particular contract, and in the last two columns the
excess or deficiency between the realised profit and the estimate
is stated. It is interesting to note that the statements show
a continual deficiency in the estimates of roughly between
£300 and £1700 up to the year 1807, when the first excess
appears. The actual net premium realised varied, of course,
in some proportion to the output, and amounted during the
years 1801 and 1812 to between £6000 and £10,000. It is
not quite clear on what basis the distinction between the
manufacturing profit and the " premium " was made ; but,
since the total profit included both, it must be assumed that
the figures for the " Metal Materials," which were deducted
from the agreed selling price in order to ascertain the " premium," did not represent the manufacturing cost only, but
already included a manufacturing profit.

The significance of the conclusions which can be drawn
from all these figures is supplemented considerably by various
other factors illustrative of the development of the business.
As already stated, a certain devolution of functions had set in,
and, although the control of business policy was still very auto-
cratic, the owners' powers, as far as technical and commercial
details were concerned, had been delegated to the experienced
assistants. Technical problems were considered by a committee of the partners and the engine erectors ;[1] and, since

[1] M. R. Boulton to J. Watt, jr., 1798, Dec. 13. B. & W. Colln.

prices were practically fixed, the routine of answering enquiries, making out invoices and supervising the despatch of goods, was carried out by the office staff. Judging from the copies of letters in the firm's letter books and the account books, the organisation of the office and the work performed by the staff appears to have been extremely satisfactory ; and, in general, the position of the firm had been put on such a sound basis that, among other reforms, Boulton, jr., suggested that they should themselves erect their engines, as did their competitors.[1]

Financial difficulties had long since ceased to trouble the Soho business. When, in 1802, Mrs. Matthews, the widow of Boulton & Watt's banker in London, who had continued her husband's business, died, a new firm was set up in London under the style of M. & R. Boulton, J. & G. Watt & Co.[2] On the death of Gregory Watt, this was changed to M. R. Boulton, J. Watt & Co., and this partnership continued until 1833, when an account was opened with the Bank of England. The concern worked quite profitably [3] and considerably helped the Soho firm in its financial transactions.

The great growth in the firm's capital resources is well shown in a statement of M. R. Boulton's capital account, drawn up by Pearson in 1806. The following were the items :

	£	s.	d.
Balance carried forward . . .	15,783	19	2
One year's interest . . .	793	0	0
Transfer from M. Boulton's A/c. . .	16,643	2	8
Estimated share of year's profits . .	1,779	18	2
	£35,000	0	0

---

[1] M. R. Boulton to J. Watt, jr., 1799, Jan. 30. B. & W. Colln.

[2] Documents relating to the setting up of a banking house in London, *ibid.*

[3] See Appendix XXII.

It is also noteworthy that in 1804 part of the capital of the firm was transferred to the London House, the details being as follows :

	£	s.	d.
M. Boulton	9,050	o	o
M. R. Boulton	3,650	o	o
J. Watt, jr.	7,300	o	o
	£20,000	o	o

In September, 1805, Boulton's capital in the firm was transferred to his son, who thus became joint partner with James Watt, jr., and was credited with both his own share of the profits and with what had previously been his father's. The Soho Foundry, too, had prospered ; and from 1801 onwards its share of the output was always greater than that of the Engine Manufactory. By the year 1812, the debt to the parent firm of over £21,000, incurred for the erection of buildings and for machinery, had been repaid together with interest at the rate of 5 per cent. per annum.

Apart from the reputation which they enjoyed, the most important factor which helped Boulton, jr., and Watt, jr., to establish a very prosperous business in spite of the rise of competition, was the circle of experienced and reliable assistants which they had at their disposal. Amongst them three stand out—Southern, Lawson, and Murdock ; and the rise of their status in the firm is very interesting. Southern had originally been engaged as draughtsman, with an initial salary of about £100 per annum. In 1800 he was made virtually a partner in the business by being given a two-year contract, stipulating a 2¼ per cent. commission on all goods manufactured at Soho, with a guaranteed yearly minimum of £600.[1]

[1] Agreement with John Southern, 1800, June 18. B. & W. Colln.

Lawson, who had for many years acted as the firm's supervising engineer, was also given a new contract in 1800.[1] He was engaged for five years as engineer and agent in Scotland at an annual salary of £250 for the first half of the period and £300 for the second half; and he undertook to make over and assign to the firm " the full use of and property in any invention which may be made by him, tending to the improvement of the manufacture or construction of steam engines." In addition to his salary he was to have 1 per cent. commission on all goods sent to Scotland and a further ½ per cent. commission on all orders procured by him in England, Wales, or Ireland. An annual minimum of £350 during the first half of the period of his contract and £400 during the second was guaranteed to him. Lawson proved one of the firm's most capable and valuable employees.[2] On several occasions he was

[1] Agreement with James Lawson, 1800, Oct. 1. B. & W. Colln.

[2] Lawson seems to have been an extremely shrewd observer of the economic affairs of his time, and this somewhat lengthy but highly interesting account of the position of the Lancashire cotton industry, contained in his letter from Manchester to Boulton, dated Feb. 27, 1803 (A.O. MSS.) may be quoted :

" In the year 1765, cotton as an article of commerce was scarcely known in this country. Soon after this time, Mr. Arkwright got his patent. . . . In 1782 the whole produce of Cotton Manufacture—about two million sterling—import about five millions of lbs. In 1801, the import of cotton wool was 42 millions of lbs., value about 4 millions, and the estimated value when manufactured, 15 million sterling. In 1802, the import has been 54 millions of lbs., the value in proportion, say 19 million sterling. The trade is calculated to employ 800,000 individuals, to take 30,000 tons of shipping and 2000 seamen to bring the raw cotton home and exporting the manufactured goods. The present year, from all appearances, is going on in an increasing ratio, such is the apparent state of the trade at present, and so many new works are going on that all calculation or conjecture where or when there will be sufficient for the demand, is unknown, yet should a change come, as frequently happens in this trade (tho' never for a long time) there must be a sad crash—as every one is on the full stretch—and many must be extending much beyond their real capital."

sent out on rounds of inspection to the various customers who had installed Boulton & Watt engines, and he usually returned with many useful suggestions for improvements. These examinations of engines, it is interesting to note, were carried out entirely free of charge to the customers.

Murdock, the best known of the firm's employees, experienced a very romantic rise to fame and fortune. He started at a wage of fifteen shillings per week, and for many years this never rose above two guineas. In 1800 he was engaged for five years in the capacity of engineer and superintendent.[1] The same provision, as in the instance of Lawson, regarding inventions made by him was included in his contract. His salary was to be £300 a year with a commission of 1 per cent. on the sales price of all goods manufactured at Soho. In this way he, too, was given a share in the business; and in 1804 a sum of £3000 was placed to his credit with the London banking house of the firm.

Southern was made a partner in the firm in 1810, receiving one-sixth of the profits, and he remained at Soho until his death in 1815. Lawson left the firm in 1811 to take up an appointment as superintendent of machinery to the Royal Mint; but he continued to do some work for his former employers until his death.[2] Murdock remained until nine years before his death in 1839. From 1810 onwards he was in receipt of an annual salary of £1000 which he chose instead of a partnership.[3]

[1] Agreement with W. Murdock, March 30, 1800. B. & W. Colln.
[2] Dickinson & Jenkins, *op. cit.*, p. 288.
[3] William Murdock (1754-1839) was the inventor of many contrivances; but he is usually remembered as the first to use coal-gas for lighting purposes. In a paper read to the Royal Society on the 25th of Feb., 1808, he gave the history of this invention. In 1792 he lighted up his house at

We have followed the history of the steam-engine business at Soho until the first years of the nineteenth century, and we leave it at a stage when subsequent changes must be of a less spectacular character than those that took place during the first thirty years of its life. The history of the firm's development during the first half of the century up to its end, in 1850, would certainly provide interesting illustrations of the economic history of that period ; and from the abundant records available it would be possible to construct it. It is, however, probable that all the changes which followed after the closing date here chosen would, in most respects, be nothing more than those caused by the ordinary expansion of a prosperous business. One can expect that, after that date, the course of the firm's fortunes would run more smoothly and that the control of its prosperity would depend more and more on outside factors and less on the efforts of its owners. Soho had reached a standard of efficiency far above that of the " representative firm " of the time and, in all probability, progress by leaps and bounds was no longer possible.

For this reason it seems advisable here to conclude the history of the first factory in the engineering industry.

Redruth with gas ; but it was not until six years later that the first gas-lighting apparatus was installed at Soho. From the beginning of the new century onwards the manufacture of lighting apparatus formed a regular feature of the Soho business. See Hunt, C., *A History of the Introduction of Gas Lighting* (1907).

CONCLUSION.

THE development of the steam-engine business has been outlined and we are now in a position to summarise the main changes in its organisation as well as the reasons for these changes, and we may also attempt to draw conclusions from this survey. Broadly speaking, two phases can be distinguished in the history of the firm, one sharply contrasted with the other. During the first of these up to about 1795, Boulton & Watt remained consulting engineers whose object was to supply plans and supervise their execution, while they themselves manufactured only a small range of more intricate engine parts. Throughout that period Soho exhibited all the traits of a pioneer business. The system of production gave rise to a peculiar system of payment; and the two together made advances in organisation unnecessary. It has been shown that the division of functions between designing engineer, executive engineer, and iron-master was due to a variety of causes, the most important being the lack of large capital resources which a combination of these functions would have demanded.

Slowly, however, more and more of the functions were combined, and progress was effected in the same measure as the initial obstacles were overcome; but the increase in the number of engine parts manufactured at Soho was only partly due to an increase in the available capital resources, and in this respect technical considerations were more important than those of an economic nature.

The Watt engine was designed originally without reference to the possibilities of its practical applications. It was a theoretical invention, and the possibility of applying it to practice was demonstrated only after protracted and laborious experiments on a small scale, and these did not definitely establish it as a " commercial proposition." Unlike his predecessors in the engine field, Watt paid no attention to the insufficiency of the executive skill and machinery available at the time ; and not the least of his achievements is the fact that, by demanding the seemingly impossible, he created and stimulated forces which made it ultimately possible.

The firm of Boulton & Watt was started before machinery and skill had developed to the desired degree ; and during the early years of its existence Soho became the training centre for skilled workmen and the laboratory for new processes. These were, however, confined to those engine components which were required by the continual introduction of the new technical improvements on which the success of the engine depended. Such technical considerations, therefore, were mainly responsible for changes in the organisation of the firm and in its fortunes ; but it is only right to point out that technical progress was in itself the result of economic causes. Once the superiority of the new engine had been demonstrated beyond doubt, the demand for it rose rapidly and the problem of satisfying this demand became pressing. This was especially the case after the great Cornish market had been opened up, of which the difficulties of serving have already been described.

Up to the year 1782 the period was one of experiment. Notwithstanding technical improvements and the widening of the market the system of production and that of payment remained the same ; and the only outstanding change of these years was the evolution and final emergence of a small but highly-skilled class of workmen. Boulton & Watt had gathered round them a band of assistants whom they trained carefully and whose reliability increased rapidly. One of the results of this was that the function of executive engineers got more and more into the hands of the Soho firm whose engine erectors were so superior to the engineers of the localities where engines were put up that the services of the latter were often dispensed with altogether.

Great changes arose in the year 1782. The introduction of an effectual appliance for the production of a rotative movement caused not only a shifting but also a considerable widening of the market ; and it became necessary to produce an even greater number of engine parts at Soho, whose products, although more expensive, were of a superior quality to those of other suppliers. The changed market was also responsible for an alteration in the system of payment and for a change in the status of the firm in relation to its customers. It was no longer possible to describe the superiority of the performance of the new engine in terms of saving of fuel or to measure the royalties in this manner. More important still, it was no longer possible to leave the customer at liberty to secure the supply of the components from whomsoever he pleased. Further, the customers in the new industries were unable and unwilling to assume any responsibility and insisted on leaving the execution of the entire contract in the hands of Boulton & Watt. Although the seeds were thus sown for the change which occurred in the years 1795 and 1796, the internal organisation at Soho was not immediately affected. The heavier engine parts were still ordered from outside, and this arrangement continued for a surprisingly long time. The financial position of the firm, however, shortly afterwards began to undergo an important change. The output increased and the income derived from premiums grew in proportion; also, since the latter was easily measured and was, moreover, paid by buyers who enjoyed the prosperity of the great industrial expansion, it became more regular and reliable.

On the administrative side progress continued. Greater use was made of supervision by delegates, foremen and clerks; and the partners' time was less taken up by details of office routine. They began to interest themselves more and more in broader questions of economic policy. Some of their activities in this direction have been indicated. At the same time the previously noticed tendency of diminishing reliance on outside executive engineers continued with greater force during the eighties. Another development also made its first appearance during those years—that of standardising, or as it was termed " methodizing " the production. Originally this was caused through the necessity of producing duplicates of various parts for the engines supplied to the Cornish mines, a necessity arising out of the frequent breakdowns which, combined with the distance from Soho and the precarious nature of mining, often caused emergencies. After 1782, the rising demand resulted in a desire to restrict production to a certain number of standardised sizes, and this rule was enforced more and more strictly.

Most of the factors which led to the establishment in 1795 of Soho Foundry had been in evidence long before that date. Difficulties such as lack of capital and skilled labour had been eliminated, and it is indeed surprising that the change should not have taken place earlier than it did. Apart from *vis inertiæ* the explanation is to be found in the constant expansion of the business, especially on the technical side, which made its owners reluctant to incur the great delay which a change in the organisation of production would have caused. In the year 1795 a kind of climax in this expansion had been reached, and, at the same time, the older partners were relieved of some of their duties by the entry of their sons into the business. In a way, however, their hand was forced by the quarrel with Wilkinson, their principal supplier, which jeopardised the timely execution of their orders. Thus, Soho Foundry was built and the foundation laid for the first engineering factory.

With the concentration of the entire production in one concern, a gradual change in the price policy set in. The system of royalties was abolished and an ordinary price-fixing system adopted in its stead. The last years of the eighteenth century and the first of the nineteenth saw also the introduction of entirely new methods which closely combined technical and economic considerations. It has been related how the new factory was planned and executed, how the application of machinery was extended and how both the production processes and the workmen engaged in them were subdivided into different classes. It has been shown what progress was made in the subdivision and specialisation of labour and how the standardisation of the products was carried to an even higher degree than before. Of all these changes that which commands perhaps the greatest interest relates to the remuneration and conditions of labour. The scientific attitude to problems of organisation which is claimed for those then responsible for the Soho firm found its most striking expression in the many attempts to introduce payment by result. This was facilitated by the higher degree of specialisation of functions with its consequent gradation of workmen by the greater use of machinery and by the standardisation attained in the variety of products.

All these factors led to an intense pre-occupation with problems of time study, evidenced by the exceedingly elaborate records that were kept. These records of time taken for different jobs were necessitated by the decision to apply, to a greater extent than formerly, payment by result to which they formed an important preliminary. At the same time the new method of remuneration reacted, in its turn, on the specialisation and gradation of labour, which had, to some extent, been responsible for its introduction ; and greater progress in both was thus achieved. On the whole the attitude of the partners of the firm to labour became more detached and, although welfare experiments, begun in the age of " paternalism," were continued for reasons different from those which had created them, it seems, indeed, quite safe to impute to the young partners at Soho in matters affecting organisation of production, no less than in those affecting the treatment of labour, motives essentially similar to those of enlightened big business of to-day.

The change in internal methods had also important effects on the business policy of the firm and on its financial position. Once the final stage in the evolution of the price policy had been reached, the firm could, until the expiration of its monopoly in 1800, exercise its privileged position to enforce price discrimination, a procedure which was abolished only gradually as the fatal year approached. From the new system of payment, it was only a small and natural step to the adoption of a system of costing which would be as satisfactory as that of the production to which it referred. Methods of book-keeping became more exact and, in addition to improvements in accounts already in use before, a great number of statistical books and records were introduced the purpose of which was, largely like

269

that of similar methods of to-day, to lay the foundations for the evolution of new reforms. At the same time a considerable strengthening of the firm's finances can be observed and, when we leave off the survey of its development, it presents the picture of a prosperous going concern.

Since the organisation of Soho during the first period of its history does not differ largely from the general conception of eighteenth-century business organisation and practice, it is to the second phase that we have to turn for the material for our conclusions. To be sure, even under Matthew Boulton and James Watt, Soho was an exceptional enterprise ; but what distinguishes those twenty years from the following five is the absence of any deliberate, preconceived and recorded attempt at efficient organisation in all its aspects. Boulton & Watt had made steam engines a commercial possibility. Their successors manufactured them. The fathers had been builders, the sons were organisers ; and, although the older generation had laid the foundations, the new built a super-structure of such unique elaboration that it becomes difficult to balance the merit of the two generations. " For large inventions and other advancements," says Marshall,[1] " are seldom completed by a single man ; and not always by a single generation. In fact they are often named after those who have planted the flags of conquest on the crests of the battle-ments ; while those who led the way, but did not live to partake in the ultimate victory, are forgotten." This has certainly not been so in the present instance, and it is time that a revaluation was made and due credit given to Matthew Robinson Boulton and James Watt, jr.

The first impressions of an account of the experiments in business organisation carried out by this firm tend to evoke

[1] *Op. cit.*, p. 199.

a desire to revise the general belief in a comparatively recent introduction of such experiments which have lately been invested with all the glamour of a science. It is commonly supposed that problems such as those of scientific works design, subdivision and specialisation of labour in conformity with the greater use of machinery, more accurate methods of wage payment, keeping of records and of systems of cost accounting did not arise until thirty or forty years ago during the era of what is termed the " new industrial revolution." Mass production, with its use of automatic machinery, is made responsible for a revolution in industrial methods with social repercussions equally or even more profound than those of a hundred years ago.

The history of Soho does not encourage such generalisations ; and even when it is admitted that Soho was an exception—although the lack of evidence regarding other enterprises may be due merely to the absence of records—the presence of experiments in scientific management shows that these are not exclusively a product of the era of mass production but were apparent from the very beginning of machine industry. The problems, partly technical and partly economic, which evoke them to-day were in evidence then ; and there is no reason to assume that the degree of common sense required to solve them was not as easily forthcoming one hundred years ago as it is to-day, even though it was not then systematised into a science.

The procedure adopted to solve problems of organisation and administration was, taking them one by one, in no way different from that laid down by management experts at the present time ; and the cause necessitating changes was then, as now, mainly economic. Demand pressed on supply ; and the assurance of an extensive and steady market stimulated inventive ability. The machine-designer was called into play, and it was not long before he had improved or invented such machines as were required to ensure regular satisfaction of the demand. Once, however, the technical expert became of importance in industry his part assumed an ever-growing dominance, and his postulates, no less than those of the business man, would tend to mould industrial organisation. Although it is true enough that " changes in business organisation revolutionised machinery," [1] it must not be forgotten that in the second place the reverse would also be the case. In the designing of the works the engineer demanded avoidance of waste caused by intervals in the production processes. Soho was planned accordingly ; and if the difference between its layout and that which conforms to modern theories should be taken as an indication of less efficiency, it must be pointed out that it went as far as the contemporary degree of the development of industrial technique demanded. The degree of application of machinery cannot serve as a basis of comparison. Soho was essentially a machine-operated concern, limited, of course, by the resources of the time. It possessed all the features of machine production, and the finished article which it produced arose " thanks to a series of interdependent processes and manipulations." [2] This fact is substantiated by the results which the mode of production had on the class of labour employed ; and it is, perhaps, in this respect that the Soho of 1800 presents the most striking contrasts both to itself before that date and to the usual broad generalisation concerning the period.

The records of the firm make it abundantly clear that problems connected with changes in the nature and degree

---

[1] Rowe, *op. cit.*, p. 92.   [2] Marx, K., *op. cit.*, vol. 1, p. 360.

of the workers' skill were in evidence from the very dawn of the modern industrial age. In the infancy of the engineering industry one of the greatest difficulties had been the finding of workers sufficiently skilled to produce the complicated new machines required. Yet, immediately such a class of workmen came into being the simultaneous increase in the use of machinery presented the problem of keeping a balance between the skilled and semi-skilled men. Since, at Soho, the greater use of machinery went hand in hand with a general pressure for greater efficiency, the need for specialisation and subdivision of labour was felt at once ; and, although it is commonly supposed that the breaking up of different classes of workmen, such as turners, borers, and fitters, into many subdivisions of varying degrees of skill, began only thirty or forty years ago with the introduction of automatic machinery, evidence has been given of a high degree of specialisation in the case of one well-organised firm one hundred and thirty years ago. One may therefore be led to question the common assertion that the skilled worker is gradually dying out, an assertion usually accepted without any convincing evidence. If the elimination of the skilled worker is taken as one of the results of the use of machinery, then it must be evident that he has taken a very long time in dying, since the tendency for his skill to diminish has been in operation very much longer than is generally assumed.

As regards labour remuneration also, a knowledge of the practices at Soho will discourage sweeping generalisations about the " modernity " of economic measures to ensure efficiency ; nor will it be safe to point to a too abrupt gradation of the stages through which methods of wage payment have passed. It has been shown that incentives were introduced in a very elaborate and well thought out form in one of the earliest organised factories ; and it has also become apparent that a certain chronological overlapping of various methods of labour remuneration has to be admitted. This applies especially to the presence at Soho of a revised form of the journeyman system which was, and still is to some extent, characteristic of the Birmingham district. To-day, however, the pure " contract " system which gave to the journeyman full control over his men not only in the matter of engaging or dismissing them but also in that of wage-fixing, has almost completely disappeared. Where it has survived it has taken on a different form by wresting to a large extent from the sub-contractor his unlimited wage-fixing power. A similar system was in existence at Soho at a time when out-and-out sub-contracting was flourishing ; and a skilful blending of various systems was introduced to suit the peculiar requirements of the place.

Closely bound up with changes in remuneration is the question also of the general attitude towards labour. On this point, however, evidence among the firm's records has been found to be very scanty. There is reason to believe that, measured by contemporary standards, the workers at Soho were tolerably well-off ; but whether or not this was due to an exceptional benevolence on the part of their employers must largely remain a matter of speculation. The experiments with wages in themselves indicate that a change was taking place ; and on the whole, what evidence there is seems to point to the fact that the fate of the workers was gradually becoming independent of any good or ill-will on the part of the employer. Even then one could have expected that at no very distant date the worker would enjoy only that well-being which was allowed him by the degree of efficient organisation in force and by the principles underlying it. This, however, need not be taken to imply that under the new management at Soho the conditions of life of the workers were harsher than they had been hitherto. In fact they were, in many ways, improved ; and, as far as earnings were concerned, the wages books show their monetary position to have become much more favourable. The fact seems to be that only the motives which dictated the employers' attitude were changed ; and this implies that although, broadly speaking, the advancing industrialisation created previously undreamt of misery through-out the country, Soho had, in a few years, bridged the gulf of a century and more that separated it from the " enlightened self-interest " of to-day, and had established conditions for its workers far superior to those prevailing at the time.

Of all the causes which led to the changes brought by the new century one deserves to be emphasised again before this summary is concluded, namely, the sudden transformation of a state of monopoly into one of competition. The menace of it was the most powerful external factor leading to efficiency ; and from it the factor of personal ability received its strongest impetus. The analysis of the figures showing the trading results, although in many ways inconclusive, does at least sub-stantiate that point emphatically ; for as long as the business of the firm was mainly that of collecting royalties the manu-facturing side was carried on at a loss. This had to be remedied when, with the expiration of the patent, the income from royal-ties ceased, when the production was concentrated at Soho, and when this production had, moreover, to stand the strain of competition. It is not easy, in retrospect, to divorce economic from personal factors ; but at least it can be said that problems arising from similar causes, did, in essence, find the same solution as they would find to-day if they commanded the same degree of personal ability.

On the whole the main conclusion from this survey of an

individual business is to guard us once more against broad generalisations in economic history. For those, however, who wish to generalise the history of this pioneer firm may provide interesting morals.

The optimist will point with pride to the energetic methods adopted once the firm's position was challenged ; and he will apply this example to the reorganisation of a pioneer country which has since lost its predominance. The sceptic, on the other hand, may be forgiven for being confirmed in his nothing-new-under-the-sun attitude. He will prefer to emphasise the fact that there is, after all, little originality in scientific management, and this, he will maintain, must seriously detract from its curative value. He will, therefore, be inclined to question the wisdom of those who regard efficiency alone as the panacea for the ills of the industrial system.

APPENDICES.

1. The Summary Page from James Watt's private Account Book.
2. Table showing number of Engines produced, Men employed, and Profits and Losses for the years 1787 to 1801.
3. Engine Manufactory. Composite Trading Account for the years ending September 30th, 1787-1794.
4. A Valuation of Soho Foundry.
5. Resolution proposed to a meeting of Manufacturers regarding the mode of Assessment of Poor Rates.
6. Extracts from James Watt's suggestions for a new Patent Law.
7. Letter from Boulton & Watt to Mr. Thomas Kevill.
8. Cast Iron Goods supplied by outside Founders during the years 1791 to 1794.
9. Goods sent from Soho during the years 1791 to 1794, with the proportions of work done by outside Founders.
10. Arrangement of Workmen and distribution of work at Soho Foundry, September 14, 1801.
11. Specification of the fitting of Engine Materials and the Shops where it is to be done, December 3, 1801.
12. Account of the work done by the Day and by the Piece in the Engine Yard, Soho, June, 1800.
13. Particulars of the work done by Piece at Soho Foundry, 1800.
14. Calculations for ascertaining Piece-rates for the fitting of Steam Cases.
15. Proposed Piece-prices for the fitting of different sizes of Steam Cases.
16. Table and Calculations for proposed Premiums to the Borers. Table for the Cylinders.

17. Table for Air Pumps.
18. List of Premiums upon various sizes of Air Pumps and Cylinders proposed to be paid to the Borers.
19. Prices for Rotative Engines.
20. Summary Abstract of the Wages paid at Soho Foundry for the week ending September 26th, 1801.
21. Engine Manufactory. Composite Trading Account for the years ending September 30th, 1795 to 1801.
22. Abridged Balance Sheet of the London House: M. & R. Boulton, J. & G. Watt & Co.

Photographic Copies of a Memorandum entitled " Arrangement of Soho Engine Manufactory, December, 1801."

(1) Machinery.
(2) Arrangement of Soho Engine Manufactory.

APPENDIX I.

THE SUMMARY PAGE FROM JAMES WATT'S PRIVATE ACCOUNT BOOK.

(*Muirhead Papers—Boulton & Watt Collection.*)

BOULTON & WATT.

		£	s.	d.			£	s.	d.
1776					1775	By cash from scale at Soho	72	7	0
Dec. 9th	To sundry charges paid this year	34	6	11	1776	By cash from B. & F.	235	14	6
1777					1777				
Oct.	To draught on Boulton Kendall & Co.	27	17	3	Sep. 27th	By act. on Chacewater small engine recd.	45	14	3
Dec. 20th	To charges paid this year	39	3	5	Dec.	By cash from B. & F.	336	11	8
1778					1778				
July 6th	To draught on B. K. & Co.	80	0	0	July 6th	By Tingtang Act. recd.	507	5	0
Aug. 7th	To draught on B. K. & Co. in London	386	10	0	Nov. 19th	By Wheal Union in part	88	2	3
Oct.	To draught on B. K. & Co. in London	120	15	0	July 6th	By Chacewater Comp.	80	0	0
Nov. 19th	To draught on Thos. Wood in London	88	2	3	Dec.	By Chacewater Comp. at sundries	203	13	2
Dec.	To charges paid this year	67	19	10		By cash from B. & F.	224	11	2
	To furniture of house in Cornwall	109	19	5½	1779				
	To housekeeping there on company; and	71	10	11	Dec. 31st	By balance of cash from Utd. Mines insurance	9	9	0
1779	To charges paid this year	24	9	6		By cash from B. & F.	322	5	2¼

APPENDIX II.

TABLE COMPILED FROM STATEMENTS CONTAINED IN THE "ORDER BOOK" OF THE MUIRHEAD PAPERS.

(Boulton & Watt Collection.)

Year Ending.	New Engines Made.	Men Employed.		Gross	
		In the Yard.	Erectors.	Profit.	Loss.
				£ s. d.	£ s. d.
1787	16	15–22	9		588 0 4¼
1788	10	21–22	14		576 17 9½
1789	12	19–22	9		707 14 1¼
1790	14	18–24	9		762 17 1¼
1791	15	25–38	12		1884 1 0¼
1792	26	35–42	12		299 9 9½
1793	23	40–50 later reduced to 32	18	104 19 10½	
1794	17	32–26	11		1499 3 7
1795	9	26–45	11		880 16 10½
1796	30	50–55		1585 19 0	
1797	30				123 2 7½
1798	25			611 17 0	
1799	34			2345 12 8½	
1800	41			1929 14 11½	
1801	52			4030 2 0	

APPENDIX III.

ENGINE MANUFACTORY.

Composite Trading Account for the Years Ending September 30th, 1787-1794.

Dr.

To	1787. £ s. d.	1788. £ s. d.	1789. £ s. d.	1790. £ s. d.	1791. £ s. d.	1792. £ s. d.	1793. £ s. d.	1794. £ s. d.
Inventory c/f . . .	2,319 0 8¼	2,565 2 11½	3,445 5 10	3,593 8 9¾	4,637 5 1	3,933 12 3	5,947 10 10	6,447 5 0
Goods bought during the year	2,145 0 9¼	3,369 10 0¾	2,420 11 1¼	3,340 0 5¾	8,140 12 10½	8,400 6 2½	9,660 19 3	6,877 5 3
Workmen's wages and petty cash paid during the year	1,688 12 0	1,560 1 0	1,368 14 8	1,468 9 7	1,914 15 8¾	2,595 1 8	2,967 9 8½	1,897 14 2
Salaries paid during the year	386 14 2¾	450 5 10¾	383 3 0	400 15 0	491 12 4	521 12 9	550 6 3	570 15 9
Decrease in the value of buildings (interest at 5 per cent. per annum) .	28 13 6	27 10 0	27 10 0	98 6 6½	44 2 0	68 3 0	32 15 0	62 0 0
Interest on the capital required at 5 per cent. per annum . . .	225 0 0	250 0 0	250 0	300 0 0	450 0 0	600 0 0	750 0 0	600 0 0
Balance (gross profit) .	—	—	—	—	—	—	104 19 10½	—
	6,793 1 2¼	8,222 9 11	7,895 4 7¼	9,201 0 5	15,678 8 0	16,118 15 10½	20,014 0 9	16,455 0 2

Cr.

By	1787. £ s. d.	1788. £ s. d.	1789. £ s. d.	1790. £ s. d.	1791. £ s. d.	1792. £ s. d.	1793. £ s. d.	1794. £ s. d.
Inventory c/f . . .	2,565 2 11½	3,445 5 10	3,593 8 9¾	4,637 5 1	3,933 12 3	5,947 10 10	6,447 5 0	5,195 14 10
* Goods sold during the year . . .	3,639 17 10½	4,200 6 3½	3,594 1 8¼	3,800 18 2¾	9,858 14 8¾	9,871 15 3	13,566 15 9	9,810 1 9
Balance (gross loss) .	588 0 4½	576 17 9½	707 14 1¼	762 17 1¼	1,884 1 0¼	299 9 9½	—	1,499 3 7
	6,793 1 2¼	8,222 9 11	7,895 4 7¼	9,201 0 5	15,678 8 0	16,118 15 10½	20,014 0 9	16,455 0 2

The above table gives in composite form a series of trading accounts taken from the Order Book—Muirhead Papers (*Boulton & Watt Collection*).

* The figures for the years 1790 and 1791 include £435 and £525 respectively for new buildings, while that for the year 1794 includes the following items :—
" Goods B.W.S. No. 2 got up last year but delivered in this £2,052 17 11
" Goods for B'ham Navigation Co., delivered in 1787 but not charged till this year £340 4 3
Corresponding entries appear on the debit side.

APPENDIX IV.

A VALUATION OF SOHO FOUNDRY.

(S. Wyatt—Boulton & Watt Collection.)

"Valuation of Soho Foundry and the different Buildings belonging to it, taken comparatively with the rest of the Parish for an Assessment of Poor Rates."

Foundry stores and furnaces	.	.	80 sq.
Boring mill, etc.	. .	abt.	44
Turning shop	.	. .	10
Fitting „	.	. .	9
Magazine	.	. .	12
Carpenters' shop	.	. .	13
Boiling house	.	. .	4

abt. 172 sq. at 24£ = £4,128 0 0

Smiths' shop and coalshed	.	.	32 sq.
Pattern shop	.	. abt.	18
Shed for sand	.	. .	5
Drying kiln for boards	.	.	3

abt. 58 sq. at 10£ = 580 0 0

Making the dock and bridge for
towing path . . . abt.   50 0 0

Total value £4,758 0 0

£4,758 at 5 p. Ct., £237. For the rate according to
custom, ⅔ of above £158 0 0
1800, thirteen houses for workmen . . abt. 60 0 0

£218 0 0

APPENDIX V.

MANUSCRIPT ENDORSED BY BOULTON.

(Boulton & Watt Collection.)

" *Sketch of Resolution to be proposed to a Meeting of Manufacturers, Monday, January 14, 1799, respecting the mode of assessment of Manufactories to the Poor Rates.*"

After reciting the circular letter convening the meeting :

. . . " and the said letter having been occasioned by a deviation from the general practice of rating Manufacture to the Poor Rates in the instance of Messrs. Boulton & Watt's Foundry in the parish of Harborne, which from documents laid before the meeting by Mr. Boulton, appears to include a valuation of the Machinery employed in the same :

" Resolved : That the principle of subjecting the Stock profits and implements of Trade to the payment of parochial Taxes if carried into practice would prove of the utmost prejudice to the Manufacture and Trade of this town and this neighbourhood and to the nation at large and greatly tend to damp that spirit of enterprise and expenditure which is the great source of our Wealth and importance as a commercial and manufacturing country by subjecting every ingenious Manufacturer to the exposure of secrets upon which his success and reputation in life may principally depend and by exposing him to the arbitrary exercise of the Caprice of a parish officer and affording pretence for his prying into the concerns and workshops of every Individual.

" That the Stock in Trade of a merchant or trader must necessarily be in a continual state of fluctuation and much of it be purchased on Credit Terms, consequently can form no just criterion of his capital or ability to pay and that a compulsory exposure of his books in a public Court for the purpose of ascertaining the amount of his assessment would be a measure pregnant with the most ruinous consequences to every Trader. Whereas the long established practice of assessing Buildings and Manufactories at a valued Rent affords a plain, permanent and equitable standard of assessment.

" That the rise and increase of this populous town may be principally attributed to the protection and freedom under which every inhabitant has hitherto been able to carry on his Trade without any vexatious intrusion, but if this detrimental practice of Taxation is once introduced, there is the greatest reason to believe from instances, which have already occurred in other parts of the Kingdom, that our manufactories would be induced to emigrate to other places where so prejudicial a system has been wisely discontinued.

" That such a tax cannot be laid upon Stock in Trade and profits arising from the machinery used in our manufactories without ultimately falling upon the numerous poor persons employed by that machinery and by attaching to the same articles of Manufacture in various hands must considerably advance their price and thereby operate as a Bounty to our competitors in commerce, whom our Machinery alone has hitherto enabled us to outvie under the pressure of our National Debt, dear provisions and high price of labour.

" Resolved that in the opinion of this meeting it is highly expedient to avoid the agitation of a question envolving consequences of such serious consideration to the manufacturing and commercial interest of this Kingdom and therefore we recommend Messrs. —— be deputed to meet the Gentlemen of Harborne for the purpose of communicating the sentiments of this meeting and preventing if possible the subject from coming before a Court of Law."

APPENDIX VI.

EXTRACT FROM MANUSCRIPT. (Qto. 15 pp.) JAMES WATT.

(Boulton & Watt Collection.)

" Heads of a Bill to explain and amend the laws relative to Letters Patent and Grants of Privilege for new Inventions."

After reciting part of the existing law :

. . . " and whereas of late years sundry doubts have arisen in his Majesty's Courts of Law, as to the true intent and meaning of the words ' *any manner of new manufactures* ' as used in the sd. in part recited Act of Parlt. as well as to the manner of specifying or describing such new inventions as to conform to the true meaning and intent of the proviso in the sd. letters patent relative thereto, whereby many ingenious men are in danger of being harassed with law suits and eventually of being deprived of the exclusive privileges for using the various new inventions so supposed to be secured unto them and which they have attained with much labour, expense and anxiety and by which law suits or deprivation they run a risque of being totally ruined (for the prevention whereof and for the further encouragement of useful discoveries, and for the better securing to the persons making the same the benefits intended them by such his Majesty's grants as aforesaid, and for the greater advantage to the public) :

" It is therefore hereby enacted and declared that the said words ' *the sole working and making of any manner of new manufactures* ' have been understood to mean and do mean or are to the same effect, as the words used in the sd. letters patent—' the sole benefit and advantage of making, exercising, using and vending ' of any kind of new invention in the arts or manufactures comprehending

284

"(1) every new art, machine, utensil, manufacture, factitious
substance or commodity;

"(2) every new improvement of or upon any art, machine,
utensil, manufacture, substance or commodity;

"(3) every new mode, manner, method or way of applying,
constructing or using any art, machine, utensil, substance,
material or commodity;

"(4) every new process for making, preparing, compounding or
producing any manufacture, substance, material or commodity, whereby the same may be rendered more useful
or valuable, may be made, prepared or used in a more
commodious or less costly manner, may be improved in
its quality or otherways rendered cheaper, more profitable
or beneficial.

"Lastly and generally, every new and useful philo-
sophical, chemical or mechanical art or invention whatever
is hereby declared and enacted to have been and to be
a subject properly entitled to be secured by patent to the
first and true inventors thereof (as to the publick use and
exercise of the same) according to the true intent and
meaning of the said Act of Parlt. herein before in part
recited.

"And it is hereby further enacted and declared that the first
introducers into this realm of any Inventions coming under any of
the descriptions herein before contained and first practised in foreign
countries, have been and shall be considered virtually as first inventors thereof and legally entitled to the grant of the same privilege
by latters patent as the real and true inventors of new arts or manufactures."

Follow provisions about the validity of existing specifications
and detailed regulations regarding the procedure for obtaining
patents.

"And whereas the specifications of patent inventions are accessible to all manner of persons upon paying the usual fees of office
by which means other persons are enabled to pirate the inventions
to the great prejudice of the patentees and also inventions are pre-
maturely carried to foreign countries to the great loss of this nation;

Be it therefore enacted that from and after the passing of this Act, the particular or explanatory specifications of all patents for new inventions shall, during the term of the patent, be locked up in Chancery, not to be inspected except by the express order of the Ld. Chanr., to be granted whenever any dispute shall arise upon the patent rights, concerning priority of invention or otherways; but in order that all persons may know what the nature of the invention is which is secured to the patentee and may not unknowingly offend, the general specification of the nature of the said invention shall, within one month from the date of its enrollment in Chancery, be printed at length in the London Gazette at the expense of the patentee.

" Provided always and be it hereby enacted that no patent for the sole or exclusive use of any natural substance shall be good or valid but only for certain uses and applications of the same in combinations or otherways.

" And it is hereby enacted and declared that in all questions which may hereafter arise in any of his Majesty's Courts of Justice concerning the validity of a Patent for any meritorious invention, this law shall be construed in the most beneficial sense for the said patentee and according to the true intent and meaning hereof."

APPENDIX VII.

LETTER FROM BOULTON & WATT TO Mr. THOMAS KEVILL, TREASURER OF COOKS KITCHEN MINE.

Soho, August 10th, 1798.

SIR,

We trust the tenor of our letter will prove to you more effectually than any apology, that your favour of the 24th ult. has not remained unanswered from inattention to its contents.

In fact both of us have latterly been absent from home and engaged by avocations of considerable moment, which have thrown us back in our correspondence. We readily acknowledge our obligations to the advrs. in Cooks Kitchen for the friendly disposition manifested by them, nor are we insensible of the justice of the reasons you assign for modifying the premium upon their Engine.

It was our intention to have anticipated your application by an unsolicited concession of one-third, but the very ungenerous acquittal of the Whl. Abraham advrs. to our proposed abatement was, you will allow, a considerable discouragement to the further pursuit of our design and induced us to believe the motives of it would be misconstrued.

We shall not, however, follow an example we condemn in retorting upon our friends the injustice of our adversaries, or like them consider our power to resist your demand, rather than its equity.

Mr. Wilson will therefore be instructed to settle the arrears due from Cooks Kitchen advrs. upon the same footing as the other mines alluded to in your letter, as soon as a suitable memorandum of agreement is entered upon the mine books and for which purpose we shall request him to consult with you and beg your kind assistance in bringing this business to a speedy close.

We remain with great respect, Sir,

your obdt. humble servants,

(Sgd.) BOULTON & WATT.

Note.—Thomas Kevill had applied to B. & W. for a reduction of one-third of the monthly premium (about £18) on the ground that the mine was losing. The above is a copy of the reply sent by Matthew Robinson Boulton to James Watt, jr., who was then in London. It affords an interesting example of the firm's business correspondence.

APPENDIX VIII.

STATEMENT OF THE QUANTITY OF CAST IRON GOODS EXECUTED FOR BOULTON & WATT BY DIFFERENT FOUNDERS IN THE YEARS 1791, 1792, 1793 & 1794.

(Boulton & Watt Collection.)

	Cwts. Qrs. Lb.	£ s. d.	Cwts. Qrs. Lb.	£ s. d.
1791				
Dearmans .	1765 2 25	1322 19 3		
Bradley . .	820 1 9	676 7 11		
Seager (& 1792)	838 0 6	583 14 0		
Bersham .	3433 1 4	125 12 9		
			6,857 1 16	6,708 13 11
1792				
Dearmans .	1823 0 14	1388 13 7		
Bradley . .	1256 2 2	1004 5 10		
Bersham .	1923 2 22	2699 5 8		
			5,003 1 10	5,092 5 1
1793				
Dearman & Co.	1370 1 8	1007 8 1		
Bradley . .	518 0 3	406 19 5		
Seager . .	321 0 21	236 2 1		
Bersham .	1377 1 23	1980 16 2		
			3,586 3 27	3,631 5 9
1794				
Dearman & Co.	968 1 27	777 18 1		
Bradley . .	306 0 17	250 0 4		
Seager . .	63 1 15	45 13 7		
Bersham .	970 2 19	1419 18 4		
			2,308 2 22	2,493 10 4
			17,756 1 19	£17,925 15 1

289

APPENDIX IX.

STATEMENT OF GOODS SENT FROM SOHO IN THE YEARS
1791, 1792, 1793, 1794, WITH THE PROPORTION OF WORK
DONE BY THE DIFFERENT FOUNDERS EMPLOYED BY
BOULTON & WATT.

(Boulton & Watt Collection.)

					£	s.	d.
1791.	Goods sent from Soho	.	.	.	11,895	6	9
	Deduct founders' account		.	.	7,300	17	3
					4,594	9	6
1792.	Goods sent from Soho	.	.	.	10,552	11	11
	Deduct founders' account		.	.	6,155	4	5
					4,397	7	6
1793.	Goods sent from Soho	.	.	.	10,819	15	9
	Deduct founders' account		.	.	4,007	6	1
					6,812	9	8
1794.	Goods sent from Soho	.	.	.	6,329	13	2
	Deduct founders' account		.	.	3,104	7	3
					3,225	5	11

Year.	Founders.			Soho.		
	£	s.	d.	£	s.	d.
1791	7,300	17	3	11,895	6	9
1792	6,155	4	5	10,552	11	11
1793	4,007	6	1	10,819	15	9
1794	3,104	7	3	6,329	13	2
	20,567	15	0	39,597	7	7
				20,567	15	0
				19,029	12	7

Note.—The figures of founders' accounts include, in addition to cast-iron work, brass and wrought-iron work and fitting.

290

ARRANGEMENT OF WORKMEN AND DISTRIBUTION OF
WORK AT SOHO FOUNDRY, SEPTEMBER 14TH, 1801.

Wells and two assistant men, one lad.	To be employed constantly in fitting nozzles.
Man and two assistants.	Fitting safety valves, reserve valves, feeding valves, blowing valves, stop valves on end of steam pipes, glands and brasses of stuffing box of cylinder and air pump lids.
Anthony Bunting and assistant man and boy.	Fitting parallel motions.
One man and boy (Wm. Badelly).	Fitting governors, throttle valves.
Man and assistant (Wm. Buxton, John Mincham).	Turning, draw filing and finishing piston and air pump rods, either by hand or machine.
Hughes.	Fitting air pumps ; A. P. buckets and pistons.
Bissaker and boy.	Working gears.
John Allport and John Hunt, or great lathe turner.	Turning cylinders, stuffing boxes, etc. Air pump lids, pistons, air pump buckets, main gudgeons, rotative wheels, rotative shafts.
Man and assistant (Thos. Marson).	Fitting screws to gland of cylinder top ; fitting screws to false lid and making joint of dto. ; fitting cover to foot valve of air pump ; making bottom joint, fitting top and bottom of plug rod.
One foreman and three assistants, viz. : J. Hacket. S. Hughes. J. Mason. J. Hadeley.	Fitting steam case, viz., drilling flanges of cylinder top ; dto. of steam case ; chipping and fitting it to cyl. ; fitting inner and outer bottoms to cyl., and drilling flanges of dto. ; fitting side pipes ; drilling flanges of top and bottom branch of cyl. ; fitting in steady pins and bolt with nut of the outer bottom and top joint of cyl. ; drilling holes in outer bottom and fitting dto, ready to join comms. and syphon pipes.

ARRANGEMENT OF WORKMEN (*cont.*).

Foreman and three assistants, with lad to grind chisels.	Sundry chipping, viz., cold water pumps, main gudgeons and others and shaft ends, manhole pipe and cover ; chipping and fitting fire apparatus, boiler steam pipes—fly wheels.
John Taylor and John Stephen.	Fitting and gearing buckets and clacks of cold water, hot and other pumps.
Man and boy.	Chipping, fitting and lapping of brasses, viz., saddle plate, connecting link, plummer blocks, stops and nuts of saddle plates.
Man and assistant.	Turning outer end gudgeons all below 16 horse. Top pin of connecting rod. Fitting sun and planet wheels with staples and turning centre pin of dto. Fastening wheel on rotative shaft or crank on shaft.
Man and boy (Isaac Ball).	Injection rod handle, etc. Hot and cold water pump bracket, steam gauges, barometer pipes, feed apparatus, stop pipe plugs and handle, syphon.
Six men.	Weighing, packing, loading and unloading of goods and labouring work.
One borer and assistant (Wm. Nelson).	Boring—large and small rods.
One man to each (S. Eales and F. Evans).	Drilling—large and small drills.

Eight men and four boys wanted.

APPENDIX XI.

SPECIFICATION OF THE FITTING OF ENGINE MATERIALS AND THE SHOPS WHERE IT IS TO BE DONE, DECEMBER 3RD, 1801.

DISTRIBUTION OF WORK AT SOHO ENGINE MANUFACTORY.

CYLINDER.

Cylinder Lid.	Goes to steam case fitting shed (E) and is then finished ready to be sent away.
Facing.	To large turning lathe No. 3—drilling machine—Heavy fitting shop (C).
Centring the lid.	
Turning dto.	
Drilling dto.	
Boring out stuffing box	
Boring the gland.	
Turning and Fitting Brasses, viz. :	
Turning and boring brass bush for gland.	To piston rod lathe No. 4 or lathe in upper fitting shop (G).
Turning and boring brass of stuffing box.	
Turning the gland itself.	
Fitting the bush into gland.	
Fitting Screws to Gland and Cover to Lid, viz. :	
Drilling false cover, etc.	Drill—Heavy fitting shop (C).
Fitting cover to lid.	
Fitting screws of the gland.	

Fitting Steady Pins in Top Flanch and Drilling Holes.

Piston and Cover.	
Boring and Fitting ditto, viz. :	
Boring out the case.	Large turning lathe No. 3.
Centring piston and cover.	Drill—Heavy fitting shop (C).
Turning dto.	
Drilling cover.	
Turning pins for dto.	
Fitting with screws, lockers and brasses.	

293

CYLINDER *(cont.).*

Fitting Plate and Spanners, viz. : Fitting spanners. Drilling piston for plate. Drilling plate. Fitting plate.	Drill—Heavy fitting shop (C).
Piston Rod. Centring. Turning. Labour. Filing.	Piston rod lathe No. 4—Heavy fitting shop (C).
Fitting Rod to Piston, viz. : Drilling, cutting and filing hole.	Drill and heavy fitting shop (C).
Steam Case. Drilling and Fitting, viz. : Drilling. Chipping and fitting it to cylinder.	Fitting shed (E). *N.B.*—At present the drilling must be done at Drill No. 1.
Sundries, viz. : Fitting inner and outer bottoms to cylinder. Fitting stand plate to cylinder.	

AIR PUMP.

Air Pump. Facing. Drilling. Chipping.	Drill—either No. 1 or in Fitting shed (E).
Fitting Piece Work, viz. : Fitting top and foot valve bucket and steady pins to top flanch. Boring out stuffing box and gland of lid.	Fitting shed (E).
Turning and Fitting the Brasses, viz. : Turning and boring brass bush for gland. Turning and boring brass of stuffing box. Turning the gland itself. Fitting the bush into gland.	Turning lathes Nos. 8 and 9.

294

AIR PUMP (*cont.*).

Air Pump Lid, viz. :	
Centring.	Large lathe No. 3—Drilling machine.
Turning.	
Drilling.	

Fitting the Bottom Plate.

Bucket.	
Boring the case.	Turning lathe No. 3—Fitting shed
Turning.	(E).

Air Pump Bucket Rod.	
Centring.	Piston rod lathe—Fitting shop (G).
Turning.	
Filing	

Fitting Cap and Bracket to Rod.

COLD WATER PUMP.

Boring.	Drilling machine No. 1.
Drilling flanches.	
Chipping.	

Fitting Bucket and Clack, viz. :	
Turning bucket and clack and fitting	Light fitting shed (G).
them with valves.	

HOT WATER PUMP.

Boring.	Drilling machine.
Drilling flanches.	
Chipping.	

Fitting Bucket and Clack, viz. :	
Turning bucket and clack and fitting	Fitting shop (G).
them with valves.	

NOZZLES.

Drilling flanches.	Drilling machine.
Boring.	
Chipping ditto and side pipes.	

Fitting Piece Work, viz. :	
Fitting spindles, valves, racks, sectors,	Nozzle shop (D).
seats and guides.	Fitting shed (E).
Use of machinery in turning.	
Putting them together and making	
joints.	

MAIN GUDGEON.

Chipping and filing (large ones). Turning or dressing.	Large lathe No. 3 or piston rod lathe No. 4.
Fitting Plummer Blocks and Brasses, viz. Chipping blocks. Filing or lapping brasses. Fitting ditto into blocks. Fitting pins into blocks.	Heavy fitting shop.

OUTER END GUDGEON.

Chipping (large ones). Turning.	Piston rod lathe (No. 4), or lathe No. 8.
Fitting Saddle Plate and Brasses, viz. : Chipping plate. Filing or lapping brasses. Fitting them to saddle plate. Fitting stops to the nuts.	In heavy fitting shop (C).
Fitting hoop straps to gudgeon and connecting rod ; or Boring connecting rod and gudgeon. Turning the pin and fixing ditto with rod and cutter.	Drilling machine. P.R. lathe (No. 4)—Heavy fitting shop (C).

ROTATIVE WHEELS OR CRANK.

Centring. Turning out centre and rim. Finishing ditto by hand. Chipping.	Large lathe No. 3.

CONNECTING ROD.

Boring, Drilling and Chipping, viz. : Boring. Drilling. Chipping.	Drilling machine No. 1. Heavy fitting shop (C).
Turning Conn. Link Pin or Crank Pin. Fitting Planet Wheel and Pin to Rod or Crank, viz. : Fitting planet wheel to rod and staples.	P.T. lathe No. 4 or great lathe No. 3. Heavy fitting shop (C).
Fitting with Brasses, viz. : Conn. link or conn. rod.	Do. do.

CONDENSER.

Fitting ditto, viz. :	
Drilling.	Drilling machine.
Chipping.	
Fitting plate to bottom.	Heavy fitting shop (C) or yard.
Fitting Blow Pipe, viz. :	
Drilling ditto and valve seat.	Drilling machine.
Chipping.	
Fitting valve and seat (piece work).	Light fitting shop (G), lathes Nos. 8 and 9.
Fitting Injection Cock, viz. :	
Drilling.	Drilling machine—Light fitting shop
Fitting pipe and valve.	(G), lathes Nos. 8 and 9.
Fitting rod and handle and do. to cock.	

BOILER FURNITURE.

Safety Pipe.

Boring, etc., viz. :	
Boring.	Drilling machine.
Drilling.	Light fitting shop (G).
Chipping.	Lathes Nos. 8 and 9.
Fitting with valve (piece work).	
Use of machinery in turning, etc.	

Throttle Pipe.

Boring, etc., viz. :	
Boring pipe and turning brass bush.	Drilling machine.
Drilling.	Light fitting shop (G).
Fitting with valve (piece work).	Lathes Nos. 8 and 9.
Use of machinery in turning, etc.	

Manhole Pipe.

Drilling it and its cover.	Drilling machine—Yard.

Stop Pipe.

Drilling, etc., viz. :	
Boring.	Drilling machine.
Drilling.	Lathes Nos. 8 and 9.
Turning valve.	Light fitting shop (G).
Fitting ditto.	
Use of machinery.	

Fire Apparatus.

Fitting, viz. :	
Chipping.	Drilling machine.
Fitting damper and frame.	Heavy fitting shop (C).
Fitting fire door.	
Fitting feeding mouth.	

BOILER FURNITURE (*cont.*).

Feeding Apparatus.
Fitting, viz. :

Turning and fitting valve and seat.	Drilling machine.
Use of machinery.	Lathes Nos. 8 and 9.
Drilling stuffing box.	Light fitting shop (G).
Fitting ditto with pipe and chipping top.	

Reverse Valve.

Boring valve and seat.	Drilling machine.
Fitting with levers, standard and weight.	Turning lathes Nos. 8 and 9.
Use of machinery.	Light fitting shop (G).

Steam Gauge.

Fitting (piece work).	Light fitting shop (G).

PERPENDICULAR PIPES.

Drilling, etc., viz. :

Chipping (when in separate pieces).	Drilling machine—Yard.
Drilling.	
Boring ends.	

Boiler Steam Pipes.
Drilling, etc., viz. :

Chipping.	Drilling machine—Yard.
Drilling.	
Boring ends.	

Socket Pipe.
Drilling, etc., viz. :

Drilling.	Drilling machine.
Chipping.	Turning lathes Nos. 8 and 9.
Boring end.	Light fitting shop (G.)
Fitting with valve (piece work).	
Use of machinery.	

ROTATIVE SHAFT.

Turning, etc., viz. :

Centring.	Large lathe No. 3.
Turning.	
Labour.	

Fitting Plummer Blocks and Brasses, viz. :

Chipping blocks.	Heavy fitting shop (C).
Filing or lapping brasses.	

298

Rotative Shaft (*cont.*).

Fitting them into blocks.
Fitting pins into blocks.

Fitting End of Rotative Shaft, Wheel, or Crank, viz. :	
Drilling end and fitting pins.	Heavy fitting shop or Yard.

Fly Wheel.

Drilling, etc., viz. :	
Drilling.	
Chipping.	
Fitting with pins.	

Governor.

Fitting, viz. :	
Fitting (piece work).	Parallel motion shop (F).
Fitting with top and bottom brakes.	Lathes Nos. 6 and 7.
Use of machinery.	

Parallel Motion.

Boring or rhymering holes.	Drilling machine—Parallel motion
Fitting (piece work).	shop (F)—turning lathe Nos. 6 and
Use of machinery in turning.	7 or, in the case of very large ones,
Fitting wood and making wooden gauges.	at the lathe No. 3.

Working Gear.

Boring levers, etc.	Drilling machine—Fitting shop (G).
Fitting (piece work).	Lathes Nos. 6 and 7.
Use of machinery.	

General Fitting.

Fitting nozzles to cylinder.	Fitting shed (E).

Labour.

Weighing goods.	Magazine and yard.
Blacking goods.	
Packing goods.	

Note.—In the original document the left-hand column is printed and the shops, etc., where the processes were to be carried out are entered in ink. This fact would indicate that several copies were made, probably for distribution among the foremen, although only one has been discovered.

APPENDIX XII.

ACCOUNT OF THE WORK DONE BY THE DAY AND BY THE PIECE IN THE ENGINE YARD, SOHO, JUNE, 1800.

(Boulton & Watt Collection.)

Day Work.	Piece Work.

CYLINDER.

Day Work.	
Facing . .	Soho foundry.
Turning the lid and boring stuffing box . .	Tongue.
Drilling . .	Pearson.
Turning and boring gland and brasses . .	Wright & Spooner.
Fitting lid or false face . .	Lads.
Fitting nozzles to cylinder . .	Sundry people.

PISTON.

Day Work.	
Turning . .	Tongue
Fitting . .	Lads.
Fitting plate and spanners .	Pearson.
Fitting rod .	,,
Turning rod .	Tongue and Lawrence.

AIR PUMP.

Day Work.	
Facing . .	Soho foundry.
Turning the lid and boring stuffing box . .	Tongue.

300

AIR PUMP (*cont.*).

Drilling . .	Pearson.	Air pump and bucket with valves, 3s. per inch done by Brown & Scuttar.
Turning and boring gland and brasses . .	Wright, etc.	
Turning bucket .	Tongue.	
Chipping pump .	Thompson and Morgan.	
Turning rod .	Lawrence.	
Fitting plate to bottom . .	Thompson.	
Fitting cap to rod and the rod and bracket that carried the plug.		

STEAM CASE.

Drilling . .	Pearson.
Chipping . .	Salmon.
Fitting the cylinder	Sundry people.

NOZZLES.

Chipping . .	Salmon.	Fitting them with double sets of valves, etc., 22s. per inch. When single, 18s. per inch. Done by Joseph Turner & Co.
Boring . .	Meadows.	
Drilling . .	Pearson.	

CONDENSER.

Drilling . .	Pearson.
Chipping . .	Thompson & Co.
Fitting plate to bottom . .	,,

BLOW PIPE.

Drilling . .	Pearson.	Blowing valves, 2s. 6d. each.
Fitting rod and handle to injection cock and flanch to blow pipe . .	Lads.	

PERPENDICULAR PIPES.

Chipping . .	Thompson and others.
Drilling . .	Pearso .
Boring ends .	Meadows.

301

Working Gear.

Boring levers .	Meadows.	4 Horse . .	£2 18 6
		6-12 Horse . .	£3 3 0
		14-20 Horse . .	£3 13 6

Done by Willis & Moseley.
Fitting brasses to perpendicular pipes and brasses to brackets, 5s.

Parallel Motion.

Boring or rhymer-
   ing holes . Meadows. | Fitting 3s. per inch of the diameter of the cyl., John Ready.

Main Gudgeon.

Turning. . Lawrence and
           Tongue.

Plummer Blocks, etc.

Chipping . . Lads.
Fitting the brasses
   and pins . „

Fly Wheel.

Drilled and fitted at Soho foundry.

Cold and Hot Water Pumps.

Boring . . Meadows.
Drilling . . Pearson.

Bucket and Clacks.

Fitting . . Lads.

Manhole Pipe.

Drilling it and its
   cover . . Pearson.

Fire Doors.

Fitting . . Biddle.

Eduction Pipe.

Drilling . . Pearson.

Safety and Socket Pipe.

Boring . . Meadows.   Fitting, 8s. to 12s. each, done by
Drilling . . Pearson.   James Wright.
Chipping . . Sundry people.

APPENDIX XII

Throttle Pipe.

Boring . . Meadows. | Fitting, 10s. 6d. each, James Wright.

Governor.

| Fitting, 18s. each, Willis & Moseley.

Feeding Apparatus.

Fitting . . Lads. | Feeding and reverse valves, 2s. each, James Wright & Lawrence.

Outer End Gudgeon.

Turning . . Lawrence.

Saddle Plate, etc.

Chipping and fit-
 ting it with
 brasses and
 pins and fitting
 the brasses to
 gudgeon . Lads.

Connecting Rod.

Boring . . Meadows.
Drilling . . Pearson.
Chipping . . Sundry people.
Fitting planet
 wheels to rod .   „
Fitting pin to top
 of rod . . Lads.

Crank.

Boring . . Meadows.
Turning pin . Lawrence.
Fitting „ . Lads.
Chipping crank . „
Fitting brasses . „

Rotative Wheels.

Turning out centre Tongue.
Drilling . . Pearson.
Chipping . . Thompson and
      others.
Fitting pin to planet
 wheel . . —
Turning pin . Lads.

303

CONNECTING LINK.

Fitting it with
brasses, gib,
and cutter and
brasses to necks
of rotative shaft
and connecting
link pins . Lads.

ROTATIVE WHEELS.

Turning . . Tongue.

PLUMMER BLOCKS, ETC.

Chipping them and
fitting the brasses Lads.

Note.—A similar document, dated 1801, is in existence, which, with one small exception, is identical with the present one.

APPENDIX XIII.

PARTICULARS OF THE WORK DONE BY PIECE AT SOHO FOUNDRY, 1800.

(Boulton & Watt Collection.)

CYLINDER GLANDS.

Boring and turning the gland. Bushing the gland. Boring and turning brushes for the gland.	Done by Bunting for 5s. per cwt. for all sizes.

PISTON.

Fitted with cover, spanners and bottom plate.	Done by Hughes at 4s. 6d. for each pin screwing down the cover.

PISTON RODS.

Turned and filed (but not fitted into the piston).	Done by Bunting at 1½d. per lb. net weight.

AIR PUMP.

Fitting the pump and bucket with valves, rod to bucket, pins to gland, and steady pins to top flanch.	Done by Hughes at 3s. 3d. per inch, as far as a 2H., and 3s. for all above that size.

AIR PUMP BUCKET RODS.

Turned and filed.	Done by Bunting at 1½d. per lb. net weight.

PARALLEL MOTIONS.

Fitted (exclusive of rhymering).	Done by Bunting at 3s. per inch of cylinder and 1 day for repairing tools.

WORKING GEARS.

Fitted (exclusive of rhymering). | Bissaker.

THROTTLE PIPES.

Fitted (exclusive of boring, rhymering | W. Badalley at 10s. 6d. for all below
and putting in collars). | 30H., and 11s. for all above that.

BAROMETERS.

Hughes at 1s. 3d. each.

BAROMETER CASES.

Alex. Pope at 1s. 6d. each.

APPENDIX XIV.

CALCULATIONS FOR ASCERTAINING PIECE-RATES FOR THE FITTING OF STEAM CASES.

(*Boulton & Watt Collection.*)

Diameter of Cylinder.	Number of Days.	Amount per Theorem.			Reduced Amount.			Panels.	Average.		
		£	s.	d.	£	s.	d.		£	s.	d.
16	14·2	1	9	11	1	3	3	4			
17⅜	16·2	1	16	6	1	7	1	4	1	7	0
19¼	18·1	2	0	10	1	10	3	4			
20¾	19·9	2	4	9	1	13	2	6			
21⅜	20·65	2	6	6	1	14	5	6	1	17	2½
23¾	23·5	2	12	6	1	19	2	6			
25¼	25·3	2	16	9	2	2	0	6			
27⅛	27·55	3	5	11	2	6	7	6			
28⅛	28·78	3	4	9	2	7	11	6			
29	29·8	3	7	0½	2	9	8	6	2	9	3¾
30¾	31·9	3	11	9	2	13	1½	6			
31½	32·8	3	13	10	2	14	9	8			
33⅓	35·0	3	18	9	2	18	4	8			
34	35·8	4	0	6	2	19	8	8	2	19	1½
36	38·25	4	6	1	3	3	9	8			
40	43·0	4	16	9	3	11	3	8			
42	45·4	5	2	2	3	15	8	8			
44	47·8	5	7	5	3	19	9	8	3	18	7
48	52·6	5	18	4	4	7	8	8			
52	57·4	6	9	2	4	15	8	10	4	15	8
60	67·0	7	10	9	5	10	0	12			
63	70·6	7	18	10	5	17	8	12	5	19	10½
66	79·2	8	18	3	6	12	0	12			

Note.—The "Theorem" is: d (diameter) $\times$ 1·2 -5 = time in days. The rate of wages is 2s. 3d. per day.

The above table shows a number of clerical errors which have been left to conform with the original.

APPENDIX XV.

PROPOSED PIECE-PRICES FOR THE FITTING OF DIFFERENT SIZES OF STEAM CASES.

(Boulton & Watt Collection.)

Diameter of Cylinder.				Proposed Prices.		
Ins.	£	s.	d.	£	s.	d.
16 to 19¼	1	7	0	1	1	0
20¾ ,, 25¼	1	17	2½	1	10	0
27⅛ ,, 30¾	2	9	3¾	2	2	0
31½ ,, 36	2	19	1½	2	12	0
40 ,, 48	3	18	7	3	15	0
52	4	15	8	4	15	0
60 to 66	5	19	10½	5	10	0

APPENDIX XVI.

TABLE AND CALCULATIONS FOR PROPORTIONING PREMIUMS TO YE BORERS. TABLE FOR THE CYLINDERS.

(Boulton & Watt Collection.)

(This document is endorsed on the back : " Table of the Times of boring Cylinders with Observations thereon, 1800.")

Length.		Diam.	Horse-Power.	Average of Time from Accounts.	Surface.	Average of Time for each Size per Calculation from Surface.	Average of Time according to the Theorem Below.	Gratuity upon each Size of Cylinder.	
ft.	ins.	ins.		days.		days.	days.	s.	d.
4	0	12⅛	4	4	48·5	2·13	4·02	1	8
4	0	14¾	6	4	50·0	2·6	4·37	1	10
5	1	16	8	4·72	81·5	3·6	5·12	2	1
5	1	17⅞	10	4·5	90	3·95	5·4	2	3
5	1	19¼	12	5·15	98	4·32	5·67	2	4
6	2	20	14	5·75	108	4·75	6·0	2	6
6	2	21⅜	16	5·6	134	5·9	6·87	2	10
6	3	23¾	20	5·93	149	6·5	7·37	3	0
7	4	25¼	24	6·8	185	8·15	8·57	3	6
7	4	26⅛	26	—	—	8·3	—	—	
7	4	27½	28	8·25	202	8·8	9·13	3	9
7	4	28⅛	30	9·0	206	9·1	9·27	3	10
7	4	29	32	9·2	213	9·4	9·5	3	11
8	5	30¾	36	12·5	225	9·9	9·93	4	1
8	5	31½	—	12	265	11·6	11·23	4	8
9	5	34	50	19·75	267	11·7	11·3	4	8
11	0	64	—	27·5	760	33·5	27·33	11	4
				144·65	3091				

" 3091)144 = 21·465, but as the times of facing the cylinders and some other parts of the operation are not in the ratio of their diameter and length, the above factors should be modified and the following theorem substituted :

" To the surface add 72 and divide by 30—gives the number of days."

Note.—The above table, together with the two following, shows the calculations carried out in order to compute a bonus for the borers, and their results. Clerical errors have not been corrected.

309

APPENDIX XVII.

TABLE FOR AIR PUMPS.

(Boulton & Watt Collection.)

Horse-Power.	Diameter.		Bored Length.		Surface.	Average of Time According to Theorem.	Gratuity Money at 3d.	
	ft.	ins.	ft.	ins.			s.	d.
4	0	$8\frac{1}{2}$	2	$6\frac{1}{4}$	21·25	3·1	0	9
6	0	$10\frac{1}{2}$	2	$6\frac{1}{2}$	26·25	3·3	0	10
6	0	$9\frac{3}{4}$	3	$1\frac{3}{4}$	—	—	0	11
8	1	$0\frac{1}{8}$	3	$1\frac{3}{4}$	38	3·66	0	11
10-12	1	1	3	$2\frac{1}{4}$	42	3·8	0	$11\frac{1}{2}$
14-16	1	$2\frac{3}{4}$	3	$9\frac{5}{8}$	56	4·3	1	1
18-20	1	4	3	$10\frac{1}{8}$	62	5·1	1	3
22	1	$4\frac{3}{4}$	4	$4\frac{5}{8}$	73	4·8	2	0
26	1	$5\frac{2}{3}$	4	$4\frac{5}{8}$	77	5·0	2	1
28	1	$7\frac{1}{4}$	4	$4\frac{5}{8}$	84	5·2	2	2
32	1	8	4	$4\frac{5}{8}$	87	5·3	2	$2\frac{1}{2}$
40	1	$10\frac{5}{8}$	5	0	113	6·2	2	7
50	1	$11\frac{3}{4}$	5	7	134	6·8	2	10
60	2	6	5	$2\frac{1}{2}$	157	7·7	3	$2\frac{1}{2}$
Hebbn.	3	0	6	$2\frac{1}{2}$	223	9·8	4	1

APPENDIX XVIII.

LIST OF PREMIUMS UPON VARIOUS SIZES OF AIR PUMPS AND CYLINDERS, PROPOSED TO BE PAID TO THE BORERS.

(*Boulton & Watt Collection.*)

Table of Air Pumps.						Table of Cylinders.					
Diameter.		Bored Length.		Gratuity Money at 3d.		Diameter.		Bored Length.		Gratuity Money at 5d.	
ft.	ins.	ft.	ins.	s.	d.	ft.	ins.	ft.	ins.	s.	d.
0	8½	2	6¼	0	9	1	1⅛	4	0	1	8
0	9¾	2	6¼	0	10	1	2¾	4	0	1	10
0	10½	2	6¼	—		1	4	5	1	2	1
1	0⅛	3	1¾	0	11	1	5⅔	5	1	2	3
1	1	3	2¼	0	11½	1	7¼	5	1	2	4
1	2¾	3	9⅝	1	1	1	8	6	2	2	6
1	4	3	10⅛	1	3	1	9⅜	6	2	2	10
1	4¾	4	4⅝	2	0	1	11¾	6	3	3	0
1	5⅔	4	4⅝	2	1	2	1¼	7	4	3	6
1	7¼	4	4⅝	2	2	2	2⅛	7	4	—	
1	8	4	4⅝	2	2½	2	3⅛	7	4	3	9
1	10⅝	5	0	2	7	2	4⅛	7	4	3	10
1	11¾	5	7	2	10	2	5	7	4	3	11
2	6	5	2½	3	2½	2	6¾	8	5	4	1
3	0	6	2½	4	1	2	7½	8	5	4	8
—		—		—		2	10	9	5	4	8
—		—		—		5	4	11	0	11	4

APPENDIX XIX.

PRICES FOR ROTATIVE ENGINES.

(Boulton & Watt Collection—probably August, 1795.)

Stroke.	Horse-Power.	Metal Materials.	Iron Boiler.	Total of Metal Materials.	Premium for Five Years.	Total Charge including Premium.	Total Charge with 50 per cent. on Metal Materials.	Carriage to Hull.		Total.
ft.		£	£	£	£	£	£	£	s.	£
4	8	295	40	335	155	490	502	23	0	525
4	10	320	50	370	192	562	555	25	5	580
4	12	342	60	402	232	634	603	27	0	630
5	14	434	70	504	270	774	756	34	0	790
5	16	460	80	540	310	850	810	36	5	846
5	18	480	90	570	350	920	855	38	0	893
5	20	500	100	600	388	988	900	39	10	940
6	24	620	115	735	466	1201	1102	49	0	1151
6	28	660	130	790	544	1334	1185	52	0	1237
7	32	845	150	995	622	1617	1492	62	0	1554
7	36	885	170	1055	700	1755	1582	64	10	1646
7	40	927	195	1122	776	1888	1668	67	10	1735
8	45	1060	220	1280	874	2154	1920	78	0	1998
8	50	1112	240	1352	970	2322	2028	81	0	2109

APPENDIX XXI.

ENGINE MANUFACTORY.

Composite Trading Accounts for the Years Ending September 30th, 1795 to 1801.

	1795.	1796.	1797.	1798.	1799.	1800.	1801.
	£ s. d.	£ s. d.	£ s. d.	£ s. d.	£ s. d.	£ s. d.	£ s. d.
Inventory brought forward (less debts)	5,195 14 10	5,000 5 6	7,069 14 7	4,829 18 3	5,119 12 7	8,501 7 11	8,523 18 9
Goods bought	3,094 12 1½	12,364 9 3¼	9,605 15 7¼	13,931 7 1½	15,706 16 7 }	24,221 5 10½	7,310 14 11
Materials bought	—	—	—	—	3,810 5 11½ }		
Transfer of goods	—	—	—	—	3,014 9 6½		
Goods manufactured	—	—	—	—	—	—	26,505 16 4
Tools of various sorts	—	—	—	—	—	—	299 0 7½
Boilers	—	—	—	—	—	—	3,780 18 2
Workmen's wages and petty cash	2,142 10 8½	3,145 9 10¼	3,033 8 6	2,860 1 11	{2,224 8 10½ 289 8 5	2,559 8 1½ 242 15 1 }	3,407 7 7
Engine Erectors' wages	—	540 2 4	752 18 8½	402 6 2	820 5 10½	682 8 2½	1,249 18 3½
Salaries	505 7 2	497 15 0	597 4 2	722 19 2	255 16 0	282 7 3	
Interest (less interest received)	—	—	—	853 10 11¼	672 5 1	1,195 17 10	
,, on inventory	259 15 9	—	—	—	—	—	
,, on buildings (decrease in value)	60 0 0	65 14 3	123 12 0	111 5 0	100 3 0	102 2 0	
,, money advanced	77 11 0	—	—	—	—	—	
,, B. & W.	—	617 1 2	381 15 8	—	—	—	
,, partners	—	41 11 8½	525 5 7	—	—	—	
,, foundry	—	—	45 8 6	63 14 0	—	—	
,, N. Boulton	—	—	—	295 2 7	—	—	General ex-
,, Boulton, jr.	—	—	—	213 18 0	—	—	penses :
,, J. Watt	—	—	—	45 16 1¼	—	—	1,973 6 4½
,, J. Watt, jr.	—	—	—	157 4 2	—	—	
,, G. Watt	—	—	—	226 15 8	—	—	
Wear and tear of machinery	—	—	—	—	154 0 0	108 11 7	
Expense of procuring cash	6 13 5	—	—	—	—	—	
Insurance and taxes	1 11 6 }	40 1 1	50 2 1½	43 1 8	—	—	
Postage	2 5 0 }						
Repairs	—	—	—	—	—	327 12 9	
One year's rent	—	—	—	—	76 0 0	70 0 0	
Pencils and papers	—	—	35 0 0	—	—	—	
Miscellaneous expenses	—	87 13 7	165 8 11	39 3 0	3 16 1	—	
Balance (gross profit)	—	1,585 19 0	—	611 17 0	2,345 12 8½	1,929 14 11½	4,030 2 0
	11,343 16 6	23,986 3 7	22,385 14 4¼	24,396 10 3	34,422 10 8½	40,123 11 7	57,081 3 0½

	1795.	1796.	1797.	1798.	1799.	1800.	1801.
	£ s. d.	£ s. d.	£ s. d.	£ s. d.	£ s. d.	£ s. d.	£ s. d.
Inventory carried forward (less debts)	5,000 5 6	7,069 14 7	4,829 18 3	5,611 4 7	6,485 19 9	8,523 10 9	10,189 12 9
Goods sold including :	5,281 12 9½	—	—	—	—	30,501 10 4	45,121 14 3
Carriage	—	16,394 5 0	16,532 4 3	18,319 5 5½	22,725 7 7	—	67 8 0
Pneumatic account	—	—	—	—	—	156 15 9	145 11 3
And sundries	181 1 4	—	—	—	—	189 6 1	142 14 3
Miscellaneous charges	—	—	—	—	129 7 9	—	—
Transfer of goods	—	—	—	—	4,237 1 6½	—	—
Charges for Engine Erectors' time	—	522 4 0	900 9 3	466 0 2½	886 18 8	752 8 8	1,414 2 6½
Commission upon foundry engines	—	—	—	—	157 15 5	—	—
Balance (gross loss)	880 16 10½	—	123 2 7¼	—	—	—	—
	11,343 16 6	23,986 3 7	22,385 14 4¼	24,396 10 3	34,422 10 8½	40,123 11 7	57,081 3 0½

Note.—This table was compiled from the trading accounts in the "Order book" (Muirhead Papers, *Boulton & Watt Collection*). Unlike the table for the preceding years, changes of minor importance had to be made for the purpose of drawing up this composite table. It will be seen that the nomenclature is not the same for all years, and as far as possible the different names for the various items have been preserved. Sometimes an item would be analysed, at other times it would include a number of items. This difference arises out of the fact that the accounts were either abstract statements by M. R. Boulton, or taken from the books of either Foreman or Lodge.

APPENDIX XX.

SUMMARY ABSTRACT OF THE WAGES PAID AT SOHO
FOUNDRY FOR THE WEEK ENDING SEPTEMBER 26TH,
1801.

(From the Firm's " Wages Book."   Boulton & Watt Collection.)

"ABBREVIATURE."

	£	s.	d.
Foundry Current Expenses	48	13	8½
Fitting ,, ,, ...	40	13	3
Smithy ,, ,, ...	16	12	3½
General Expenses	1	9	9½
New Building	12	9	10½
Coal and Coak Account	1	1	0
Lime and Sand Account	0	4	4
Farm Account	0	3	3
Timber Account	0	10	3½
Thos. Middleton	4	0	0
Wages—Sept. 26th, 1801 .	£125	15	9½

ABRIDGED BALANCE SHEET OF THE LONDON HOUSE, 1804.

"STATEMENT OF BALANCES AND PROFITS IN THE CONCERN OF MATTHEW & ROBINSON BOULTON, JAMES & GREGORY WATT & CO., DECEMBER 31ST, 1804."

(Boulton & Watt Collection.)

Debts owing to M. & R. B., J. & G. W. & Co.

Sundry Debtors		£1,562	2 11
B. Walker & Collins		4,286	15 10
M. Boulton Coinage		4,492	9 1
Boulton Watt & Co.		2,255	7 8
Sundries, viz.:—			
6000 3 p.c.t. Consols	£4,166 5 0		
House in London St.	1,230 2 8		
Discount to receive			
Bills in hand	16,536 6 4		
Cash	1,621 8 7	23,554	2 7
		£36,150	18 11

Debts owing by M. & R. B., J. & G. W. & Co.

Sundry Creditors		£1,293	14 11
M. R. Boulton		4,606	0 9
M. Boulton Lodgement		4,762	8 3
Boulton & Watt		1	0 6
James Watt & Co.		379	16 10
J. Watt, Lodgement		3,525	17 0
M. Boulton & Button Co.		111	4 5
M. Boulton		2,557	10 10
M. Boulton & Plate Co.		897	17 4
James Watt, junior		7,870	1 3
Boulton & Smith		604	14 4
William Murdock		3,000	0 0
		£34,857	4 0
Balance		1,293	14 11
		£36,150	18 11

Note.—A number of smaller items have been summarised under the headings "Sundry Debtors" and "Sundry Creditors."

NOMINAL ACCOUNTS.

Profit and loss to 1803 Cr.	.	.	.	.	.	.	£863 17 11
Commission .	.	.	.	.	.	£554 13 5	
Discount Profit	.	.	.	.	597 6 6	
Insurance Commission	.	.	.	.	173 19 0	
Shipping Charges Profit .	.	.	.	16 10 4	

	£1,342 9 4
Deduct General Charges	912 12 4
	429 17 0
	£1,293 14 11

Arrangement of Soho Engine Manufactory
Dec.r 1801

Machinery

No 1. Large Drill — *An upright one to ... convenient ... of cylinder hold in front ...* Present speed 8 p.m. proposed speed — 8	to bore hot & cold water pumps, Nozzles, connecting ... a steam pipes. Blow & Valve seat. Nozzle pipes. Safety pipes ... & .. uneven valve seats — Parallel Motion of Nozzle & Gear
No 2. Small Drill — *an upright one for the same convenient ... present ...* present speed 50 p.m. proposed 75 - 75	to drill air pumps, condensers, pistons, steam ... pannels & most of the foregoing articles —
No 3. Large Turning Lathe — *Both ... & chuck* present speed 2 p.m. proposed speed ... 3 ... 4½ ... 18 f. m. 18	to turn cylinder lids. Pistons, Air pump buckets & lids. Main gudgeons of large size. Rotative Wheels & shafts of all descriptions. large sized parallel Mot. Gudgeons & Crank pins —
No 4. Piston Rod Lathe *with ... & dead ...* present speed 10. 30. 60. proposed speed 10. 20. 30. 60 (10. 30. 50. 60)	Piston & Air pump rods — Outer end Gudgeons & Main ... of common size. Crank pins. Connect.g Link pins — occasionally Pistons & Cylinders —
No 5. Nozzle Lathe *Chuck & dead Center* present speed 12 3/4 h. proposed speed 85 . 00 . 130	Valves & other work for Nozzles —
No 6 & 7. Parallel Motion *Lathe ... & dead center* first speed at 16. ... speed 12. 40. 60	Parallel Motion gudgeons & other articles belong.g to D.o Working gear work — governor D.o —
No 8 & 9. Lathe in use for *... Chuck ... dead center ...* proposed d.o 50. 80. 120	Reverse, safety & other Valves. Buckets & clacks of hot & cold water pumps. Injection Rod Handles & Valves small gudgeons & bushes — Air pump Valves ...
No 10. Small Lathe — proposed speed 200. 300	turn.g small pins of work & gear & generally all small pins used —
No 11. Lapping Machine &c.	for Lapping all brasses of plummer block &c.
No 12. Pattern Maker *...speed from 120. 63 ...*	for ye use of ye pattern makers —
No 13. Steam Case Drill —	proposed to be in fitting shed —

INDEX.

Crowley Ironworks, 227, 228.
Cylinders, boring of, 209-11.
— fitting of, 179-80.
— supply of, 25, 34.
— transport of, 58.

Dartmouth, Lord, 51, 131, 136.
Dartrie, Lord, 131.
Darwin, Dr. E., 8.
Dearman Foundry, 56-7, 152, 166.
Depreciation, 123-4, 254-5.
Dickinson and Jenkins, 15, 19, 77, 78, 108, 111, 114, 163, 190, 262.
Drawing Office, 155, 224.
Drillers, wages of, 211-16.
Drilling machines, 173, 175.
Drunkenness, 61-2, 64, 191, 232.
Dudley, Thomas, 68, 73, 81-2.

Eden, Sir F. M., 228.
Efficiency, 187, 250-1, 263.
Emigration, 137.
Engine erection, charges for, 247-9.
— — delay in, 57, 60, 82-3.
— — directions for, 186.
— — expenses of, 32.
— parts, fitting of, 154, 172, 176, 178-80, 202-5.
— — supply of, 55-6, 121, 150-2, 266.
— — transport of, 58-9.
— performance, 29, 116.
— — comparison of, 31, 39, 78-80, 116.
— — guarantee of, 33.
Erectors, charges of, 65-6, 122-3, 254.
Ermanski, J., 187.
Evans, Francis, 183, 212-15.
Ewart, Peter, 159, 162, 167.
Export, prohibition of, 32.

Factory system, at Soho, 9, 60, 186-8, 200, 220.
— — origin of, 1.
Financial difficulties, 100-7, 259.
Fitters, 181-3.
— wages of, 197-206.
Fleming and Brocklehurst, 1.
Flour mills, 111.
Fordyce Bros., failure of, 11.
Foreign business, 47-54, 239-40.
Foremen, function of, 200-1, 204, 233.
Fothergill, John, 7, 17, 99, 107.
France, engines for, 48-54, 240.
Free trade, 139.
Friendly societies, 227-8.

Fuel consumption of Newcomen engine, 3.
— — of Watt engine, 29, 41, 67, 77-8, 242.
Funeral benefits, 233.

Gang work, 198, 200, 202, 207, 219-20.
Garbett, S., 39, 137.
Gas lighting, 262-3.
Grand Trunk Canal, 58.

Hallamanin engine, 74.
Hamilton, G., 91.
Hamilton Jenkin, A., 68, 90, 93, 145.
Harper's Hill, 155-6.
Harrison, Joseph, 29, 43, 62, 74.
— William, 184, 202-3, 247-8.
Hasbach, W., 226, 227, 228.
Heathfield, Hall, 165.
Henderson, Lieutenant Logan, 63.
Hornblower, 56, 69, 81-2, 144-5.
Horse-power unit, 116.
Hull, freight to, 239.
— Waterworks, 31, 32.

Insurance society at Soho, 223, 225-6, 228-36.
Interest charges, 123, 254-5.
Ireland, engines for, 240.
Irish resolutions, 138.

Jary, 50-1.
Jones, E. D., 171, 185.
Journeyman system, 5, 200-1, 274.

Keir, James, 104, 130.
Knowles, L. C., 4.

Labour conditions at Soho, 191, 220-2, 274-5.
— disputes, 61, 222-3.
— division of, 155, 180-4, 189, 197.
— hours of, 223-4.
— problems, 60-1, 235.
— scarcity of, 13, 60, 66, 191, 233.
— skill of, 9, 21, 60, 62, 265-6, 273.
Lawson, James, 63, 144, 162, 192, 223, 260-2.
Levy, H., 91, 145.
Lord, J., 30, 47, 55, 226, 233.
Lowe, Vere & Co., 100-7.
Lowmoor Ironworks, 141, 166, 168.
Ludlow, J. M., 227.

Manchester, cotton trade, 261.
— wages at, 190.

318

For Product Safety Concerns and Information please contact our
EU representative GPSR@taylorandfrancis.com, Taylor & Francis
Verlag GmbH, Kaufingerstraße 24, 80331 München, Germany